I0825343

THE

LIFE

OF

THOMAS PAINE

AUTHOR OF

Common Sense, The Crisis, Rights of Man,
&c., &c., &c.

BY

James Cheetham

"Speak of me as I am"—William Shakespeare

London
Spradabach Publishing
2022

Spradabach Publishing
BM Box Spradabach
London WC1N 3XX

The Life of Thomas Paine
Originally published in 1809.

First Spradabach edition published 2022

Interior design by Alex Kurtagic

ISBN 978-1-909606-32-6

British Library Cataloguing-in-Publication Data:
A catalogue record for this book is available from the British Library.

TO GEORGE CLINTON,

VICE-PRESIDENT OF THE UNITED STATES

SIR,

Without asking your permission, allow me to dedicate to you, as a tribute of my admiration of your private and public virtues, the following Life of the Author of *Common Sense*. I know not, indeed, that a work, which necessarily treats in some respect of revolutions, could more properly be dedicated than to one, who, in the struggles of the colonies for independence, animated his countrymen by his patriotism, encouraged them by his firmness, and supported them with his sword. "Had it," said Mr. Burke, "adverting with pious resignation to the death of his son; had it pleased God to continue to me the hopes of succession, I should have been a sort of founder of a family." You, sir, have been more favoured by Providence. You have not only the great felicity of being the founder of a family, every branch of which I hope but dare not believe will emulate your virtues, but you have also the glory of being enrolled amongst the most conspicuous founders of a great empire.

In whatever light we contemplate your character, it is worthy of all imitation. When, at the commencement of the war of independence, irresolution, like a pestilence, shook the nerves of the state; when, awed by hostile appearances, by the power of a formidable enemy, by the absence of preparation for defence, and the want of adequate resources, not a few of your contemporaries shrunk from the responsibility, the suffrages of your fellow citizens called you to the chair of the state, and, evincing an intrepidity which the exigencies of the times required, you obeyed their voice. Your country beheld you with enthusiasm and joy in the triple character of an unyielding patriot, an enlightened governour, a gallant general. At that period, pregnant with consequences to posterity the most baneful or the most happy, no *caucuses*[1] were held to cheat you out of the affections of the people. Those who applauded your heroick defence of Forts Montgomery and

1 A cant term, used amongst us to designate a political cabal; an assemblage of intriguers, privately convened to plot their own elevation, upon the ruin, not unfrequently, of better men.

Clinton, against a greatly superior force, although they envied you the glory, were far from courting the danger of the command. The steadiness of your course, the prudence of your measures, the bravery of your conduct, the sagacity of your councils, civil and military, attracted the notice of WASHINGTON, your illustrious companion in arms, and pointed you out in the event of his death as commander in chief of the American army. Never were the civil and military functions, mingled by necessity, more mildly, more faithfully, or more ably executed. The peace, which gave you a nation and crowned you with immortality, did not efface from the minds of your fellow citizens the just impressions which your meritorious services had stamped upon them. For twenty-one years you administered the government of the state! There is no eulogium of language that can equal the eulogium of the fact. He who in a republick like ours, where a revolution had let loose the passions where the press is licentious beyond all example—where suffrage, with few exceptions, is in every man's hands—where the popular will is almost without restraint—where demagogues, greedy of money, avaricious of popular honour, are numerous and ambitious, and, like all other demagogues, hypocritical, perfidious, remorseless; in such a republick, under such circumstances, his merit must be great, who, without flattering the vanity of the multitude, without courting their capricious favours, dignifiedly retains a station so elevated for a period so long. "I like," said Lord Mansfield, "that popularity which follows, not that which is run after." That great man liked, I fear, what he never enjoyed. You, sir, more happy, enjoyed, in plenitude, that which he liked.

From the chief magistracy of the state you were elected, in the year 1805, almost without your know ledge, certainly without your agency, to the second office in the national government. Here, maintaining the solid reputation you had acquired, it was expected, from your services and experience, from your capacity and the gradations of office, that you would have succeeded to the presidency, when Mr. Jefferson retired from it. This expectation would have been realized, had the election been free. Popularity still followed you, and, in its course and current, gained both rapidity and strength. But, although you were the favourite of the people, you were not the choice of the reigning president, and strange as it may seem, the president and his party, (and the president is too often the president of a party) by intrigue and manoeuvre, by trick and stratagem, can elude the principles of the constitution, and render them nugatory. Ill, sir, in this regard as you have been treated, prominent as the injustice and ingratitude of the nation are, I do not complain entirely on your account. If the example of Mr. Jefferson is to be followed; if it is to be "omnipotent" and "binding," leaving us, as has been contended for by his friends, no "option," the constitution is a dead letter; it is worse; it is a mockery; for whilst it *deludes us with the show,* and thrills us with the sound of freedom, it ingeniously, and almost without the possibility of a peaceful remedy, reduces us to a state of vassalage. Between this doctrine and practice, and the nature of an hereditary executive, I cannot perceive any essential difference.

The president and vice president are chosen by electors, who in some of the states are elected immediately by the people; in others, by the state legislatures. The constitution excludes, in terms, members of Congress and persons holding places of honour and profit under it from the electoral functions. The excluding provision was intended to keep out of the election the *influence* of gentlemen of both descriptions, but how easily is it dispensed with in practice!

Your locks, sir, are whitened in the service of your country. You have the age of ripe experience, and the experience of mature age. Yet Mr. Madison was the choice of Mr. Jefferson, for he was committed, it was thought, to his singular system of administration.

To Mr. Jefferson, a re-election had been offered by his party, but declined by him. In his circular letter of declension to the several states, he assigns, as reasons for declining, that he had served two terms; that as the constitution had not limited the duration of the service of a president, and evils of great magnitude might grow out of long incumbency, it was an act of patriotism to make a voluntary resignation of the office. In a popular government, professions so fair, concealing a purpose so foul, are sure to be applauded. The sage spoke like an angel, and it was therefore concluded that his actions must be angelick.

But forgetting, in the course of writing his circular, the reasons he had assigned for his voluntary retirement, perhaps in the intenseness of his purpose to strike a blow in favour of Mr. Madison, he unnecessarily went out of his way to deliver an homily on *old age*. In this he mentioned, in very pathetick terms, that the cares of office were too great for his advanced years; that his exhausted nature, sinking under those cares, urged tranquillity and ease; and he artfully pointed every one to the inference which he meant to be drawn, and which was drawn; that a gentleman, as far advanced in years as himself, (and you, sir, it was known was one or two years older) was unfit to be president of the United States!

He who under our system of government and management of parties obtains, no matter by what means, a nomination to an elective office, is sure to be elected, if his party, of the two parties into which the nation is divided, be the stronger. Every thing, therefore, depends upon *starting*, and the adroitness with which the candidate is *started*. When the candidate is nominated, (and the nomination is always made by a few) party doctrine and discipline are, that he must be supported. Party vengeance is next denounced against the noncomformist, and though he may not, perhaps, be consumed by fire and faggot, he is put out of the pale of the political church, and it becomes dangerous to give him encouragement in his business, or countenance in any other way.[2] By party law it cannot be asked, whether the candidate be a good moral man, or qualified by capacity and acquirements for the business of legislation. Questions of this nature, when nominations are made, are heresies, which, if obstinately persevered in, never fail to be punished.

Aware, when he composed his elegy on the cares of office and the quiet of old age, of this overbearing doctrine and overwhelming practice, Mr. Jefferson was sensible, that nothing was essential to the election of Mr. Madison, but the nomination of Mr. Madison, and that nothing was necessary to that nomination, but the expression of his own wish, however indirectly, that Mr. Madison should be nominated.

Accordingly, soon after the publication of his circular, a *caucus* of members of Congress, whose influence the constitution excludes from the elec-

---

2 The *republican* process is this. A meeting is publickly called at an ale-house. Resolutions, denouncing the dissenter by name, are drawn up; passed; signed by the chairman and secretary, and published in the newspapers. A person holding an office, or some way dependant on popular favour, is asked to officiate as chairman. If from the iniquity of the act which is about to be committed, he refuse, he is himself deemed recreant, and deprived of office, or of the popular favour, as the case may be. But there is no danger of this. A demagogue cares nothing about means but in their adaptation to his sinister purposes.

tion, was suddenly convened, at Washington city, under his own eyes, and by this caucus, Mr. Madison was nominated for the presidency.

The old, uniform, and slavish doctrine, was now again brought forth in all its horrours. The republicans were sorry, very sorry, they said so, and I believed them, that you, sir, were not nominated by the caucus; but, shrugging up their shoulders in token of regret, these champions of freedom, or rather, I must say, for I will speak out, these ignorant tramplers on constitutional law, or deliberate assassins of constitutional principles, mournfully added, that the nomination must be supported, or the party would be undone. They felt no solicitude for the cause; none for the principle; all was for the party; that is, in respect to the party chiefs, for immediate personal interest.

This act of intrigue on the one side, slavishness on the other, and ingratitude on all; this violation of the constitution, was carried triumphantly into effect by force of the logick which is frequently employed to preserve it. THE PEOPLE, in whom the power of delegation resides, and to whom, at short stated periods, the power having been exercised, it reverts, are the arbiters of political life and death. *Wheresoever the elective power is not with the intelligence of a nation, and it is not nor can it be where suffrage is universal,* the exertion of power will often be capricious, and not seldom in the highest degree tyrannical. In such a country, parties are more distinctly marked, more rancorous, more vindictive, more really hostile to each other, than in those nations, where liberty lives, moves, and has her being in a medium. And the more clearly parties are divided, the more cordial with each other the members of each are; the more mutual in their efforts; the more narrow and despotick in their opinions and practices. Hence it is that when the republican party succeeds against the federal in the election of a president, his administration must be, without exception, in gross, implicitly and zealously supported by his party; whether it be wise or foolish, weak or wicked, for the interest or against the interest of his country. It will be perceived, that in a state of things so discouraging, a republican president is in practice, though not in theory, of greater weight and consequence in the republick, than the royal personage is in a limited monarchy, and that he is backed by a force—the force of the press—the force of zeal—the force of popular assemblages—the force of inexorable party discipline, greater and less yielding than a king of England can even hope for. And that which is a rule out of Congress is a rule in it, for the popular will, dealing out rewards and punishments, commands in the representative, if he desire to retain his seat, the most rigid and humiliating obedience. Thus corroborated by a victorious party in the national legislature, to which the law, never openly, is yet always given by the president, is it surprising that Mr. Jefferson, wrapped up in popular mummy, in effect nominated his successor, controuled the national elective power, and broke down the national constitution; or that his party, that it might be entire, supported and applauded the violence?

Having witnessed the success of this combination of criminal intrigue and reprehensible acquiescence, my hopes of the duration of the republick are, I acknowledge, much less sanguine than they were wont to be. The substance of the constitution is essentially gone; the name, the unessential name, I may say only, is retained. The late practice is to be the permanent one; party has had it so; party will have it so: all argument has been derided.

Behold then the mode of election which is now established! See to what a shadow our boasted liberty is reduced!

The president, having gratified his own ambition, is about to retire: a successor is to be elected. The majority of Congress, elected by the dominant party, are assembled at Washington, in the character of legislators. The president, to whom more deference is paid by his party, and therefore by his party's representatives in Congress, than is usually paid to a king of England, indicates the person whom he wishes for his successor. The party members of Congress assemble in caucus, nominate the favourite of the retiring president, publish the nomination, and the party at large, which under all circumstances must be united, assemble in popular meetings. These meetings, which, whether visibly or not, are always directed and governed by two or three leading men, pass resolutions, applauding the nomination as *truly* republican, pledge themselves to its support, and intimate anathemas against those of the party who by speaking or writing manifest opposition to it: all this is matter of routine. A legislator who dissents cannot, but by a miracle, be re-elected; he loses his popularity; and where popularity is so precious, who will risk it? A disobedient placeman forfeits his place, and as office and emolument are every thing, it will not be inferred, that nonconformists amongst this class of citizens will be numerous.

Such is the rule; such the practice. The president may therefore appoint his successor. The presidency, therefore, though not in name, is yet in party management and detail next to hereditary: it is not elective for such a process cannot amount to any thing more than a mockery of election.

In addition to party influence on party representatives, (and they are all party representatives) other motives dispose them to gratify the wishes of the retiring president. In appointments to office, the national executive has very extensive patronage. Several members of the caucus by which Mr. Madison was nominated, resigning their seats in Congress seemingly for the purpose, were immediately appointed to distinguished and lucrative places by Mr. Jefferson. Nor can the new president be unmindful of those to whom he is indebted for his election. He will not be ungrateful.

These evils are reluctantly confessed by the friends of a nomination of the president by Congress; by those who fiercely support it; by those who outrage freedom of opinion to carry it successfully into effect; but they at the same time contend, in a manner that leaves no hope of a mitigation of the practice, that there is no other commodious or feasible rule. This is thought fully dispensing with the constitution as *visionary and impracticable.* It is true that the constitutional method might sometimes put party prevalence in jeopardy; I admit the possibility, but if this were an evil, it should be remembered, that national freedom may best be maintained by an alternate succession to power of the rival parties.

By executive management, by party obedience, by that inordinate love of popularity and place which characterize the more intelligent part of our citizens, the constitution has suffered a severe shock, and you, venerable patriot, who were the choice of the people for the presidency, have been deprived of their support for that office.

You have lived, sir, to see two revolutions; one from a monarchy to a republick; the other from a republick to something very like a monarchy. In the first you acted, acted nobly; in the second, you and the nation have been acted upon; acted upon unworthily. Perhaps there never was a nation, enjoying lights like those of the present age, and possessing a government whose elements are free, which in so short a period after its establishment was in such imminent danger of losing its freedom.

In other nations, governments, by force or by fraud, have abridged the liberty of the people, but, dividing ourselves into two parties, each more intent upon its preservation against the other than watchful over the liberties of the whole, we knowingly recede from freedom, and offer our necks for the yoke.

Every thing is inverted. Party is not modelled by the constitution, nor does it yield to its force. If the preservation of constitutional principles be incompatible with the maintenance of party maxims, drawn from party animosity, from party struggles, from party convenience, of which the personal aggrandizement of a few demagogues is the main spring, constitutional principles are no longer estimable. That a retiring national executive, co-operating with expectant members of Congress, should avail themselves of this delirium to impose upon the nation a president of their own choice, suiting their own views, answering their own purposes, can excite no surprise. A people that invites slavery cannot long be free.

I have the honour to be,
With the greatest respect,
Your most obedient
Humble servant,
JAMES CHEETHAM.

New York, October, 1809.

Table of Contents

Foreword

Never meet your heroes, they say, and the dictum has seldom been better embodied than in this volume, the first full account of the life of Thomas Paine, written by a contemporaneous author. Unlike the two hostile biographies published in his lifetime—George Chalmer's, in 1791, and William Cobbett's, 1793, both with the same title—this one was authored by someone who had known him personally; who had once been his admirer, disciple, and friend. For, indeed, James Cheetham, originally a hatter by trade, had known of him since his own days as a Manchester radical, when, as a member of the Constitutional Society, he engaged in anti-government agitation and had his own brushes with the law.

The biography appears to have been written in a rage: hardly had the Thetford pamphleteer's corpse gone cold in June 1809 when Cheetham applied quill to paper, bent on breaking down his subject before the maggots had their chance. He managed to complete, proof, and publish the text before the year was out—an astonishing celerity in an era when editing was done by hand and printing was laborious, time-consuming, and back-breaking work. It was done with movable type, one character at a time, after all. However, 37-year-old Cheetham was then responsible for two partisan periodicals, *The American Citizen* and *The American Watchman*, in which capacity he had frequently been sued for libel, so he was a stranger neither to writing fast nor to doing so insultingly.

Since then, Paine has received largely hagiographical treatment, even in Britain, whose government once indicted him for treason, and where he became second only to Guy Fawkes' as the personage most frequently burnt in effigy. Paine's native Thetford, in Norfolk, has seen it fit to put a guilded statue of him, by an American sculptor and in a dramatic pose, on permanent display. The statue in Lewes is equally idealised. And whatever paintings and engravings we have, even by contemporaries, were clearly produced by admirers. At worst he is described euphemistically as having been 'complex'.

Cheetham's contemptuous narrarative, which presents in *haut relief* all the negative features of Paine's prickly character, retells every gross anecdote retrievable from memory or from others who had known him; it sets out to record every tut, every eyeroll, and every exasperated sigh Paine might have caused, thus bringing us closer to the man behind the legend, and painting a much more relatable picture of the times in which he lived. We encounter him here as a deeply flawed human, with less than pristine motivations, whose company, never pleasant to begin with, became ever more intolerable with age. But then this his how the author knew him: as a cantakerous old man twice his age. And Cheetham does not appear to have been pleasant himself; like Paine, he had a penchant for burning bridges. Is this surprising? Revolutionaries make their careers out of being a pain in the neck and, however high-flown or 'enlightened' their rhetoric, their reasons are invariably personal, as much a consequence of their character and background as of whatever grievances originally impelled them into action. They are not generally known for their agreeableness.

Thus, the irritation of Paine's contemporaries is as much a valid and necessary historical document as is the admiration of their successors. A well rounded understanding of history and its movers demands that the hagiography be always counter-balanced by a demonography. In each case, we may either learn directly about the subject, or indirectly about the author, because even 'neutral' biographers cannot but project themselves onto their subjects. What is more, can we really trust these putatively neutral biographers? Their apparent balance, reasonableness, and calm tone arguably offers better concealment for their inevitable biases, omissions, framing, allegiances, selective emphases, etc., than do the airy panegyrics of friends or the frothing vituperation of enemies. At least with the latter we know where they stand and to seek further if we want the whole story. There is no such thing as neutrality or objectivity and a consensus offers only the illusion of protection: everyone has, albeit to different degrees, a position, an emotional response, an axe to grind, an ideology; all we have are competing perspectives, some more meritorious than others.

Whether vindictive or brutally honest—and even amiable biographers like John Keane interpret or explain rather than deny some of the unsavoury episodes—Cheetham's account remains classic 'history from below'.

Note on This Edition

The text herein presented is based on the 1809 edition printed in New York by Southwick and Pelsue. Said text is here reproduced in its entirety.

Punctuation and spelling, including archaic ones and variants on common words, have been left as in the original. This includes words like 'spunging', vs common 'sponging'; 'antedeluvian', vs 'antediluvian'; 'monarchial' vs 'monarchical'; 'politicks', etc. A few obvious typographical errors, however, have been corrected. Book titles cited by Cheetham, which in the original appear between quotation marks, or in plain Roman type, have been rendered in Italics. Proper names that appeared uncapitalised have been capitalised. So have military and office titles, and the names of various committes. Long quotations have been set as block quotes. A complement of editorial footnotes have been added to the author's own and marked accordingly. Where the author's footnotes have given a bibliographical citation, these have been reformatted according to modern convention, and whenever possible missing information been added. An index has been generated. The original appendix, which was some forty pages long and contained a variety of material, has been split into four appendices, with the contents grouped by category.

Preface

Two lives of Mr. Paine have been published; one by "Francis Oldys, of Philadelphia," a large octavo pamphlet, printed by Stockdale, London, 1792;[1] and an *Impartial Sketch*, an anonymous pamphlet of ten pages, published by T.

1 I have not seen a London copy of Oldys's *Life*, nor is there one either in our bookstores or in our city library. Mr. Cobbett says, that it was published in London in 1793, but as the *Impartial Sketch*, which was avowedly written to correct some of the extravagancies of Oldys, bears upon its title-page the London imprint of 1792, I conclude from that circumstance, and from Paine's *Rights of Man*, part second, having been published in February of the same year; that Mr. Cobbett was mistaken in the date.

Brown, Drury Lane, in the same year. To these may be added a continuation of Oldys's *Life*, by William Cobbett, Philadelphia, 1796.

Francis Oldys is, I believe, a fictitious name;[2] "of Philadelphia," was probably subjoined to give interest and authenticity to the work. The French revolution, that terrible concussion which had perniciously affected all Europe, and particularly England, had prepared the clubs for the unhinging doctrines of the *Rights of Man*. Never did the parched earth receive refreshing rain with more welcome, than that with which the revolutionary people of England admitted amongst them the tumultuous writings of Paine. To that which was his object; to commotion, to the overthrow of the government, and to blood shed, in all its horrid forms, they were rapidly hastening. Thus predisposed, the cordiality and enthusiasm with which the first part of the *Rights of Man* was greeted, although flattering to the vanity and encouraging to the hopes of the author, were not surprising. The clubs, zealous to a degree of frenzy; always vigilent, always alert, published a great edition of thirty thousand copies of the work, which was distributed amongst the poor, who could not afford to purchase. In the great manufacturing towns, Paine was considered by the ignorant as an apostle

2 It was: the author's real name was George Chalmers (1742-1825), a Scottish antiquarian and political writer, who was paid £500 by the British government to write a hostile biography of Thomas Paine. —Ed.

of freedom.[3] The government, alarmed, knew not how to meet the evil.[4] BURKE did, however, by his successive and impressive appeals, animate them to precautionary measures. In these, Oldys's life may, I think, be included. To deprive Paine of the momentary and undeserved popularity which he had acquired amongst the illiterate, whose passions were to have been worked up to a revolutionary pitch, was no doubt esteemed by the cabinet an object of some importance. To effect this purpose, Oldys's life was written; and perhaps I am not mistaken in ascribing it to the agency of the ministry. With many facts, such as Paine's birth, his education, his employment in the excise, his dismission from it, and his separation from his wife, are mingled more misrepresentations and distortions. On a work so evidently of a party nature, one cannot implicitly draw.

The *Impartial Sketch*, written by a friend of Paine, is not worthy of particular remark. It is a compilation from such parts of Oldys's narrative

3 A song was privately circulated, beginning with—

> God save *great* Thomas Paine,
> His Rights of Man proclaim,
> From Pole to Pole!

4 Mr. Burke, alluding to the language of the cabinet, says, "But I hear a language still more extraordinary, and indeed of such a nature as must suppose or leave us at their mercy. It is this; "you know their promptitude in writing, and their diligence in caballing: to write, speak, or act against them, will only stimulate them to new efforts." Appeal from the new to the old Whigs.

as suited the views of the writer, stripped of Oldys's exaggerations.

Mr. Cobbett's is really a continuation of Oldys's life. His superadditions are in the spirit of the original. His vigourous pen was wielded against Paine by passions yet more vigourous. Roused by the confusion which the author of the *Age of Reason* was endeavouring to raise all over the world, and dreading the prevalence of it in the United States, he censured to excess; censured, perhaps, without judgment, censuring without discrimination.

My information respecting Paine before he left England in 1774, is derived from persons who knew him when he was a boy—when he was at school—when he worked with his father at stay making—when he was in the excise—when he was married, and when he separated from his wife: much of this agrees with Oldys's facts referring to the same time.

Of his career in the colonies after his arrival in 1774, my sources of information, in addition to the journals of Congress, histories of the revolutionary war, &c. are gentlemen of the highest political standing, several of whom were members of the revolutionary Congress.

When the *Rights of Man* was first published, I was in England, involved in politicks, and tolerably well acquainted with political parties.

Respecting the conduct of Paine while in Paris, I draw the chief part of my information from notorious facts: and gentlemen equally distinguished in diplomacy and in literature, have favoured me with their correspondence.

After his return to the United States from France, I became acquainted with him on his arrival in New York, in the year 1802. He introduced himself to me by letter from Washington City, requesting me to take lodgings for him in New York. I accordingly engaged a room in Lovett's Hotel, supposing him to be a gentleman, and apprised him of the number. On his arrival, about ten at night, he wrote me a note desiring to see me immediately. I waited on him at Lovett's, in company with Mr. George Clinton, jun. We rapped at the door: a small figure opened it within, meanly dressed, having on an old top coat without an under one; a dirty silk handkerchief, loosely thrown round his neck; a long beard of more than a week's growth; a face, well carbunckled, fiery as the setting sun,[5] and the whole figure staggering under a load of inebriation. I was on the point of inquiring for Mr. Paine, when I saw in his countenance something of the portraits I had seen of him. We were desired to be seated. He had before him a small round table, on which were a beef-stake, some beer, a pint of brandy, a pitcher of water, and a glass. He sat eating, drinking, and talking, with as much composure as if he had lived with us all his life. I soon perceived that he had a very retentive memory, and was full of anecdote. The Bishop of

5 Falstaff's description of Bardolph's nose, would have suited Paine's.

Llanda[6] was almost the first word he uttered, and it was followed by informing us, that he had in his trunk a manuscript reply to the Bishop's *Apology*. He then, calmly mumbling his stake, and ever and anon drinking his brandy and beer, repeated the introduction to his reply, which occupied him near half an hour. This was done with deliberation, the utmost clearness, and a perfect apprehension, intoxicated as he was, of all that he repeated. Scarcely a word would he allow us to speak. He always, I afterwards found, in all companies, drunk or sober, would be listened to, but in this regard there were no *rights of men* with him, no equality, no reciprocal immunities and obligations, for he would listen to no one. Having repeated the introduction to his manuscript reply, he gave us the substance of the reply itself. He then recited from memory, in a voice very plaintive, some Asiatick lines, as specimens of morality equalling at least the sublime doctrines of the New Testament. He had read but little in the course of his life, much less than may have been supposed, but that little he had sorted, laid up in his intellectual store-house with care, and could deal it out with a facility and discrimination, which, however hated or despised, or on whatever account, was truly admirable.

My acquaintance with him continued, with very various views, two or three years. My intercourse

6 In 1796 Richard Watson (1737- 1816), Bishop of Llandaff, had published a rebuttal to Thomas Paine's *Age of Reason*, titled *An Apology for the Bible*. —Ed.

with him was more frequent than agreeble, but what I suffered in feeling from his want of good manners, his dogmatism, the tyranny of his opinions, his peevishness, his intemperance, and the low company he kept, was perhaps compensated by acquiring a knowledge of the man. The latter part of his life was spent in the city of New York, in a great measure under my own eye, but I have yet made particular inquiries of the persons in whose houses he successively lived, as to his manner of living, his temper, and his habits. The facts respecting his death and burial, and the opinions which he obstinately maintained on his death-bed, I have from a sensible and humane Quaker gentleman; from Doctor Manley, his kind and attending physician, and from his nurse, a woman of intelligence and piety.

The object of my labour is neither to please nor to displease any political party. I have written the life of Mr. Paine, not his panegyrick.

Life, &c.

Over families not distinguished by birth, by fortune, or by extraordinary talent, time throws an obscurity that cannot be removed. Of the grand-parents of Mr. Paine, we know little; of his ancestors still more remote, nothing. It is in intimated, possibly as imparting respectability, that his grand father was a small but respectable farmer.[1]

His father, who bore a good character, was a staymaker by trade, and a Quaker by religion, His

1 [Anonymous, *An*] *Impartial Sketch* [*of the Life of Thomas Paine* (London: T. Browne, 1792).]

mother, the daughter of a country attorney, was of the Church of England.

THOMAS PAINE was born at Thetford, in the county of Norfolk, England, in January, 1737. Whether he was baptised or not, is uncertain. Oldys affirms, that, probably owing to a religious disagreement between his parents, he was not, but that, through the care of his aunt, he was confirmed at the customary age by the bishop of Norwich.

The penury of his parents did not enable them to give him a college education. He was taught reading, writing, and arithmetick, at the Thetford free school, under the care of the Rev. Mr. Knowles.[2] His education was merely and scantily English. He left school at the age of thirteen. The few ordinary Latin phrases which we meet with in his works, he picked up when he found them either convenient or ostentatious.[3]

From school he was taken to his father's shop board, where he was taught staymaking. He worked with his father several years: Oldys and the *Impartial Sketch* say five.[4]

---

2 "My parents were not able to give me a shilling beyond what they gave me in education, and to do this they distressed themselves." *Rights of Man*, part 2.

3 He was, however, of opinion, towards the close of his life, that the old languages are superfluous. "As there is now nothing new to be learned from the dead languages, all the useful books being already translated, the languages are become useless, and the time expended in teaching and learning them is wasted." *Age of Reason*, part 1.

4 "When little more than sixteen years of age, I entered on board

From his father's, perhaps without his father's permission, he went, when sixteen, to London, whither Scotchmen and provincial adventurous English flock to make or mar their fortunes.

But necessity obliged him to work a few weeks at his trade, with a Mr. Morris, a staymaker, in Hanover street. From London he journeyed to Dover, where he worked at staymaking with a Mr. Grace.

About this time he entered on board the *Terrible*,[5] from which adventure, he observes, "I was happily prevented by the affectionate and moral remonstrance of a good father, who from his own habits of life, being of the Quaker profession, must begin to look upon me as lost."[6]

The effects of the moral remonstrance were not, however, durable. Disliking his trade, we may presume, he soon after entered in the "*King of Prussia* privateer, and went to sea."[7] How long he was at sea, or what the fruits of his cruise were, we do not learn. Brave in political warfare at his desk, he

---

the *Terrible* Privateer, Captain Death." *Rights of Man*, part 2. Oldys remarks, that the *Terrible* "not fitted out till some years afterwards;" but it is probable that Paine's statement is correct, and if it be, he could not have worked with his father more than two or three years. [Concerning Captain William Death and the Terrible privateer, see *A genuine and faithfull narrative of the unfortunate Captain William Death Commander of the Terrible Privateer* by Joseph Hart (London: Thomas Bailey, 1757). —Ed.]

5 Paine's Conversation.

6 *Rights of Man*, part 2.

7 *Rights of Man*, part 2.

was not made to *seek the bubble reputation in the cannon's mouth.*

In the year 1759, he settled at Sandwich, as a master staymaker.[8]

At Sandwich he married *Mary Lambert*, daughter of an exciseman, who shortly after went with him to Margate, where, in the year 1760, she died.[9] From Margate he went to London, and from London to his father's, at Thetford.

Perhaps his marriage with Miss Lambert led him to wish for a place in the excise, which, aided by the recorder of Thetford, he obtained, after much preparatory study for it, in the year 1761. It is not probable that the recorder would have used his influence for him, if his conduct towards his wife had been as atrocious as Oldys represents it. I am right in this conclusion, or the recorder could not have been acquainted with him, a circumstance which is not probable.

He retained his station in the excise until August, 1765, when, being guilty, Oldys says, of scandalous misconduct, he was dismissed from the office. The same author admits that he was restored to the excise the following year. This restoration

8 Oldys asserts, that ten pounds which he had borrowed of Miss Grace upon a promise of marriage, daughter of Mr. Grace, staymaker, of Dover, with whom he had worked, enabled him to commence business, but that he neither repaid the money nor married the girl. He adds, that at Sandwich, Paine preached at his lodgings as an independent minister.

9 Oldys insinuates that she died of a premature birth, occasioned by ill usage.

does, I think, disprove that fact. If he had been dismissed for gross misconduct, it is not probable that he would have been restored. The offence was no doubt a venial one. During his dismission, he resided in London, where he taught English, in an Academy, at a salary of twenty five pounds a year.

In March, 1768, he was stationed as an excise man at Lewes, in Sussex, where he lived with Samuel Ollive, grocer and tobacconist. Mr. Ollive died the following year. Shortly after his death, Paine, probably with the approbation of his widow and daughter, opened the grocery and worked the tobacco mill, in his own name. In 1771, he married ELIZABETH OLLIVE, daughter of Samuel.

It is mentioned that he this year wrote an electioneering song for one of the candidates for the honour of representing New Shoreham, in parliament, for which he got three guineas, and that in the next year he wrote the case[10] of the excisemen, who, united throughout the kingdom, were applying for an increase of salary. Whether the song and the case were written by him or not, is very problematical. In the *Crisis*, No. 3, he says:—"I never troubled others with my notions till very lately, and never published a syllable in England in my life;" but he was not always veracious.

In April, 1774, sinking under accumulated misfortunes, the effects of his shop were sold to pay his debts. In the same month, having dealt as a grocer in exciseable articles, and being suspected, I know

10 Said to be an octavo Pamphlet, of 21 pages.

not how justly, of mal-practices in the excise,[11] he was a second time dismissed. He petitioned to be restored, but without success.

In May of the same year, Paine and his wife entered into articles of separation, which, in the following June, probably in consequence of a defect in formality, were redrawn.[12]

---

11 Oldys says, that availing himself of his place in the excise, he smuggled tobacco for the use of his mill.

12 Mr. Carver, of this city, who when a boy went to school with Miss Ollive, and was well acquainted with her and Paine when they were married, relates to me, as having been notorious in Lewes, the following extraordinary fact. From some cause which Paine would not explain, and which is yet unascertained, he never, Mr. Carver affirms, had *sexual intercourse with his wife*. This almost incredible circumstance, which became the subject of the borough conversation, Mr. Carver adds, was stated by Mrs. Paine in answer to a question which had been put to her by her friend, Mrs. Tibott, on observing, some weeks after their marriage, the gloominess of her mind. Despised by the women, jeered by the men, and charged with a want of virility, Paine submitted, Mr. Carver continues, to a professional scrutiny. He was examined by Doctors Turner, Ridge, and Manning, who pronounced that there was no natural defect. On Doctor Turner's inquiring into the cause of his abstinence, Paine answered, that it was no body's business but his own; that he had cause for it, but that he would not name it to any one. It appears that he accompanied his wife from the altar, but that, though they lived in the same house for three years after their marriage, they had from the day of their nuptials separate beds, and never cohabited together. Of these facts Mr. Carver has offered me an affidavit, but I have thought it unnecessary. He stated them all to Paine in a private letter which he wrote to him about a year before his death; to which no answer was returned: Mr. Carver showed me the letter soon after it was written.

Paine lived with Mr. Carver in this city: they were bosom friends. Mr. Carver kept his company three or four years,

His little property having been sold—himself a second time dismissed from the excise—the separation from his wife completed, and being reduced almost to beggary, Paine, in want of every thing that makes life agreeable, travelled, mournfully no doubt, from Lewes to London. What he had recourse to in the metropolis for a livelihood, neither Oldys nor the *Impartial Sketch* offers a conjecture, but a member of the revolutionary Congress told me, that when Dr. Franklin first knew him, which was about the middle of the year 1774, he was a garret writer. In this situation, he procured an introduction to Dr. Franklin, who advised him to go to America.[13] He accordingly sailed from England in September, 1774, and arrived at Philadelphia just before the affair at Lexington, which happened April 19, 1775.[14] Here his political career commences. While in England, we find him struggling, indeed, with poverty, buts with regard to politicks, not at all discontented.[15] No opposition is mentioned either by his partial or his impartial biographer. Nor did he, if in conversation he ever recurred to this infelicitous period of his life, speak

---

which was perhaps as long as any body could keep it.

13 "The favour of Dr. Franklin's friendship I possessed in England, and my introduction to this part of the world, was through his patronage." *Crisis*, No. 3.

14 "It was my fate to come to America a few months before the breaking out of hostilities." *Crisis*, No. 7.

15 "I had no disposition for what was called politicks." *Age of Reason*, part 1, p. 66, New York, 1795. He alludes to the time when he was a second time dismissed from the excise.

of him self as having meddled with government.[16] His only opposition to it seems to have been that of an exciseman, who naturally enough wanted additional pay. If he had been reinstated in the excise after his second dismission, and could have retained his place, it is probable that he would have lived and died in his native land. But he was abandoned, it may be said, by man and woman, and he did well to change the scene. England had no longer any enjoyment for him. Poor, resourceless, and almost without hope, from government he expected nothing, and if he turned his thoughts upon his wife, upon that which should have been his home, and upon all their endearing and inappreciable ties, what would have been his feelings had he possessed the ordinary sensibility of an ordinary man?

His first engagement in Philadelphia was with Mr. Aitkin, a reputable Bookseller. In January,

---

16 The following anecdote, which in conversation he related himself, first turned his thoughts, he remarked, to government, "After playing at Bowls, at Lewes, retiring to drink some punch, Mr. Verril, one of the Bowlers, observed, alluding to the wars of Frederick, that the king of Prussia was the best fellow in the world for a king, he had so much of the devil in him. This, striking me with great force, occasioned the reflection, that if it were necessary for a king to have so much of the devil in him, kings might very beneficially be dispensed with."

The thought was not, however, in England, followed up by action. *There*, he was neither a ministerialist nor an antiministerialist. Whenever he turned his attention to government, it was only for a place, or for an increase of the salary of that which he held: he was thirty seven when he left England.

1775, Mr. Aitkin commenced the publication of the *Pennsylvania Magazine*, and Paine's business was to edit it. His introduction to the Magazine, dated January 24th, 1775, is thus concluded:

> Thus encompassed with difficulties, this first number of the *Pennsylvania Magazine* entreats a favourable reception; of which we shall only say, [that,] like the early *snow drop*, it comes forth in a barren season, and contents itself with foretelling, that CHOICER FLOWERS are preparing to appear.

To the politeness of Dr. Rush, of Philadelphia, who was a member of the memorable Congress, which, on the 4th July, 1776, declared the colonies "*Free and Independent States*," I am indebted for the following interesting letter.

Philadelphia, July 17th, 1809,

SIR,

In compliance with your request, I send you herewith, answers to your questions relative to the late Thomas Paine.

He came to Philadelphia about the year 1772,[17] with a short letter of introduction from Dr. Franklin to one of his friends. His design was to open a school for the instruction of young ladies in several branches of knowledge, which, at that time, were seldom taught in the female schools of our country.

---

17 Dr. Rush is mistaken. It was 1774.

About the year 1773,[18] I met him accidentally in Mr. Aitkin's bookstore, and was introduced to him by Mr. Aitkin. We conversed a few minutes, when I left him. Soon afterwards I read a short essay with which I was much pleased, in one of Bradford's papers, against the slavery of the Africans in our country, and which I was informed was written by Mr. Paine. This excited my desire to be better acquainted with him. We met soon afterwards in Mr. Aitkin's book store, where I did homage to his principles and pen upon the subject of the enslaved Africans. He told me the essay to which I alluded, was the first thing he had ever published in his life. After this Mr. Aitkin employed him as the editor of his Magazine, with a salary of fifty pounds currency a year. This work was well supported by him. His song upon the death of Gen. Wolfe,[19]

18 1775.

19 I have procured this beautiful Song, and as some groundless doubts have been expressed whether or no Paine was the author of it, I will here insert it.

GENERAL WOLFE.

In a mouldering cave where the wretched retreat
Britannia sat wasted with care;
She mourn'd for her Wolfe, and exclaim'd against fate,
And gave herself up to despair:
The walls of her cell she had sculptur'd around
With the feats of her favourite son;
And even the dust as it lay on the ground
Was engrav'd with some deeds he had done.

The sire of the gods from his Crystalline throne
Beheld the disconsolate Dame;
And mov'd with her tears he sent Mercury down

and his reflections upon the death of Lord Clive, gave it a sudden currency which few works of that kind have since had in our country.

When the subject of American Independence began to be agitated in conversation, I observed the publick mind to be loaded with an immense mass of prejudice and error relative to it. Something appeared to be wanting, to remove them, beyond the ordinary short and cold addresses of newspaper publications. At this time I called upon Mr. Paine and suggested to him the propriety of preparing our citizens for a perpetual separation of our country from Great Britain,

---

And these were the Tidings that came:
Britannia, forbear, not a sigh or a tear
For thy Wolfe, so deservedly lov'd;
Your tears shall be chang'd into triumphs of joy,
For Wolfe is not dead, but remov'd.

The sons of the east, the proud giants of old,
Have crept from their darksome abodes;
And this is the news, as in Heav'n it was told,
They were Marching to War with the Gods;
A Council was held in the Chambers of Jove
And this was their final decree:
That Wolfe should be call'd to the Army above,
And the charge was intrusted to me.

To the plains of Quebec with the orders I flew,
He begg'd for a moment's delay;
He cry'd, oh forbear, let me Victory hear,
And then thy command I'll obey:
With a darksome thick film I encompass'd his eyes
And bore him away in an urn;
Lest the fondness he bore to his own native shore
Should induce him again to return.

by means of a work of such length as would obviate all the objections to it. He seized the idea with avidity, and immediately began his famous pamphlet in favour of that measure. He read the sheets to me at my house as he composed them. When he had finished them, I advised him to put them into the hands of Dr. Franklin, Samuel Adams, and the late Judge Wilson, assuring him, at the same time, that they all held the same opinions that he had defended. The first of those gentlemen saw the manuscript, and I believe the second, but Judge Wilson being from home when Mr. Paine called upon him, it was not subjected to his inspection. No addition was made to it by Dr. Franklin, but a passage was struck out, or omitted in printing it, which I conceived to be one of the most striking in it. It was the following— "A greater absurdity cannot be conceived of, than three millions of people running to their sea coast every time a ship arrives from London, to know what portion of liberty they should enjoy."

A title only was wanted for this pamphlet before it was committed to the press. Mr. Paine proposed to call it "plain truth." I objected to it and suggested the title of *Common Sense*. This was instantly adopted, and nothing now remained, but to find a printer who had boldness enough to publish it. At that time there was a certain Robert Bell, an intelligent Scotch bookseller and printer in Philadelphia, whom I knew to be as high toned as Mr. Paine upon the subject of American Independence. I mentioned the pamphlet to him, and he at once consented to run the risk of publishing it. The author and the printer were immediately brought together, and "*Common Sense*" bursted from the press of the latter in a few days with an effect which has rarely been produced by types and paper in any age or country.

Between the time of the publication of this pamphlet, and the 4th of July, 1776, Mr. Paine published a number of essays in Mr. Bradford's paper, under the signature of "The Forester," in defence of the opinions contained in his *Common Sense.*

In the summer and autumn of 1776, he served as a volunteer, in the American army under General Washington. Whether he received pay and rations, I cannot tell. He lived a good deal with the officers of the first rank in the army, at whose tables his "*Common Sense*" always made him a welcome guest.

The legislature of Pennsylvania gave Mr. Paine 500 *l.*[20] as an acknowledgment of the services he had rendered the United States by his publications.

He acted as clerk to the legislature of Pennsylvania about the year 1780. I do not know the compensation he received for his services in that station. He acted for a while as secretary of the Secret Committee of Congress, but was dismissed by them for publishing some of their secrets relative to Mr. Dean.

Mr. Paine's manner of life was desultory. He often visited in the families of Dr. Franklin, Mr. Rittenhouse, and Mr. George Clymer, where he made himself acceptable by a turn he discovered for philosophical, as well as political subjects.

After the year 1776, my intercourse with Mr. Paine was casual. I met him now and then at

20 Approximately, £71,000 in 2021 money. —Ed.

> the tables of some of our Whig citizens, where he spoke but little, but was always inoffensive in his manner and conversation.
>
> I possess one of his letters written to me from France upon the subject of the abolition of the slave trade. An extract from it was published in the *Columbian Magazine*.
>
> I did not see Mr. Paine when he passed through Philadelphia a few years ago. His principles, avowed in his *Age of Reason*, were so offensive to me that I did not wish to renew my intercourse with him.
>
> I have thus briefly and in great haste endeavoured to answer your questions. Should you publish this letter, I beg my testimony against Mr. Paine's infidelity may not be omitted in it.
>
> From, sir,
> Yours,
> Respectfully,
> BENJN. RUSH.
>
> MR. CHEETHAM.

Paine continued his superintendence of the magazine several months. In one of his lucubrations, adverting to the riches of the earth, the diligence which is necessary to discover, and the labour to possess them, he thus elegantly invites us to industry and research.

> Though nature is gay, polite, and generous abroad, she is sullen, rude, and niggardly at home: Return the visit, and she admits you with all the suspicion of a miser, and all the reluc-

> tance of an antiquated beauty retired to replenish her charms. Bred up in antideluvian notions, she has not yet acquired the European taste of receiving visitants in her dressing-room: She locks and bolts up her private recesses with extraordinary care, as if not only resolved to preserve her hoards, but to conceal her age, and hide the remains of a face that was young and lovely in the days of Adam. He that would view nature in her undress, and partake of her internal treasures, must proceed with the resolution of a robber, if not a ravisher. She gives no invitation to follow her to the cavern.—The external earth makes no proclamation of the interior stores, but leaves to chance and industry, the discovery of the whole. In such gifts as nature can annually re-create, she is noble and profuse, and entertains the whole world with the interest of her fortunes; but watches over the capital with the care of a miser. Her gold and jewels lie concealed in the earth in caves of utter darkness; the hoards of wealth, heaps upon heaps, mould in the chests, like the riches of a necromancer's cell. It must be very pleasant to an adventurous speculatist to make excursions into these Gothic regions; and in his travels he may possibly come to a cabinet locked up in some rocky vault, whose treasures shall reward his toil, and enable him to shine on his return, as splendidly as nature herself.

At what period he left the employ of Mr. Aitkin, who died some years since, I have not been able to ascertain, but probably not until early in the year, 1776.

Of the independence of the colonies, for some time after the affair at Lexington, few thought and no one wrote. Here and there it was indistinctly mentioned, but no where encouraged. Never were a people more attached to a government and nation, than were the colonists to the government and people of England. Reconciliation so adjusted as to have left them the right of granting their own money by their Provincial Assemblies, would have been universally satisfactory. There was no wish for a separation; none for a republick. That indulgence which might have been allowed, which was compatible with the British constitution, and essential to freedom, would have retained the colonies to the Crown, we know not how long, but probably for a century at least.[21] In this spirit of cordial affection, Congress, on the 8th of July, 1775, petitioned the king, most humbly imploring his majesty to devise some method by which English freedom might be extended and secured to the colonies.

---

21 Alluding to the predominant wishes of the colonists soon after his arrival, Paine says:—"I found the disposition of the people such, that they might have been led by a thread, and governed by a reed. Their attachment to Britain was obstinate, and it was at that time a kind of treason to speak against it; they disliked the ministry, but they esteemed the nation. Their idea of grievance operated without resentment, and their single object was reconciliation." *Crisis*, No. 7.

"Independence was a doctrine scarce and rare even to wards the conclusion of the year '75. All our politicks had been founded on the hope or expectation of making the matter up; a hope, which though general on the side of America, had never entered the head or heart of the British court." *Crisis*, No. 3.

Attached, they say, to your majesty's person, family, and government, with all the devotion which principle and affection can inspire; connected with Great Britain by the strongest ties that can unite societies, and deploring every event that tends in any degree to weaken them, we solemnly assure your majesty, that we not only most ardently desire the former harmony between her and these colonies may be restored, but that a concord may be established between them upon so firm a basis as to perpetuate its blessings, uninterrupted by any future dissentions, to succeeding generations in both countries.

We therefore beseech your majesty, that your royal authority and influence may be graciously interposed to procure us relief from our afflicting fears and jealousies, and to settle peace through every part of your dominions; with all humility submitting to your majesty's wise consideration, whether it may not be expedient, for facilitating these important purposes, that your majesty be pleased to direct some mode by which the united applications of your faithful colonists to the throne, may be improved into a happy and permanent reconciliation.[22]

---

22 *Journals of Congress.*

Mr. Burke has a passage respecting Dr. Franklin which evinces the Doctor's attachment to the British government how strongly soever he may have been opposed to some of its acts,

"What might have been in the secret thoughts of some of their leaders, it is impossible to say. As far as a man, so looked up as Dr. Franklin, could be expected to communicate his ideas, I believe he opened them to Mr. Burke. It was, I think, the very day before he sat out for America, that a very long

Congress directed the petition, on which the hopes of the colonists principally rested, to be presented to the king by Mr. Penn, who was sent to England on purpose, accompanied by the colony agents residing in London. On the first of September, 1775, it was presented, and on the fourth of the same month, Mr. Penn was told, by Lord Dartmouth, that "no answer would be given to it." The king's haughty and contumelious decision was received by Congress at the close of October, and the effect of it on the colonists was inconceivable. From the top of expectation they were all at once precipitated down to the lowest abyss of despondency. All prospect of relief from England had vanished.

---

conversation passed between them, and with a greater air of openness on the Doctor's side than Mr. Burke had observed in him before. In this discourse Dr. Franklin lamented, and with apparent sincerity, the separation which he feared was inevitable between Great Britain and her Colonies. He certainly spoke of it as an event which gave him the greatest concern. America, he said, would never again see such happy days as she had passed under the protection of England. He observed, that ours was the only instance of a great empire, in which the most distant parts and members had been as well governed as the metropolis and its vicinage; but that the Americans were going to lose the means which secured to them this rare and precious advantage. The question with them was not whether they were to remain as they had been before the troubles, for better, he allowed, they could not hope to be, but whether they were to give up so happy a situation without a struggle? Mr. Burke had several other conversations with him about that time, in none of which, soured and exasperated as his mind certainly was, did he discover any other wish in favour of America than for a security of its ancient condition. "Appeal from the new to the old Whigs", works, vol. 6, p. 121-2, London, 1803.

With the images of their brethren slaughtered at Lexington fresh in memory, their condition was a defenceless one. Called upon for unconditional submission, they were menaced with military execution in case of disobedience. Still, even now, few thought seriously of independence. The mind was over powered by fear, rather than alive to safety.

Paine, like Milton's vanquished fiend, looking back malignantly on England as a Paradise lost to him; availing himself of this awful pause, and joyously turning to his account the high handed measures of an infatuated cabinet, wrote his *Common Sense*; probably in revenge for his expulsion from the excise. This pamphlet, of forty octavo pages,[23] holding out relief by proposing INDEPENDENCE to an oppressed and despairing people, was published in January, 1776. Speaking a language which the colonists had felt but not thought, its popularity, terrible in its consequences to the parent country, was unexampled in the history of the press.[24] At first, involving the

23 Philadelphia ed. 1797.

24 "*Nothing could be better timed than this performance.* In union with the feelings and sentiments of the people, it produced surprising effects. Many thousands were convinced, and were led to approve and long for a separation from the mother country: though that measure, a few months before, was not only foreign from their wishes but the object of their abhorrence, the current suddenly became so strong in its favour that it bore down all before it." *Ramsay's Rev.*, vol. 1, p. 336-7, London, 1793.

"The publications which have appeared, have greatly promoted the spirit of independency, but no one so much as the

colonists, it was thought, in the crime of rebellion, and pointing to a road leading inevitably to ruin, it was read with indignation and alarm, but when the reader, (and everybody read it) recovering from the first shock, re-perused it, its arguments, nourishing his feelings and appealing to his pride, reanimated his hopes and satisfied his understanding, that *Common Sense*, backed by the resources and force of the colonies, poor and feeble as they were, could alone rescue them from the unqualified oppression with which they were threatened. The unknown author, in the moments of enthusiasm which succeeded, was hailed as an angel sent from heaven to save from all the horrours of slavery, by his timely, powerful, and unerring councils, a faithful, but abused, a brave, but misrepresented people.[25]

---

pamphlet under the signature of *Common Sense*, written by Mr. Thomas Paine, an Englishman. *Nothing could have been better timed than this performance*: it has produced most astonishing effects." *Gordon's Rev.*, vol. 2, p. 78. New York, 1794.

25 When *Common Sense* arrived in Albany, the Convention of New York was in session. General Scott, a leading Member, alarmed at the boldness and novelty of its arguments, mentioned his fears to several of his distinguished colleagues, and suggested a private meeting in the evening, for the purpose of writing an answer. They accordingly met, and Mr. Mc Kesson read the pamphlet through. At first it was deemed both necessary and expedient to answer it without delay, but casting about for the requisite arguments, they concluded to adjourn and meet again. In a few evenings they re-assembled, but so rapid was the change of opinion in the colonies at large, in favour of independence, that they ultimately agreed not to oppose it.

As a literary work, *Common Sense*, energetically as it promoted the cause of independence, has no merit. Defective in arrangement, inelegant in diction, here and there a sentence excepted; with no profundity of argument, no felicity of remark, no extent of research, no classical allusion, nor comprehension of thought, it is fugitive in nature, and cannot be appealed to as authority on the subject of government. Its distinguishing characteristicks are boldness and zeal; low sarcasm and deep-rooted malevolence. It owed its unprecedented popularity, on the one hand, to the British cabinet, which sought to triumph by bare-faced force instead of generous measures; and, on the other, to the manly spirit of the colonists, which, though often depressed, could not be conquered.

Yet Paine, vain beyond any man I ever read of,[26] or ever knew, was of opinion, in which indeed he was partly correct, that he was not only an efficacious agent in effecting the independence of the colonies, the very *prop and stay of the house*, but that the revolution, of which he was in a great measure the parent, "led to the *discovery* of the principles of government:" The assertion was undoubtedly a dictate of gross ignorance. "One of the great advantages of the American revolution has been, that it led to the discovery of the principles,

26 "I possess more of what is called consequence in the world, than any one in Mr. Burke's catalogue of Aristocrats." *Rights of Man*, part 2.

and laid open the impositions of government."[27] He might have correctly said that it led, in some respects, to a new *practice*, but certainly no new *principle* was discovered.

But if a new principle had been discovered, it is obvious that Paine, the chief if not the only writer who with success supported the revolution, considered himself as a second Columbus, and that as we owe the discovery of the land to the genius of the one, so we are indebted for the principle to the researches of the other.

Common Sense treats of the "origin and design of government; of monarchy and hereditary succession; of the ability of America" to become independent.

On the first two heads, which alone afforded scope for the discovery of a new principle, he is brief and feeble. He had, indeed, thought on the subject, but not deeply; perhaps he had read, though he affirms that he had not.[28] If this be so, as no force of genius can adequately supply the defects of study, so no probable degree of vanity could have flattered him with the high expectation of being ranked in history with the Harringtons, the Sydneys, and the Lockes of England; men who have enlightened the

27 *Rights of Man*, part 2.

28 Adverting to the commencement of his revolutionary labours in America, he remarks: "I saw an opportunity in which I thought I could do some good, and I followed exactly what my heart dictated. I neither read books nor studied other peoples' opinions." *Rights of Man*, part 2.

world with their works; enlightened England; England, whence we have drawn all that is excellent in our constitution and worthy in our practice.

His observations on the origin of government, but lightly touching the subject, are trite; those on monarchy and hereditary succession, of no greater solidity, are not new: it was on the latter, however, that he valued himself. Here, if he had not discovered a new principle, he fancied he had applied a new argument. Let us examine his pretensions.

> To the evils of monarchy we have added that of hereditary succession; and as the first is a degradation and lessening of ourselves, so the second, claimed as a matter of right, is an insult and imposition on posterity. For all men being originally equal, no one by birth could have a right to set up his own family in perpetual preference to all others forever, and though himself might deserve some decent degree of honours of his contemporaries, yet his descendants might be too unworthy to inherit them. One of the strongest natural proofs of the folly of hereditary right in kings is, that nature disapproves it, otherwise she would not so frequently turn it into ridicule by giving mankind an ass for a lion.[29]

This is the *only* argument contained in *Common Sense* against hereditary succession. The conclusion, that which he terms the "strongest natural proof," although, the period of its publication con-

29 *Common Sense*, p. 13, Phil. 1797.

sidered, perhaps very popular, is an impertinent and vulgar sarcasm altogether unworthy of the subject. The first part, that which alone is entitled to the appellation of an argument, I should have judged he had clandestinely taken from Locke, had he not told us that he "read no books, studied no man's opinions."

"Men being, as has been said, by nature, all free, equal, and independent, no one can be put out of his estate, and subjected to the political power of another without his consent."[30]

> It is true, that whatever engagement or promises any one has made for himself, he is under the obligation of them, but cannot, by any compact whatever, bind his children or posterity; for his son, when a man, being altogether as free as his father, an act of his father can no more give away the liberty of his son than it can of anybody else.[31]

His strictures on the ability of the colonies to become independent, contain nothing remarkable. A very ordinary writer might have written them.

Accident directed the thoughts of the Americans to a republick. When *Common Sense* was written, the friends of independence were not re-

30 Locke, "Of Government", *Works of John Locke*, 10 vols. (London: J. Johnson, 1801) vol. 5, p. 394

31 Locke, "Of Government", *Works of John Locke*, 10 vols. (London: J. Johnson, 1801) vol. 5, p. 407-8

publicans. Paine's invectives against monarchy were intended against the monarchy of England, rather than against monarchy in general, and they were popular in the degree to which the measures and designs of the British cabinet were odious.[32] The question, when no alternative but colonial vassalage or national independence presented it

32 "For a long course of years, my amiable young friends, before the birth of the oldest of you, I was called to act with your fathers in concerting measures the most disagreeable and dangerous, not from a desire of innovation, not from discontent with the government, *under which we were born and bred*, but to preserve the honour of our country, and vindicate the *immemorial liberties of our ancestors*. In pursuit of these measures, it became, not an object of predilection and choice, but of indispensable necessity, to assert our independence."—President Adams's reply to the address of the young men of Philadelphia, 1798. Boston Ed.

Here he plainly says that he was indeed in favour of independence, but not of a form of government different from that of England. He was attached "to the immemorial liberty of his ancestors!" What liberty? That which, according to the constitution of England, is allowed by the king, the house of lords, and the house of commons.

"I have had doubts of John Adams ever since the year 1776. In conversation with me at that time, concerning a pamphlet of mine, (*Common Sense*] he censured it because it attacked monarchial governments." Paine's second letter to the people of the United States, dated Washington City, 1802.

As Paine rarely hesitated at the propagation of a falsehood, ministering either to his vanity or to his malice, I would not have quoted him in favour of my position, that the friends of independence were not originally advocates of a republick, if he were not in this instance strengthened and confirmed by a thousand facts and circumstances, Paine's remark is as applicable to the whole of the Congress of 1774-5-6, and so on, and to the colonists at large, as to Mr. Adams.

self, was one merely of independence, for as Mr. Adams truly remarked, the colonists had no wish but for the "immemorial liberties of their ancestors." To this may be added the observation of Dr. Franklin, that they could not even hope for a government under which they could enjoy liberties more precious.

On the fourth of July, 1776, Congress declared the colonies "free and independent states,"[33] which

---

33 The writer of the declaration of Independence has been applauded much beyond the merits of the composition. The declaration consists of two parts; a solemn recognition and enunciation of a principle, and an enumeration of the grievances of the colonists. To the enumeration, no extraordinary ability was necessary, and as to the principle, it is evidently taken from Locke, without the candour of an acknowledgment.

"Prudence, indeed, will dictate, that government should not be changed for light and transient causes, and accordingly all experience has shown, that mankind are more disposed to suffer, while evils are sufferable, than to right themselves by abolishing the forms to which they are accustomed." Declaration of Independence.

"It is true such men may stir whenever they please, but it will be only to their own just ruin and perdition, for until the mischief be grown general, and the evil designs of the rulers become visible, the people, who are more disposed to suffer than to right themselves by resistance, are not apt to stir." Locke, "Of Government", *Works of John Locke* (London: J. Johnson, 1801) vol. 5, p. 474-5.

"But when a long train of abuses and usurpations, pursuing invariably the same course, evinces a design to reduce them under absolute despotism, it is their right, it is their duty to throw off such government, and to provide new guards for their future safety." Declaration of Independence.

"But if a long train of abuses, prevarications, and artifices, all tending the same way, make the design visible to the people,

was as soon after the publication of *Common Sense*, Paine remarks "as the work could spread through such an extensive country."[34]

Paine now accompanied the army of independence as a sort of itinerant writer, of which his pen was an appendage almost as necessary and formidable as its cannon. Having no property, he fared as the army fared, and at the same expence, but to what mess he was attached I have not been able to learn, although, from what I hear and know, it must, I think, though he was sometimes admitted into higher company, have been a subaltern one. When the colonists drooped, he revived them with a *Crisis*. The first of these numbers he published

---

and they cannot but feel what they lie under and see 'whither they are going, it is not to be wondered that they should then rouse themselves, and endeavour to put the rule into such hands which may secure to them the ends for which government was first erected." Locke, "Of Government", *Works of John Locke* (London: J. Johnson, 1801) vol. 5, p. 472.

There is great similarity in the following sentences, excepting only the superiour energy and eloquence of Milton's style. Speaking of "reason and free inquiry," Mr. Jefferson says: "Give a loose to them, they will support the true religion, by bringing every false one to their tribunal, to the test of their investigation: they are the natural enemies of errour, and of errour only." *Notes on Virginia*, p. 236, New York, 1801.

"And though all the winds of doctrine were let loose to play upon the earth, so truth be in the field, we do injuriously to misdoubt her strength. Let her and falsehood grapple, who ever knew truth put to the worse in a free and open encounter?" Milton's speech for the liberty of unlicensed printing, *Works*, vol. 1., p. 326. Lond., 1806.

34 See his Will in the appendix.

early in December, 1776. The object of it was good, the method excellent, and the language, suited to the depressed spirits of the army, of publick bodies, and of private citizens, cheering. WASHINGTON, defeated on Long-Island, had retreated to New York, and been driven with great loss from Forts Washington and Lee. The gallant little army, overwhelmed with a rapid succession of misfortunes, was dwindling away, and all seemed to be over with the cause when scarcely a blow had been struck. "These," said the *Crisis*,

> are the times that try mens' souls. The summer soldier and the sunshine patriot will, in this crisis, shrink from the service of his country, but he that stands it now, deserves the love and thanks of man and woman. Tyranny, like hell, is not easily conquered, yet we have this consolation with us, that the harder the conflict the more glorious the triumph; what we obtain too cheap we esteem too lightly.

The number was read in the camp, to every corporal's guard, and in the army and out of it had more than the intended effect. The convention of New York, reduced by despersion, occasioned by alarm, to nine members, was rallied and reanimated.[35] Militia-men, who, already tired of the war, were straggling from the army, returned. Hope succeeded to despair, cheerfulness to gloom, and firmness to ir-

35 Mr. Gelston, now Collector of the port of New York, was one of the nine members who remained at the post

resolution. To the confidence which it inspired may be attributed much of the brilliant little affair which in the same month followed at Trenton.

On this event, elevating American confidence and breathing caution into the British army, Paine, in January, 1776, congratulated the "Free and independent States" in a second number of THE *CRISIS*. It is addressed to Lord Howe, and ridicules his proclamation "commanding all Congresses, committees, &c. to desist and cease from their treasonable doings." Against the king and his purposes, it is full of invective, but of a sort rather popular than exquisite. Fortunately for the United States the British commander in chief dealt more in impotent proclamations than in the efficacy of arms. Washington's retreat to Trenton was a compulsive one. He had not from choice and by military skill drawn the Hessians into the toil in which they were ensnared. I do not believe that even a number of THE *CRISIS* could have saved the American army and cause from annihilation, if Howe had been an active and persevering, an enlightened and energetick commander. Washington's patience and care, his admirable coolness and prudence, although often, in the course of the war, provoked to battle by a thousand irritating circumstances, by internal faction, and by British sneers, saved America to freedom, while the idle dissipation of Howe, his devotion to licentious pleasures, his unmartial spirit and conduct, lost it to the crown.

On the 19th of April, 1776, he published, at Philadelphia, the third number of THE *CRISIS*. As there had been no military operations from the capture of the Hessians at Trenton, it was devoted to an examination of occurrences since the declaration of independence, and, as he seems to have been in lack of matter, to a repetition of the arguments which he had employed in *Common Sense* in favour of independence. To these are incidentally added, as if to lengthen out the number, light immaterial observations on paper emissions. Except some sensible remarks on the utility of reflecting on past transactions, the only thing in this number worthy of observation, and that but for reprehension, is the following vulgarity.

> There is not such a being in America as a Tory from conscience; some secret defect or other is interwoven in the character of all those, be they men or women, who can look with patience on the brutality, luxury, and debauchery of the British court, and the violations of their army here. A woman's virtue must sit very lightly on her who can even hint a favourable sentiment in their behalf. It is remarkable that the whole race of prostitutes in New York were Tories; and the schemes for supporting the Tory cause in this city, for which several are now in gaol, and one hanged, were concerted and carried on in bawdy houses, assisted by those who kept them.

On the 17th of April, 1777, he was elected by Congress Secretary to the Committee of Foreign Affairs.[36] He now left the army to attend the Committee.

Bitterly as he pretended to be opposed to TITLES, when grasping the pillars of the British government he endeavoured to subvert it, he was yet so fond of them, in reality, that he not only assumed to himself a title to which he had no claim, but he seems to have gloried in the fraudulent assumption. In the title-page of his *Rights of Man*, he styles himself "Secretary for Foreign Affairs to the Congress of the United States, in the late war." The foreign affairs of the United States were conducted, as we see, by a Committee, or Board, of which he was secretary, or clerk; *clerk* more properly, at a very low salary. His business was merely to copy papers, number and file them, and, generally, to do the duty of what is now called a clerk in the Foreign Department. He

36 "Resolved, that the stile of the committee of secret correspondence be altered, and that for the future it be stiled the Committee of Foreign Affairs.

"That a secretary be appointed to the said committee with a salary of seventy-five dollars a month.

"That the said secretary, previous to his entering on his office, take an oath to be administered by the president, well and faithfully to execute the trust reposed in him according to his best skill and judgment, and to disclose no matter the knowledge of which shall be acquired in consequence of such his office, that he shall be directed to keep secret;" also the oath prescribed for the officers of the army, and passed the 21st day of October, 1776, and that a certificate thereof be given to the president, and lodged with the secretary of Congress.

"Congress proceeded to the election of the said secretary, and the ballots being taken, Thomas Paine was elected."—*Journals of Congress.*

was, however, determined to give himself a higher title. Unsubstantial in essence as superadditions to names are, he nevertheless liked them, and seemed to be aware that, universally, they possess a charm[37] to which he was by no means insensible. From this and many other circumstances we may infer, that his objections to being himself a lord of the bed chamber, or a groom of the stole, a master of the hounds, or a gentleman in waiting, would not have been stronger than were his wishes to be retained in the excise. But he was totally unfit to be secretary of state, the title which he had impudently assumed. He had neither the soberness of habit, the reservedness of deportment, the urbanity of manners, the courteousness of language, the extent of reading, nor the wide range of thought, which a station so distinguished requires. He was formed, as has often been observed, to pull down, not to set up. His forte was anarchy. Order was the perpetual and invincible enemy of his talents. In tranquillity, he sunk into the kennel of intemperance; in a commotion of the political elements, he rode conspicuously on the surge.[38]

---

37 There is perhaps no nation so fond of titles as our own. Every man in office, or who has been in office, is addressed by the appellation of it: Mr. President, Mr. Constable, colonel such-a-one, and Judge such-a-one; though the Colonel, out of commission, is working at his bench, and the country Judge, out of court, is serving his customers in a tavern. This is universal, and we feel neglected if our title be for gotten. Yet we smile contemptuously at the weakness of nations by which titles are acknowledged!

38 Madame Roland describes him admirably. "Among the per-

On the 12th day of September, 1777, he published, at Philadelphia, the fourth number of the *Crisis*. Howe, gaining some advantage at Brandywine, had nevertheless deemed it prudent to fall back on the Schuylkill. Paine's object was to convince the people that a victory so trifling, followed by a retiring march, was in fact a defeat. Exhorting the army to perseverance, and conjuring the people to reinforce it, nothing was necessary, he ingeniously urged, to drive Howe from the Schuylkill, but conduct at once prompt, spirited, and energetick.

Number five of the *Crisis*, addressed "to General Sir William Howe," was published at Lancaster, Pennsylvania, March 21, 1778. It ridicules at great length Sir William's TITLE. In this sort of writing, always successful when appealing to popular feeling, he was not always refined. He describes Sir William as a "savage, holding humanity in contempt." Deriving his commission from the "royal brute," he thinks it dishonourable.

For language so rude, some apology may perhaps be found in the nature and operations of the

---

sons whom I was in the habit of seeing, Paine deserves to be mentioned. I think him better fitted to sow the seeds of popular commotion, than to lay the foundations or prepare the form of government. He throws light on a *revolution*, better than he concurs in the making of a *constitution*. He takes up and establishes those great principles, of which the exposition strikes every eye, gains the applause of a club, or excites the enthusiasm of a *tavern*, but for a cool discussion in a committee or the regular labours of a legislator, I conceive *David Williams*, [an Englishman] infinitely more proper than *Paine*." Roland's *Appeal*, vol. 1, part 2, p. 45, New York, 1798.

war. His business was to excite and keep up a revolutionary spirit. He charges Sir William with having forged continental paper—represents him as a felon—speaks of the ease with which the offence might be dreadfully retorted upon England, "a nation of paper money," and reminds him, that the laws of his country punish forgery with death! He associates Sir William with the Indians, who had been let loose, it was said, on our defenceless inhabitants. Of the conquest of Burgoyne he writes in triumphant terms. On the military conduct of WASHINGTON he is glowingly encomiastick, but of his just eulogiums on that extraordinary man, it will be proper to pay more particular attention when we approach the defamations which he subsequently wrote in Paris. He advises Sir William to go home, and pronounces the States unconquerable. This number is the most judicious and able of the series.

Number six of the *Crisis*, without date,[39] is addressed to the "Inhabitants of America." "As a good opinion of ourselves," he observes, "is necessary to the support of a national character," he very good naturedly compares the Americans with the Greeks and Romans; thinks them equal in courage, and very superior in wisdom. This must have been an agreeable number.

Number seven of the *Crisis*, published in Philadelphia, October 20, 1778, is addressed to the "Earl

39 It is termed, with some others, an extraordinary or supernumerary *CRISIS*, but it will be less embarrassing to number them all.

of Carlisle, General Clinton, and William Eden, Esq., Commissioners at New York." These gentlemen, when the States were proudly confident of ultimate success, laughably enough revived the paper-war which general Howe had farcically commenced and vigourously prosecuted. In a proclamation, announcing the "benevolent intentions of the king," they alternately coaxed and threatened. Coaxing was now ridiculously out of character, and menacing, with the surrender of Burgoyne staring them in the face, was sufficiently impotent. Paine handled both topicks with an acuteness which the States must have admired, and a force which the Commissioners undoubtedly felt.

The *Crisis*, number eight, published in Philadelphia, November 21, 1778, is addressed "To the People of England." This is an appeal, *as a Christian*, to the justice and magnanimity of Englishmen in favour of the States, and represents, with great cogency of argument, the possible success of the ministry, which he does not however admit, as detrimental in its consequences to the freedom and prosperity of England. BURKE is, however, on this, as on all other subjects on which they write, infinitely his superiour.

> Considering the Americans on that defensive footing, he thought Great Britain ought instantly to have closed with them by the repeal of the taxing act. He was of opinion that our general rights over that country would have been preserved by this timely concession. When, instead

> of this a Boston port bill, a Massachusetts charter bill, a fishery bill, an intercourse bill, I know not how many hostile bills rushed out like so many tempests from all parts of the compass, and were accompanied first with great fleets and armies, and followed afterwards with great bodies of foreign troops, he thought that their cause grew daily better, because daily more defensive, and that ours, because daily more offensive, grew daily worse.
>
> So circumstanced, he certainly never could and never did wish the colonists to be subdued by arms. He was fully persuaded, that if such should be the event, they must be held in that subdued state by a great body of standing forces, and perhaps of foreign forces. He was strongly of opinion that such armies, first victorious over Englishmen, in a conflict for English constitutional rights and privileges, and afterwards habituated (though in America) to keep an English people in a state of abject subjection, would prove fatal in the end to the liberty of England itself.[40]

Of the philosophy of politicks, Paine chuses to think the cabinet of England totally ignorant. He considers the government as one of precedent and venality only, and, whether deservedly or not, thus pleasantly satirises its prime minister. "As to Lord North, it is his happiness to have in him more of philosophy

40 Burke's "Appeal from the New to the Old Whigs", *The Works of The Right Honourable Edmund Burke* (London: F. and C. Rivington, 1803) vol. 6, p. 123-4.

than sentiment, for he bears flogging like a top, and sleeps the better for it. His punishment becomes his support, for while he suffers the lash for his sins, he keeps himself up by twirling about."

On the 8th of January, 1779, he compulsively resigned his clerkship to the Committee of Foreign Affairs, having held it twenty-one months. As the circumstances occasioning and accompanying his resignation, have not, materially as they affect his character, been fully explained, a statement of them somewhat minute may find in its pertinence an apology for its prolixity.

Very early in the struggle for independence, before, I believe, it was declared, Silas Deane, an artful speculator on the revolution, but a man neither of solid nor splendid acquirements, was employed by the committee of secret correspondence, afterwards the Committee of Foreign Affairs, to purchase in France, as a merchant, or to obtain from the French government for Congress, certain military supplies. He was soon after named by the Secret Committee of Correspondence, with Dr. Franklin and Mr. Lee, in a commission to the court of France.

At this period, Louis the XVI. intent on a comparative aggrandizement of his power by abridging the power of his rival, and with characteristical perfidy secretly fomenting the dispute between England and the colonists, cordially and promptly granted the supplies, which Paine says, and probably in this instance he may be credited, were furnished from the king's arsenal. But as the issue of the contest on the side of America was exceedingly problematical, and his most Christian majesty was, precisely for that reason, falsely disavowing to England all connexion with the colonists, and protesting to her and for her sentiments of the purest amity, secrecy was mutually pledged by the king and the Secret Committee of Correspondence, that the supplies, which were a present from Louis, an exciting gratuity, should never be known as such. The transaction was therefore to assume the air of an ordinary mercantile one, and a Mr. Beaumarchais, a creature of Louis, or of Silas Deane, perhaps of both, was the agent in whose name the supplies were to be despatched. Three ships, the *Amphitrite*, *Seine*, and *Mercury*, loaded with supplies, were cleared for Cape Française, and consigned to Roderick Hortalis & Co. an imaginary house. After the Declaration of Independence, after the capture of the Hessians, after the surrender of Burgoyne, and when, therefore, the politick court of France concluded, that, with a little aid, the colonies might be severed forever from the British crown, the alliance between France and the States, the effect of those brilliant events, was formed and ratified.. Still, notwithstanding the alliance, as the supplies were a gratuity, as the king's word, which was the king's honour, and the word of the Secret Committee of Correspondence had been given, that they should be so considered, the alliance neither varied the transaction, nor absolved the parties from the mutual obligations of confidence.

In this state of affairs, Silas Deane, who for misconduct had been recalled from the French court, appeared before a committee appointed by Congress to audit his accounts. Deane, clearly, I think, with fraudulent designs, had left in France the principal part of his papers. Considering, however, both France and America bound not to disclose the nature of the supplies, he presented himself, in settling his accounts, as a kind of co-agent, with a Mr. Francey, for Beaumarchais, in whose name he claimed compensation for them. The auditing committee, perhaps made acquainted by the Secret Committee of Correspondence with the nature of the supplies, questioned the justice of the claim. Deane, surely a bold faced villain, appealed to the publick. With Deane, Paine entered the field of newspaper dispute, under the imposing head of "*Common Sense* to the publick on Deane's affairs." In this controversy, pursuing with ardour an empty newspaper triumph, and disregarding his official duty, he remarked:—

> If Mr. Deane or any other gentleman will procure an order from Congress to inspect an account in my office, or any of Mr. Deane's friends in Congress will take the them my attendance, and show them in handwriting which Mr. Deane is well acquainted with, that the SUPPLIES he so pompously plumes himself upon, were present-

ed and engaged, and that AS A PRESENT, before he even arrived in France.

Here Paine, "Secretary for Foreign Affairs to the Congress of the United States, who had taken an oath to disclose no matter, the knowledge of which shall be acquired in consequence of his office," not only wantonly and without any sort of necessity (and no necessity could mitigate the offence) violated his oath and embarrassed Congress, but proclaimed to the world the insidious conduct of France, and the falsities of the king's declarations to England, at and subsequent to the time when the "PRESENT" was made. Deane's accounts were not to be settled by the "publick," but by the guardians of the publick. The publick, in the gross character of a publick, had nothing to do with the transaction but quietly to receive the benefit of it. His appeal to them was consequently as unnecessary as is was reprehensible. But, he says[41] "I prevented Deane's fraudulent demand being paid, and so far the country is obliged to me, but I became the victim of my integrity." To an enormous violation of his official duty and oath, which he decks with the epithet of *integrity*, this is adding a gross, and, if he were not, which is not probable, totally ignorant of a notorious fact, a wilful falsehood. His newspaper victory[42] had not, could not have had, the effect

41 See his letter to Congress in the Appendix.

42 No doubt he obtained one, for besides being a rogue, Deane was extremely illiterate. See his defence published in London

which he ascribes to it. How could he by an appeal to the publick have prevented the payment of the demand by the auditing committee? If the committee had been disposed to yield to the collusive and nefarious claim of the sharpers, Beaumarchais and Deane, and his publications had deterred them from their purpose, then his conclusion, without varying his offence, would have been admissible. But what induced Deane's appeal, to which Paine replied, and in replying divulged the secret? The ill treatment of the committee, as Deane termed it—their rigorous scrutiny into his accounts—their refusal to pay the claim[43]—their referring him to Congress, who alone could authorise an inspection or exposition of the secret papers. A result exactly the reverse of that mentioned by Paine, was the fact. Instead of preventing by his publications the payment of Beaumarchais's claim, his publications were the means, fraudulent as it was, of compelling Congress to adopt it. The moment his publications appeared in Dunlap's paper, the minister of France, Gérard, alarmed at the developement of the secret, the exposition of his master, presented a memorial to Congress. What was the consequence? Why, that Congress, in order to quiet the fears of Gérard,

---

after the peace, and re-published by Hudson and Goodwin, Hartford, Connecticut, 1784.

43 See Gordon's *History of the Revolution*, vol. 2, page 405-6-7, where, although the transaction is inaccurately and feebly stated, it will be seen, that the conduct of the auditing committee, firm and dignified undoubtedly, was rather haughty than yielding.

and to cover as well as they could the word of honour which his most Christian majesty had given to England, *Resolved*, as appears in their proceedings below in reference to Paine, which I quote at length,[44] that the PRESENT was *not* a present; that

---

44 *Tuesday, January* 5, 1779.

A memorial from the minister of France, was read, respecting sundry passages in two news-papers annexed of the 2d and 5th inst.

Ordered, That the consideration thereof be postponed till to-morrow.

Wednesday, January 6, 1779.

A letter, of this day, from Thomas Paine, was read; whereupon,

The order of the day on the memorial of the minister of France was called for, and the said memorial being read:

Ordered, That Mr. John Dunlap, printer, and Mr. Thomas Paine, attend immediately at the bar of this house.

Mr. John Dunlap attending, was called in, and the news papers of the 2d and 5th of Jan. inst. intitled, *Pennsylvania Packet or General Advertiser*, being shewn to him, he was asked whether he was the publisher; to which he answered, yes:

He was then asked who is the author of the pieces in the said papers, under the title *Common Sense* to the public on Mr. Deane's affairs;" to which he answered, Mr. Thomas Paine: he was then ordered to withdraw.

Mr. Thomas Paine attending, was called in, and being asked if he was the author of the pieces in the *Pennsylvania Packet* or General Advertiser of Jan. 2d and 5th, 1779, under the title *Common Sense* to the public on Mr. Deane's affairs;' he answered that he was the author of those pieces; he was then ordered to withdraw.

Thursday, January 7, 1779.

Congress resumed the consideration of the subject which was under debate yesterday. And the following set of resolutions were moved;

Beaumarchais's claim should be paid, and, in ad-

That all the late publications in the *General Advertiser*, printed by John Dunlap, relative to American foreign affairs, are ill-judged, premature and indiscrete, and that as they must in general be founded on very partial documents, and consequently depend much on conjecture, they ought not by any means to be considered as justly authenticated:

That Congress never has given occasion for or sanction to any of the said publications:

That Congress never has received any species of military stores as a present from the court of France, or from any other court or persons in Europe:

That Mr. Thomas Paine for his imprudence ought immediately to be dismissed from his office of Secretary to the Committee of Foreign Affairs, and the said committee are directed to dismiss him accordingly, and to take such further steps relative to his misapplication of public papers as they shall deem necessary.

In amendment, and as a substitute to the foregoing, the following set of resolutions was moved:

Whereas Thomas Paine, Secretary to the Committee of Foreign Affairs, has acknowledged himself to be the author of a piece in the *Pennsylvania Packet* of Jan. 2d, 1779, under the title of *Common Sense* to the public on Mr. Deane's affairs, in which is the following paragraph, *viz.* "If Mr. Deane or any other gentleman will procure an order from Congress to inspect an account in my office, or any of Mr. Deane's friends in Congress will take the trouble of coming themselves, I will give him or them my attendance, and shew them in hand writing, which Mr. Deane is well acquainted with, that the supplies he so pompously plumes himself upon were promised and engaged, and that, as a present, before he even arrived in France; and the part that fell to Mr. Deane was only to see it done, and how he has performed that service the public are now acquainted with." The last paragraph in the account is, "upon Mr. Deane's arrival in France the business went into his hands, and the aids were at length embarked in the *Amphitrite*, *Mercury*, and *Seine*." And, whereas, the said Thomas Paine hath also acknowledged himself to be the author of a piece in the succeeding *Packet* of Jan-

dition, that the president of Congress be directed

---

uary 5th, 1779, under the same title, in which is the following paragraph, to wit, "and in the second instance, that those who are now her allies, prefaced that alliance by an early and generous friendship, yet that we might not attribute too much to human or auxiliary aid, so unfortunate were these supplies, that only one ship out of the three arrived; the *Mercury* and *Seine* fell into the hands of the enemy;"

Resolved, That the insinuation contained in the said publications, that the supplies sent to America in the *Amphitrite*, Seine, and Mercury were a present from France, is untrue:

That the publications above recited tend to impose upon, mislead, and deceive the public:

That the attempt of the said Thomas Paine to authenticate the said false insinuations, by referring to papers in the office of the Committee of Foreign Affairs, is an abuse of office;

That the said Thomas Paine be, and he hereby is, dismissed from his said office.

A third set of resolutions was moved as an amendment and substitute to the two foregoing sets, *viz*.

That Congress are deeply concerned at the imprudent publication of Mr. Thomas Paine, Secretary to the Committee of Foreign Affairs, referred to by the minister of France in his memorial of the 5th inst. and are ready to adopt any measure consistent with good policy and their own honour, for correcting any assertions or insinuations in the said publications, derogatory to the honour of the court of France:

That a committee be appointed to consider the said memorial and paragraphs referred to, that they confer with the minister of France on the subject, and report as soon as may be.

In lieu of the whole the following resolution was moved as a substitute, *viz*.

Whereas exceptionable passages have appeared in Mr. Dunlap's *Pennsylvania Packet*, of the 2d and 5th inst, under the character of *Common Sense*; and Thomas Paine, Secretary to the Committee of Foreign Affairs, being called before Congress, avowed his being the author of those publications:

Resolved, That Thomas Paine be summoned to appear before Congress at eleven o'clock to-morrow, and be informed

to write him a complimentary letter, thanking him

---

what those exceptionable passages are, and called upon to explain and to shew by what authority he made those publications, in order that Congress may take proper measures relative thereto.

The previous question was moved on the last amendment; whereupon, the sense of the house was taken, whether the previous question is in order on an amendment:

Resolved, That it is not in order.

On the question to substitute the last resolution as an amendment to the whole, the yeas and nays being required by Mr. G. Morris,

New Hampshire	*Mr. Whipple*	*ay*	*ay*
Massachusetts Bay	*Mr. Gerry*	*no*	*no*
	Mr. Lovell	*no*	*no*
	Mr. Holten	*ay*	
Rhode Island	*Mr. Ellery*	*ay*	*divided*
	Mr. Collins	*no*	
Connecticut	*Mr. Dyer*	*ay*	*ay*
	Mr. Root	*ay*	
New York	*Mr. Jay*	*no*	*no*
	Mr. Duane	*no*	
	Mr. G. Morris	*no*	
	Mr. Lewis	*no*	
New Jersey	*Mr. Witherspoon*	*no*	*no*
	Mr. Scudder	*no*	
	Mr. Fell	*no*	
Pennsylvania	*Mr. Roberdeau*	*ay*	*ay*
	Mr. Atlee	*no*	
	Mr. Searle	*ay*	
Delaware	*Mr. McKean*	*ay*	*ay*

for his exertions and assuring him of their regard.”

Maryland	*Mr. Paca*	*no*	*no*
	Mr. Carmichael	*no*	
	Mr. Henry	*ay*	
North Carolina	*Mr. Penn*	*no*	*no*
	Mr. Hill	*no*	
	Mr. Burke	*no*	
South Carolina	*Mr. Laurens*	*ay*	*no*
	Mr. Drayton	*no*	
	Mr. Hutson	*no*	
Georgia	*Mr. Langworthy*	*no*	*no*

So it passed in the negative.

Friday, January 8, 1779.

A letter, of this day, from Thomas Paine, was read, by which he resigns his office of Secretary to the Committee of Foreign Affairs, and in which are the following words, “finding by the journals of this house of yesterday that I am not to be heard,” &c. whereupon,

A member desired to be informed how Mr. Paine had acquired that knowledge, and the secretary was desired to inform the house whether Mr. Paine had access to the journal; the secretary answered, “that Mr. Paine had not seen the journal of yesterday, nor had any other person had access to it since the last adjournment, as he had taken it home last night, and brought it with him to Congress this morning, so that even the clerks in the office had not seen the minutes of yesterday, and that since the last adjournment he had not seen Mr. Paine, nor communicated the proceedings of Congress to any person whatever.”

A motion was then made, that Mr. Thomas Paine, Secretary to the Committee of Foreign Affairs, be directed immediately to attend at the bar of this house, to answer to certain questions respecting the contents of his letter to the president of Congress of this day.

After debate, a substitute was moved as follows:

Upon these proceedings, forced upon Congress by

That the members of Congress be separately examined by the president, on their honour, whether they have communicated the resolutions of yesterday to Mr. Thomas Paine, and if so, in what manner they have made such representation.

After debate, when the question was about to be put, Mr. Laurens arose and declared that he had informed Mr. Paine, that a motion had been made for hearing him to-morrow at eleven o'clock, which had been seconded, that the yeas and nays had been taken thereon and passed in the negative; and that he referred him to Mr. Thompson for a sight of the journals, which would inform him more certainly, and he was persuaded Mr. Thompson would readily show the journal.

Saturday, January 9, 1779.

Congress resumed the consideration of the letter of the 8th, from Thomas Paine; whereupon, Resolved, That the determination of the question of the 7th inst. for substituting the last amendment in lieu of all the sets of resolutions moved prior to it, on which the yeas and nays were called for by Mr. G. Morris, did not imply, nor can it be justly construed to imply, that Congress had determined that Mr. Thomas Paine was not to be heard.

Monday, January 11, 1779.

A memorial dated the 10th inst. from the hon. sieur Gérard, minister plenipotentiary of France, was read:

Ordered, That the subject under debate on Thursday last, be immediately taken into consideration.

On the question to substitute the third set of resolutions in lieu of the two foregoing:

Passed in the negative.

On the question to substitute the second set of resolutions in the room of the first:

Resolved in the affirmative.

The first resolution in the second set was then read: Resolved, That the consideration of the subject be postponed till to-morrow.

Paine's publications, Beaumarchais, supported by

Tuesday, January 12, 1779.

Congress resumed the consideration of the publications in the *Pennsylvania Packet* of the 2d and 5th inst. under the title of *Common Sense* to the public on Mr. Deane's affairs, of which Mr. Thomas Paine, Secretary of the Committee of Foreign Affairs, has acknowledged himself to be the author; and also the memorials of the minister plenipotentiary of France of the 5th and 10th inst. respecting the said publications; whereupon,

Resolved, unanimously, That in answer to the memorials of the hon. sieur Gérard, minister plenipotentiary of his most Christian majesty, of the 5th and 10th inst. the president be directed to assure the said minister, that Congress do fully, in the clearest and most explicit manner, disavow the publications referred to in his said memorials; and as they are convinced by indisputable evidence, that the supplies shipped in the *Amphitrite*, *Seine*, and *Mercury* were not a present, and that his most Christian majesty, the great and generous ally of these United States, did not preface his alliance with any supplies whatever sent to America, so they have not authorized the writer of the said publications to make any such assertions as are contained therein, but on the contrary do highly disapprove of the same.

Friday, January 15, 1779.

The committee, consisting of Mr. M. Smith, Mr. Ellery, Mr. Drayton, to whom was referred the letter of the 28th of November last from Mons. de Francey, having brought in a report, the same was taken into consideration; and there upon, "*Resolved*, That according to the agreement entered into with Mr. de Francey, agent of Mons. de Beaumarchais, at York, on the 7th day of April, 1778, remittance should be made with all-convenient dispatch to the said Mr. de Beaumarchais.

Resolved, That the requisition of Mr. de Francey in his letter of the 28th of November last, is reasonable, and that 3000 hogsheads of tobacco, on account of these United States, be purchased, to be laden on board the ships mentioned in the said letter. *Resolved*, That the following letter be written to Mr. de Beaumarchais:

his imperial majesty and king, Napoleon, found-

The Congress of the United States of America, sensible of your exertions in their favour, present you their thanks, and assure you of their regard. They lament the inconveniences you have suffered by the great advances made in support of these states. Circumstances have prevented a compliance with their wishes, but they will take the most effectual measures in their power to discharge the debt due to you.

The liberal sentiments and extensive views which alone could dictate a conduct like yours, are conspicuous in your actions and adorn your character. While with great talents you served your prince, you have gained the esteem of this infant republic, and will receive the merited applause of a new world.

BY ORDER OF CONGRESS,
President.
Saturday, January 16, 1779.

Resolved, That Congress agree to the report. Congress took into consideration the letters from Thomas Paine; whereupon a motion was made,

That Mr. Thomas Paine, Secretary to the Committee of Foreign Affairs, be dismissed from office.

To which an amendment was offered as a substitute in the following words,

That Thomas Paine be directed to attend at the bar of this house on Monday next, at 11 o'clock, to answer whether he had any direction or permission from the Committee of Foreign Affairs, for the publications of which, he confessed himself to be the author when he was before the house on the 6th day of January last.

Another amendment was moved as a substitute to both the foregoing propositions in the words following,

Whereas Congress were about to proceed against Thomas Paine, Secretary to the Committee of Foreign Affairs, for certain publications and letters as being inconsistent with his official character and duty, when the said Thomas Paine resigned his office; thereupon,

Resolved, That the said Thomas Paine is dismissed from

ed a substantial claim, and prosecuted it with such

any farther service in the said office, and the Committee of Foreign Affairs are directed to call upon the said Thomas Paine, and receive from him on oath all public letters, papers and documents in his possession.

A fourth amendment was moved as a substitute to the whole in the words following,

Resolved, That the Committee of Foreign Affairs be directed to take out of the possession of Thomas Paine, all the public papers entrusted to him as Secretary to that committee, and then discharge him from that office.

When the question was about to be put, a division was called for, and the question being put to adopt the first part,

Passed in the affirmative.

On the question to adopt the second part, the yeas and nays being required by Mr. Lovell,

It was resolved in the affirmative.

The question being then about to be put on the main question, a division was called for, and the yeas and nays being required on the first part by Mr. McKean,

Resolved, unanimously, in the affirmative.

On the question to agree to the second clause, namely, 'and then discharge him from that office,' the yeas and nays being required by Mr. Penn,

New Hampshire	*Mr. Whipple*	*no*	*no*
Massachusetts Bay	*Mr. Gerry*	*no*	*no*
	Mr. S. Adams	*no*	
	Mr. Lovell	*no*	
	Mr. Holten	*ay*	
Rhode Island	*Mr. Ellery*	*no*	*divided*
	Mr. Collins	*ay*	
Connecticut	*Mr. Dyer*	*no*	*no*
	Mr. Root	*no*	
New York	*Mr. Jay*	*ay*	*ay*
	Mr. Lewis	*ay*	

vigour and success, that, in the year 1808, he obtained from the Attorney General of the United States, through Congress, a report in favour of satisfying his claim. According to the report of the attorney general, more than a million of dollars are to be paid to Beaumarchais in compensation for the supplies!

Of neither of these facts could Paine have been ignorant. The one happened in the middle of his Deane-controversy, a few days after his dismission. The other, the ultimate decision of the Attorney-General, long before his death.

In the opinion of Congress, Paine, in whom it was ascertained that official trust could not be reposed, now sunk into vileness. Dismissed from his clerkship to the committee for a scandalous breach of of-

---

Pennsylvania	*Mr. Roberdeau*	*no*	*no*
	Mr. Searle	*no*	
	Mr. Atlee	*ay*	
Delaware	*Mr. McKean*	*no*	*no*
Maryland	*Mr. Paca*	*ay*	*ay*
	Mr. Carmichael	*ay*	
North Carolina	*Mr. Penn*	*ay*	*ay*
	Mr. Hill	*ay*	
	Mr. Burke	*ay*	
South Carolina	*Mr. Drayton*	*ay*	*divided*
	Mr. Hutson	*no*	
Georgia	*Mr. Langworthy*	*ay*	*ay*

So the states being divided the clause was lost.

fice, his prospects, except the popular hold which he still had on the people, to whom his misconduct was not perhaps known, were almost as discouraging as when, a second time dismissed from the excise in England, he was assailed with continuous pains of hunger. His salary for officiating as clerk to the committee, parsimonious and spunging as he was, was scarcely adequate, considering the depreciation of the currency in which it was paid, to the expenses of his board. He had therefore made no provision for the forlorn condition in which he now found himself, for as yet publick bounty had not, bating his maintenance by the army while he was with it, been extended to him for his political labours. Thus situated, thus abandoned by the assembled wisdom and patriotism of the states, he hired himself as a clerk to Owen Biddle, of Philadelphia.[45] In this clerkship, where, perhaps, he had no secrets to betray, he prosecuted his controversy with Deane, who, he remarks, "absconded and took poison" in England.[46] The poisoning, if true, but it is not, must, I have no doubt from his manner of mentioning it, from the constitution of his mind, and from the malignity of feelings which he indulged, have afforded him great satisfaction. But Deane, whatever causes he might have had in other respects for self-upbraiding and condemnation, and he must have had many, certainly had none in reference to Beaumarchais's claim, which, as he knew before he "absconded,"

45 An attorney, I believe: see his letter to Congress in the Appendix.

46 See his letter to Congress in the Appendix.

had, through the impertinent meddling of Paine, succeeded with Congress. The probability is that he triumphantly returned to Paris,[47] to receive from Beaumarchais, his colleague in the fraud, the infamous reward of his infamous conduct.

Having finished his disputation with Deane, and being, it is probable, uneasy in the service of Mr. Biddle, he somehow obtained, early in the year 1780, the subordinate appointment of clerk to the assembly of Pennsylvania.[48]

As if nothing had happened personally to himself, he now returned to the *Crisis*, and published, in March, 1780, the ninth number. This is a continuation of his address to the people of England. It is an ordinary description of the ordinary calamities of war, but mentions them as operating with almost peculiar severity on the colonists. Being well calculated to keep up the revolutionary spirit, it was probably serviceable.

In the following June, he published, at Philadelphia, the tenth number of the *Crisis*. After desolating the southern states, Charleston had fallen into the hands of the British forces. The purpose of the number was to inspire confidence by dissipating gloom. He represents the attacks in the south as so many indications of military weakness, and zealously concludes with the remark, that "the man who does not now feel for the honour of the best and noblest cause that ever a country engaged in,

47 From Paris he went to London.

48 See his letter to Congress in the Appendix.

and exert himself accordingly, is no longer worthy of a peaceable residence among a people determined to be free."

Number eleven of the *Crisis* was published, at Philadelphia, the succeeding October. The fiscal means of Congress being exhausted, from an unaccountable unwillingness in the people to bear increased burthens, he runs a consoling parallel between the expenses of England in carrying on the war, and those of her American antagonist; between the taxes of the one nation and those of the other. He points out a mode in which he thinks additional supplies, which are indispensable, maybe commensurately raised without greatly incommoding the people. Congress had recommended the funding of its paper at forty for one, and the issuing of new money in lieu of it. Against the recommendation, Pennsylvania petitioned her assembly. Paine ardently pleads in favour of a compliance, and bluntly tells the petitioners that they are unacquainted with the subject. He knew the great and urgent wants of the army, and he was for supplying them at all events, but the means were of more difficult access than he had imagined.

Amid this financial distress, Congress framed a mission to France, in order to obtain a loan. Col. Laurens, son of the late president of Congress, was appointed to fill it. Paine, at the solicitation of the colonel, he says,[49] but certainly without the agen-

49 See his letter to Congress in the Appendix. He intimates that

cy or approbation of Congress, accompanied him to France, but in what capacity is not known, as Major Jackson was the colonel's secretary. They sailed in February, 1781—arrived in France the following month—obtained a loan of ten millions of livres and a present of six, and landed in America the succeeding August, with two millions and a half in silver. According to Paine, this aid enabled the army to "move to York Town," where Cornwallis and his troops surrendered.[50]

But he was guilty of an egregious falsehood. The combined armies under Washington and Rochambeau had moved before the money arrived. Assertion so strong should be supported by proof. "We sailed from Brest," Paine observes,

> in the Resolve frigate the first of June, and arrived at Boston the 25th of August, bringing with us two millions and a half in silver, and convoying a ship and brig laden with clothing and military stores. The money was transported in sixteen ox teams to the national bank at Philadelphia, *which enabled the army to move to York Town to attack, in conjunction with the French army under Rochambeau, the British army under Cornwallis.*[51]

---

the mission originated from him, and takes to himself the credit of it, but as I knew him, my mind involuntarily doubts almost all his assertions.. He was rarely to be believed.

50 See his letter in the Appendix.

51 See his letter in the Appendix.

This is a specimen, a poor one indeed, of the almost treasonable arguments which his invincible attachment to France in preference to all other nations, not excepting his "beloved America," often prompted him to use in newspaper effusions in the years 1807-8; attachment strong enough to have led him to a base surrender of our national independence to the bloody usurper.

Now if I show that the attack on York Town was planned, not before the arrival of the money in August, but before its departure from Brest in June, and that in pursuance of the plan, and not in consequence of the supplies, the combined American and French armies had moved towards the theatre of the decisive event, I humbly presume that I shall have attached to the memory of Paine the falsehood of which I have accused him. To do this nothing more is necessary than to recur to the history of the revolutionary war.

> May 6. The plan of operations [against Cornwallis] *had* been so well digested, and was so faithfully executed by the different commanders, that General Washington and Count Rochambeau had passed the British head quarters at New York, and were considerably advanced in their way to York Town, before Count De Grasse had reached the American coast.[52]

It appears, according to Ramsay, that the plan was laid more than three months anteriour to the

52 Ramsay's *Hist. Rev.*, vol. 2, p. 264.

arrival of the money at Boston in August, and that on the 6th of May the armies had "passed the British head quarters at New York, and were considerably advanced in their way to York Town."

Gordon, perhaps generally less copious and elegant, is yet more precise to the point.

> The French and American armies continued their march from the northward till they arrived at the head of Elk. The greatest harmony subsisted between Washington and Rochambeau. The former being without *a sufficiency of money to supply his troops*, *applied* to the Count (de Grasse) for a loan, which was instantly granted. General Washington and Rochambeau, with their suites and other officers, arrived at Williamsburgh by hard travelling, on the 14th September.[53]

The loan then was applied for by Washington when he was at the head of Elk in Maryland, which was at the latter end of August, or, at furthest, on the first or second of September. At this time the money, which arrived at Boston on the 25th of August, and was from thence conveyed in ox teams to Philadelphia, must have been on its way to, for it could not have arrived at, the "National Bank." The combined armies, therefore, had not only "moved" without the money of which Paine speaks, to which he adverts as saving America, on which he vauntingly plumes himself,

53 Gordon's *Hist. Rev.*, vol. 3. p. 254.

and the credit of which he arrogantly places to his own account, but Washington had arrived at the head of Elk without a cent of it, and even then, so far from relying on, or even thinking of it, we find him applying for a loan to de Grasse to enable him to complete his march to the scene of triumph. It is probable that when Washington reached Williamsburgh, he was ignorant of the arrival of the money at Boston.

Number twelve of the *Crisis*, without date, was published early in the year 1782. The king had delivered a speech on which it is a commentary. In the speech his majesty speaks of himself as the sovereign of a free people. Paine considers the term as misapplied, ridicules it, and attributes it to fear in the king lest his people should "send him to Hanover." With wit, at whatever expence, we are pleased, but with miserable abortions of it we are always disgusted. The number contains, however, some sensible reflections.

The *Crisis*, number thirteen, published at Philadelphia in March, 1782, is on the finances of the states. It has no interest. The war was now in fact over, and Paine's pen declined with the discontinuance of military operations. He lived in a tempest. He was lost in a calm.

In the following May, he published, at Philadelphia, the *Crisis* number fourteen, on the "Present state of News." Conjecturing that England would first endeavour to detach France from America and make a separate peace with her, and that afterwards, if unsuccessful, she would make a similar attempt upon the fidelity of the states, it sets forth the reasons for the jealousy which it suggests. The astonishment and indignation which, equally overpowering the organs of speech and the faculty of the pen, the imaginary artifice of the British court excited in him, he thus forcibly describes, happily illustrates.

> We sometimes experience sensations to which language is not equal. The conception is too bulky to be born alive, and in the torture of thinking, we stand dumb. Our feelings, imprisoned by their magnitude, find no way out, and in the struggle of expression, every finger tries to be a tongue. The machinery of the body seems too little for the mind, and we look about for helps to show our thoughts by.

That which he had imagined never happened; that which he had not imagined, and of which he seems not to have thought, really occurred. France, when peace was on the tapis, endeavoured, by propositions which she made to England, but which England rejected, essentially to deprive the states of the sovereignty for which they had long and arduously struggled.[54]

In the same month he published, at Philadelphia, addressed to Sir Guy Carlton, number fifteen of the *Crisis*. Passing by indulgently some palpa-

54 See Mr. Jay's and Mr. John Adams's correspondence with Congress.

ble malice and indiscriminate aspersion, this is an able appeal to Sir Guy on the atrocious murder of Capt. Huddy, by Lippincott, a refugee, and the interesting situation of Capt. Asgill. The issue of Asgill's captivity and doom is known. After suffering all the pang's of death, diminished only by the interposition of that comforting and encouraging hope which under the pressure of events most exciting to despair never wholly forsakes us, his life was spared. The humanity of Washington could not disport in the blood of amiable innocence in revenge for a murder committed by a wretch over whose actions Asgill had no controul.

In October, 1782, he published, at Philadelphia, number sixteen of the *Crisis*, addressed to Earl Shelburne. Peace was about to be concluded, and his Lordship, who was opposed to it, had delivered a very unseasonable and silly speech preparatory to a discussion of its terms in Parliament. On this speech, Paine invectively and unprofitably animadverts.

The last *Crisis* was published at Philadelphia, April 19th, 1783. Peace was now substantially concluded, and the INDEPENDENCE of the UNITED STATES acknowledged. He who if not the suggester was the ablest literary advocate of independence, could do no less, when independence was acquired, than salute the nation on the great event. He is not, however, content with proudly reflecting on past and triumphantly revelling in present circumstances. He still looks forward; still suggests; still advises. He points to the formation of a *na-*

tional character, that broad and solid foundation of national safety, happiness, greatness, and glory, and strenuously recommends an UNION OF THE STATES.

This was not, however, though so denominated, the last *Crisis*. In the following October he published, at New York, the concluding number, which is a trifling notice of Lord Sheffield's "Observations on the Commerce of the American States;" but as he seems to have been unacquainted with commercial principles and details, his Lordship had no formidable opponent in Paine. "Public Good," a pamphlet of thirty-three octavo pages, written in the year 1780, and published it does not appear when, but probably soon after the peace, relates wholly to Virginia and her claim to the vacant Western Territory. It is an elaborate investigation of a royal patent, very local and uninteresting.

His letter to the Abbé Raynal, an octavo pamphlet of fifty-eight pages, published at Philadelphia, August, 1782, is a repetition of the arguments and facts contained in *Common Sense* and the *Crisis*. There could have been no motive for writing it but that of detecting the Abbé in some plagiarism from *Common Sense*.

In 1783, when the army was on the point of being disbanded, General Washington, at the request of Congress, removed his quarters to Rocky Hill, the seat of their deliberations. The general availed himself of this opportunity to obtain from Congress some permanent provision for Paine. One of the several members with whom he conversed on the subject, has related to me what follows. Paine, the general remarked, was at least supposed to have rendered his country some services by his writings, and that it would be pleasing to him, and perhaps obviate charges of ingratitude, if Congress would place him in a state of ease: that he had offered Paine a seat at his table, but that he would doubtless prefer something more independent. In consequence of the general's suggestion, a motion was made in Congress by my informant to appoint Paine *Historiographer to the United States*, with a salary sufficient to support him through life, but it was received by the house with such a burst of indignation, that the mover found it prudent to withdraw it. Congress had not got over the irritation which Paine's conduct in Deane's case had excited.

In 1785, Congress granted him three thousand dollars for his revolutionary writings.

> *Friday, August* 26, 1785.
>
> On the report of a committee consisting of Mr. Gerry, Mr. Pettit, and Mr. King, to whom was referred a letter of the 13th from Thomas Paine:
>
> *Resolved*, That the early, unsolicited, and continued labours of Mr. Thomas Paine, in explaining and enforcing the principles of the late revolution by ingenious and timely publications upon the nature of liberty and civil government, have been well received by the citizens of these states, and merit the approbation of Congress; and that in consideration of these services, and the benefits produced

> thereby, Mr. Paine is entitled to a liberal gratification from the United States.
>
> *Monday, October* 3, 1785.
>
> On the report of a committee consisting of Mr. Gerry, Mr. Howell, and Mr. Long, to whom were referred sundry letters from Mr. Thomas Paine, and a report on his letter of 14th of September:
>
> *Resolved*, That the board of treasury take order for paying to Mr. Thomas Paine the sum of three thousand dollars, for the considerations mentioned in the resolution of the 26th of August last. *Journals of Congress.*

As the journals of Congress do not of course contain Paine's letter mentioned in the preamble of the resolution of August 26, and I have not been able to obtain a copy of it, we are referred for its import to Paine himself. One would naturally conclude from the phraseology of the journals, that the letter was an application to Congress claiming compensation for his revolutionary writings. Upon that letter the committee report, that for his "early, unsolicited, and continued labours, in explaining and enforcing by numerous timely publications," &c. (referring undoubtedly to his *Common Sense* and the *Crisis*, for these are the only productions which, during the revolution, he published) he is "entitled to a liberal compensation." This *liberal* compensation is three thousand dollars, or about six hundred guineas! Yet as Paine asserts in his *Common Sense*, repeats in the *Crisis*, the *Rights of Man*, in almost all his subsequent European publications, in the Letters which he addressed to the citizens of the United States after his return from France, and in his letter to Congress in 1808,[55] that he never claimed, nor thought of claiming, being too disinterested, any compensation for his revolutionary writings, there is either a capital errour in the phraseology of the journals, or Paine has imposed himself upon the world for a more immaculate patriot than he really was: the latter is by much the more probable.

In his letter to Congress of 1808,[56] he claims compensation for accompanying Colonel Laurens to France, and for nothing else, and he thinks he is the more entitled to it, because the supplies which they obtained, or rather which he obtained, for he makes himself the hero of the piece, enabled Washington to attack Cornwallis. I have already noticed the supplies, and the motion which Paine affirms they gave to Washington's army.

Now if we suppose, and we cannot, I think, but suppose, his letter of 1808, to be in substance his letter of August 13, 1785, mentioned in the journals, then the latter refers to the mission of Colonel Laurens only, and we are of course in the possession of materials enabling us to judge of the propriety of his application, and of the nature of the decision of Congress upon it.

For accompanying Colonel Laurens he certainly had no claim on Congress for recompense. Did Congress employ him? No. Did Congress sanction

55 See the Appendix.

56 See the Appendix.

the employment of him by Colonel Laurens? Did they approve of it? Were they consulted about it? Certainly not, for Congress, by whom he had been dismissed for betraying official trust, could not, without forfeiting all claim to consistency and sense, have confidence in him in the mission. Congress consequently decided in August, 1785, if in his letter of that month he claimed compensation for going to France, and if he did not the case is infinitely stronger against him, that he had no title to compensation. Congress, therefore, in 1785, resolved, whatever the nature of his application at that time was, that for his revolutionary writings only, he was entitled to a liberal gratification. If Congress were really of this opinion, and we are to take it for granted that they were, so finding it on the journals, then their ideas of *liberality* were singular enough. For whether Paine was or was not a patriot, and that he was not is more than probable; whether he was or was not in the excise a dissatisfied and from it a rejected placeman, and he undoubtedly was, is out of the question in relation to the effect which *Common Sense* and the *Crisis* had on American independence. That effect was unquestionably great, and, therefore, if his "early, unsolicited, and continued labours" had been "well received by the citizens" and had "benefited" the states, the recompense should have been commensurate with the benefit. Was a grant of three thousand dollars of that character? If with great ability to reward exertions which were deemed meritorious and beneficial; with an immense domain, not indeed immediately productive; with resources capable of being called forth to the utmost amplitude of the utmost hope; with a debt worthy of consideration only as a precious bond of tranquillity and union; if with these rich possessions Congress considered three thousand dollars a *liberal* compensation, then we are acquainted with the value which they placed on the quantity and quality of his revolutionary writings.

Two only of the states noticed by gratuities his revolutionary labours. Pennsylvania, the seat of his *Common Sense* and the *Crisis*, a state which, if his productions were honourable, was most honoured, gave him, in the year 1785, by an act of the legislature, five hundred pounds currency!

New York was more liberal. They gave him the confiscated estate of Frederick Davoe, a royalist. This estate, situate at New Rochelle, county of Westchester, consisting of more than three hundred acres of land, was in high cultivation. There was upon it, besides out-buildings, an elegant stone house, one hundred and twenty by twenty-eight feet.

In 1786, he published, in Philadelphia, *Dissertations on Government, the Affairs of the Bank, and Paper-Money*, an octavo pamphlet of sixty-four pages. The bank alluded to is the bank of North America. There is an unhappy fatality attending a similar establishment. By men borne down by a heavy load of vulgar prejudice, or lamentably labouring under incurable ignorance, or utterly disregarding publick utility and faith in a vehement pursuit of sinister purposes, the bank of North America was then, as the latter has been since, and is now, systematically attacked. Paine gives at length a history of the origin of the former, which is so closely interwoven with the revolution and allied to its most distressing period, that I cannot refuse myself the pleasure of briefly describing it.

In the year 1780, when the British army, having laid waste the southern states, closed its ravages by the capture of Charleston; when the financial sources of Congress were dried up; when the publick treasury was empty, and the army of independence paralised by want, a voluntary subscription for its relief was raised in Philadelphia.[57] This voluntary fund, amounting to three hundred thousand pounds, afterwards converted into a bank by the subscribers, headed by Robert Morris, supplied the wants of the army. Probably the aids which it furnished enabled Washington to carry into execution his well-concerted plan against Cornwallis. Congress, in the year 1781, incorporated the subscribers to the fund under the title of the *Bank of North America*. In the following year it was further incorporated by an act of the Pennsylvania assembly.

57 Paine states that he drew five hundred dollars of the salary of his clerkship to the Pennsylvania Assembly, and subscribed it to the fund. As usual, he takes all the merit of the plan and subscription to himself. He proposed it. He was everything.

When the war was over—when extreme distress had ceased, and the services which the bank had rendered were forgotten, it was attacked as an institution incompatible with individual prosperity and publick safety. All those recondite arguments which we every day hear, that banks are dangerous to freedom, were, with the customary eloquence of those who use them,[58] forcibly urged in petitions to the Pennsylvania assembly against the bank of North America. The assembly, which was truly the representative of the petitioners, which thought as they thought, and was as wise as they were, was prayed to repeal the state act of incorporation. The petitions were referred to a select committee, who, recapitulating in character the deep reasoning of the petitioners, reported in favour of the repeal. Here was an attempt under the pretence of promoting liberty, happiness, and safety, to violate them all by a most tyrannical invasion of private property! Paine very unceremoniously and vigourously assailed both the assembly and its petitioners, and probably averted the act of *despotism* which the *freemen* were about to commit.

Paine is now to figure on another and a different stage. We must follow him to Europe, He had long formed the design of revolutionizing England, and

58 A sort of unread, innate republicans, who make themselves happy with thinking, that their tendency to a state of perfect freedom is determined by the near approaches which they make towards the savage condition. I must do them the justice to say that their progress is uncommonly rapid.

if he had not the arrogance to suppose he could succeed, he had the turpitude to attempt to carry his project into execution.

> During the war, in the latter end of the year 1780, I formed to myself a design of coming over to England, and communicated it to General Greene. I was strongly impressed with the idea, that, if I could get over to England with out being known and only remain in safety till I could get out a publication, that I could open the eyes of the country with respect to the madness and stupidity of its government. I saw that the parties in parliament had pitted themselves as far as they could go, and could make no new impression on each other. General Greene wrote very pressingly to me to give up the design, which, with reluctance, I did. But I am now certain, *that*, if I could have executed it, that it would not have been altogether unsuccessful.[59]

It was of importance to Paine to represent himself in England as a man of importance in the United States. Strongly impressed with this idea, and much as he ridiculed and affected to be opposed to titles, we have seen him annex to his name the appendage of "secretary for foreign affairs." In the same spirit and practice of imposture, from the same bad motive, and with a worse view, he connects himself with the skilful, enterprising, and warlike Greene. In the year 1780, Greene was probably too much employed in the

59 Note in the *Rights of Man*, part 2, Philadelphia, 1797.

southern states, the defence of which had been committed to his care, to attend to Paine's detestable scheme for revolutionizing England. Besides, Paine was then in disgrace, and almost in want of bread. It was but the preceding year that he had been dismissed by Congress with every epithet of opprobrium that legislative decorum could use. If Greene noticed him before his dismission, which is probable, after it he must have thought him unworthy of his attention. Had Paine told us, that when banished from the confidence and employ of Congress—when forced by imperious circumstances, as in the year 1780, into the ungracious service of Mr. Biddle—when all propitious scenes had closed upon him, he thought of returning to England to stir up commotion, that he might find in national uproar individual gratification, he might have been believed.

Having, in the year 1785, procured from Congress by much importunity three thousand dollars, from Pennsylvania five hundred pounds, and from the opulent and more liberal state of New York the confiscated estate of Mr. Davoe, he sailed, in April, 1787,[60] from the United States for France. In Paris, he exhibited to the Academy of Sciences the model of his bridge.

At this period the French revolutionary principles, principles which uprooted and laid waste every thing valuable, were vigourously germinat-

60 See his letter to general Washington.

ing in that ill-fated country. Upstart philosophers in Paris, then in daily intercourse with Mr. Jefferson, were plotting confusion. Men without wealth were eyeing wealth to be plundered. Atheists were sacking the churches in thought. Sanguinary wretches, with honied words issuing from their lips, were revelling by anticipation in blood. That Paine was admitted into the philosophical caverns of the philosophick banditti, is probable. What these tigers of Europe machinated for the benefit of France, of England, and of the world, is left to conjecture, but after what Europe and America have seen and suffered, we cannot, I think, conjecture amiss.

From France, Paine passed over to England with the model of his bridge: he arrived in London in September, 1787. From London, he went to Thetford to see his mother, whom he had the merit of allowing nine shillings sterling a week for her support, until his American recompense money was expended. In England, he became acquainted with my friend THOMAS WALKER, of Manchester, a man than whom one more enlightened and patriotick, more generous and noble, perhaps never lived. Mr. Walker, the friend and companion of Fox, was, what the Washingtons, the Clintons, the Hancocks, and the Adamses were before the declaration of in dependence was forced upon the colonies, an ENGLISH WHIG. He was indeed a zealous advocate of a reform in parliament that would have led, or I am now greatly mistaken, to a revolution which he would have abhorred, for he was a rational and solid friend of freedom, and had no inclination to the shedding of English blood by English hands. Principally at the expense of Mr. Walker, who was a liberal encourager of the arts, Paine went to Rotheram, in Yorkshire, where an iron arch of his bridge was cast. The bridge obtained for him amongst the mathematicians of Europe a high reputation.

Early in the year 1788, he published in London, his *Prospects on the Rubicon*, an octavo pamphlet of thirty-three pages. The United Provinces having abridged the assumed power of the Prince of Orange, and finding themselves in consequence involved with the Prussian monarch, who chose to consider the curtailment as a personal offence to him, had successfully applied for succour to Louis the XVI. England, it was thought, would embark in the war, which seemed to be threatened. The "Rubicon" was on this subject, but possessing no merit it attracted no notice. It betrays, however, his revolutionary design. "The people of France, he observes, are beginning to think for themselves, and the people of England resigning up the privilege of thinking.[61] This is both ill intentioned and false. The *people* of France were not beginning to think. A few men in France, beginning to act, were about to let loose the people from all restraint as instruments of their meditated mischief. The people of England had long

61 Page 5.

thought; nor will they ever resign their triple and undoubted privileges of freely thinking, freely speaking, and freely printing. He meant that France was approximating to a revolution, to a national hurricane of national passions, and that England was calm. He knew that revolution was intended in the one country, and he regretted, that from present appearances, tranquillity could not be disturbed in the other.

In the middle of the year 1789, he was arrested in London for debt. The books of Whiteside, a merchant who had failed, having passed into the hands of his creditors, it was found that Paine was a debtor to the bankrupt estate in the sum of near seven hundred pounds.[62] Arrested by the assignees, he was released from a three weeks imprisonment by Cleggett[63] and Murdoch, American merchants.

How he became indebted, is not and perhaps cannot be satisfactorily explained. It is alleged that Whiteside was employed to receive his remittances from the United States. Having no property but the American donatives, his remittances must have consisted of two sums only; the three thousand dollars which he had obtained from Congress in 1785, and the five hundred pounds which Pennsylvania gave him in the same year. As he remained in America a year and a half after, and

62 £91,550 in 2021 money. —Ed.

63 Clagget in the original. The merchants' name is spelled Cleggett and Murdoch in all other sources, so I have corrected the spelling. —Ed.

was probably in debt when the grants were made, it requires no extraordinary degree of credulity to believe, that the aggregate of the grants had been diminished before his departure from America upon his revolutionary expedition to England. But I deduce the inference from a supposition which is contrary to his usual practice; that if he was in debt, he paid his debts, and that when he was able to keep himself, he did not force himself upon others to maintain him.

At all events he would take his money with him, or with some of it purchase bills on Whiteside, we will suppose; in which case he would see them transmitted, or be assured that they would be by a different vessel. Whiteside receives them, and Paine has a credit with him. He arrived in London in September, 1787. Eighteen months after, he had overdrawn his merchant in the sum of near seven hundred pounds. He could not in this short time have expended that publick bounty and this private exaction, for generally he lived in holes and corners, and his diet, while I knew him, and long, I believe, before, was the poorest and filthiest; and though he was generally inebriated, yet it will be remembered that brandy was his liquor, and that if he drank a quart a day, which he did not sometimes exceed, it could not have exhausted his pecuniary funds. As to the castings for his bridge, they cost him next to nothing, the expense having been principally defrayed by Mr, Walker. If his grants were not expended, and we cannot from his grovelling and imposing habits imagine how they could have been, his unwarrantable draughts on Whiteside may be explained in a way which would not illumine the dark shades of his character.

Daily occurrences were now kind to his hopes. The French revolution, the pretended object of which, like the pretended object of all revolutions, was at first mild and beneficent reform, was advancing with accelerated velocity to its acme of spoliation and blood. Paine, peeping out of his lurking hole in the purlieus of London, watched with ecstacy every advance. The assembly of the Notables had been succeeded by the States-General, and the States-General, at the suggestion of the proteus Sieyès, without any delegation by the people, and therefore by usurpation, had declared itself the NATIONAL ASSEMBLY. The king was taken captive by men, who, vowing to each other republican attachments, were individually planning assassination and pillage to encompass and wear his crown. An unread, an unlettered populace, just enough oppressed by old masters to become the willing victims of greater oppression from new, were artfully and mercilessly freed, by those who were to be their tyrants and scourges, from those high obligations which they owed to themselves, their country, and their God, and with which they could not dispense without suffering, as they did, the greatest calamities, the most excruciating pains. Overjoyed at appearances in France, Paine, from imprisonment in London for debt, passed, while those measures were in train, to Paris for commotion.

> The edicts, he says, were again tendered to them, and the Count d'Artois undertook to act as representative for the king. For this purpose, he came from Versailles to Paris, in a train of procession; and the parliament were assembled to receive him. But show and parade had lost their influence in France; and whatever ideas of importance he might set off with, he had to return with those of mortification and disappointment. On alighting from his carriage to ascend the steps of the parliament house, the crowd (which was numerously collected) threw out trite expressions, saying, "this is monsieur d'Artois, who wants more of our money to spend." The marked disapprobation which he saw, impressed him with apprehensions; and the word *aux arms* (*to arms*) was given out by the officer of the guard who attended him. It was so loudly vociferated, that it echoed through the avenues of the house, and produced a temporary confusion: I was then standing in one of the apartments through which he had to pass.[64]

Having viewed with rapture the many mutations in the affairs of France; the sudden and magical shifting of power from the government to the people; from those who had sometimes abused it to those who could not use it well; from the few who had now and then oppressed to the

64 *Rights of Man*, part 1.

many who must necessarily and without remission grind; from those who had unfrequently devoted for days the rich to the Bastille, to those who would convert all France into a Bastille infinitely more gloomy and horrid; having whetted his keen appetite for subversion and ruin and massacre by cabals with the grand constructors of anarchy and desolation in France, the incendiary returned, to fire England.

The usurpation of the National Assembly, necessary in the process of confounding valuable, essential, and unalterable distinctions; necessary in the process of tumult and carnage; necessary in the throes which a great nation must suffer in going down from some oppression to all anarchy, and from all anarchy to what we now see and feel, all possible despotism; that act of assumption worked up all England, a few men of cool reflection, deep penetration, great experience, and greater solidity excepted, to a pitch of enthusiasm little short of madness. There was indeed something perhaps awfully grand, certainly horrour-exciting, in the ruins of an ancient and splendid government; in the transfer of all power from those who had excluded the people from any participation of it, to the people themselves, who knew not what to do with it; who could give it no form, no direction, and who, in a tumult of joy, excited by being masters, without knowing how to master themselves, could not but commit in a few months, probably in so many days, acts of tyranny and cruelty for which an age of well regulated freedom could not adequately compensate. Englishmen, whose hearts were sound, whose intentions were good, who loved their country, who idolised its solid and venerable freedom, but whose notions, as events have proved, were visionary, were in raptures at the disenthralment of a neighbouring nation, from long continued bondage. If excess of gratulation, and, to England, the danger of excess, could have been avoided, there would have been in all this a humanity of character, a generosity of feeling, a nobleness of spirit, which future ages would have admired and applauded. But men of property, men of sense, men of letters, men who therefore should not have suffered reflection to be overpowered by gorgeous novelties, by real mockeries, by changes which are productive of nothing but mischief, forgot that they were free, forgot that they were Englishmen, and, bounding in exulting thought over the precincts of their isle, became Frenchmen; not of the Notables, nor of the States-General, nor of the National Assembly, nor of its famous declaration of rights, for they had more liberty than the National Assembly could comprehend, or France enjoy, but, in the moments of frenzy, for frenzy it surely was, deposing Frenchmen; Frenchmen of the national razor stamp.[65] The world was to be-

65 All this I felt myself, but time, with the reflection and experience which time brings with it, has settled me down in that substantial medium which cannot be overstepped, whatever be the pretence, whatever the cause or the object, without vio-

come a republick of licentiousness in fact; a fraternity of incongruous and repelling atoms; a brotherhood of absurd principles and irreducible rules. This was the philosophy; this the charm; as if all nature, at the command of presumptuous and impious French men, would at once give way; as if, to use the language of Fielding's Square, the eternal fitness of things could be unfitted, recreated, and new modelled. Parisian Jacobin clubs were imitated in London. Fraternal hugs were interchanged by Jacobin plenipotentiaries. Revolution dinners were had all over England, and revolutionary toasts drank. Even Dr. Price gave for his toast at one of these jubilees of preparatory commotion, "the parliament of England; may it be come a *National Assembly!*" Could his meaning be mistaken? The National Assembly of France had declared for a limited monarchy, which England had. It had established, or rather it had prescribed upon paper, trial by jury. Was England without this palladium of safety? All the *paper* immunities which the National Assembly had allowed in its declaration of rights, which were never reduced to practice, fell vastly short of the excellence of British enjoyment. But France was only in the adolescence of her work. From limited monarchy she was verging to unlimited devastation. She was to be a spick-and-span new nation. All old things were to be done away. England too was to be new-born. The world a republick or a desart was one of the humane dog-

lating every principle and attribute of freedom.

mas. Hunted, pillaged, and blood-sucked, a desert it might be, but a republick, and least of all a republick like that to which France was hastening, it could not be.

A tempest so tremendous as that of France, in which all has been wrecked, directing its dreadful course towards England, where, as if lost to all the means of safety, the people invited its approach, rendered it necessary for some Nelson to clear the national ship, and prepare it triumphantly to resist the *pitiless peltings of the pitiless storm.* Burke, whose enlightened patriotism had been grateful to America, and whose oratory in the British senate had delighted Europe, came forth from the tranquil scenes of closing life to avert the whelming danger. His *Reflections*, uniting to profoundest sagacity unrivalled eloquence, have drawn from the world an undivided tribute of reluctant panegyrick. Who now can question its prophetick truths? All the enormities which, from the nature of the French revolution, he sagaciously predicted and admirably described, have been committed by the French people. Its never ending fluctuations but in a despotism infinitely more terrible than that which the united labours of the National Assembly and Convention over threw, he foretold and delineated with wonderful precision and force. Who, now that the events have happened which he prognosticated, can call his deep insight into human nature, rhapsody; his predictions, which have all been verified, the chimeras of a rhetorician's brain? He saw cause and effect and their connexion, and the great energy of his great mind, roused by the horrour which perfect vision had excited, was exerted to save his country. The safety of England, which is in truth the safety of the world, was his primary object. He was sure that neither the French revolution nor its deleterious effects could be kept within the limits of France. French audacity had already emboldened British presumption. From the subversion of the one government, transitions had been made to that of the other. Dr. Price had propagated from the pulpit the right of the nation to "cashier" the king for misconduct. That it has the right is indubitable, and that it has more than once practically asserted it, is certain. But as the nation was well acquainted with its right of cashiering for a deliberate, systematick, continued, and undoubted effort to destroy its freedom; and as cashiering was the daily right and practice of France, with whom he was fraternizing, could it be that no more was intended by the doctor, amiable as it is said he was, "than to remind the people of what they well knew, and of which they had not lost the recollection? The clubs and the nation, judging from the noise that was made, supported the *drum ecclesiastick*. Cashiering was in the mouths of men who had been taught nothing but that it meant violence, a deposing of the king, an extinction of the house of peers, a destruction of the whole government. Little was heard but cashiering. Nor was encouragement withheld from

France. The English spirit of English reform was to be quickened by French revolutionists.

BURKE'S *Reflections* were published early in the year 1790. Paine, who had been a Parisian spectator of Parisian scenes, went over from France to England in order to hasten the business of reform. In March, 1791, he published *The Rights of Man*, part first," in answer, as he thought fit to style it, to Burke's *Reflections*. This miserable production was, from similarity of causes, as popular in England as his *Common Sense* had been in America. France was in confusion; England was getting into confusion: rebellion was the order of the day. With Dr. Price and the clubs, Paine was for *cashiering*. He went, however, in language, a little further than they did. What he wanted of the elegance of the English reformers, he made up in impudent and vulgar boldness. In terms at once bland and fascinating, they contended for the abstract right of cashiering; Paine, coarsely and bluntly, not only for the right but for the necessity of immediate action. They did not, however, essentially differ, if at all, either in spirit or in object. The clubs patronized his work, and widely extended its circulation. Did this look like disapprobation?

Having experienced an unprecedented sale of his pamphlet;[66] having perceived the anarchial spirit

66 "Between forty and fifty thousand copies were *sold*." *Rights of Man*, part second. Probably more than a hundred thousand copies were published. This is a much greater number than

that was up; being sure that the government would be overthrown, broken into fragments, wholly demolished, and that, as in France, the wholesome doctrine of reform would be superceded by the bloody work of revolution, he returned, in the following May, to Paris, where violence was increasing in degree and swiftness far-exceeding the calculations, but not the hopes, of the most expert and sanguinary citizen of the *terrible republick.*

That he was well received at the seat of universal havock, will not be doubted. His British fame; the popular celebrity of his despicable work, had preceded him, and rendered a particular report to his co-plotters unnecessary. The fraternizing spirit in ruin which pervaded England, of whose existence he could give irrefragable assurances, must have delighted those artificers of the greatest human misery that human means ever inflicted.

Soon after his arrival, the king fled from Paris. On his return, Paine was in some danger of be coming the victim of a sedition which he had disseminated in London, and of which he was a friend in France. On the appearance of the king,

> an officer proclaimed the will of the National Assembly, that all should be silent and covered: in a minute all hats were on. Paine had lost his cockade, the *emblem* of *liberty and equality*. A cry arose; aristocrat! aristocrat! aristocrat! *à la lanterne! à la lanterne!* He was desired by those who stood near him to put on his hat, and

---

was published of his *Common Sense.*

> it was not till after some time that the mob was satisfied by explanation.[67]

The *mob*, elevated to *liberty and equality*, going *à la lanterne* with one of the most distinguished champions of disorder, would have been a scene curious enough; but he was unknown to them. Poor abused wretches they were unacquainted with his mission to England, and with what he had done for their cause, or they would not have threatened to hang him at a lamp post for neglecting to put into his hat the emblem of liberty and equality! He is dead. It may be well that the bloodhounds, whom he had assisted in letting loose upon shrieking innocence, did not add to their crimes by tearing him to pieces.

The Abbé Sieyès now perceived, and this is the fatal errour of many sensible men, that he had gone too far, but he saw it only when he could not impede the onward course of the tumult and desolation to whose motion he had greatly contributed. He now began to apprehend that the kingly office, as well as the king, was in danger; he was sure that France was unfit for a republick, and that the destruction of the monarchy and the monarch would be followed, as it was, by the destruction of civil and social order. When the disease was beyond the power of the physician, he publickly challenged all writers in defence of the monarchial against the republican system. "If it be asked," he said,

67 *Impartial Sketch*

> what is my opinion with respect to hereditary right, I answer, without hesitation, that, in good theory, an hereditary transmission of any power or office, can never accord with the laws of a true representation. Hereditaryship is, in this sense, as much an attaint upon principle as an outrage upon society: *But*, refer to the histories of all elective monarchies and principalities: is there one in which the elective mode is not worse than the hereditary succession?

Paine, elate with the rare work which was going on in France, as well as with his British success, accepted the challenge. His publick letter of acceptance is dated Paris, July 8, 1791, the moment of his departure for England. France was now in a condition to complete her own ruin without his aid. His post was England, where the work of subversion, dismay, and horrour was to be prosecuted.

On the 13th of the same month, he arrived in London, where the French revolution was to be celebrated by party feasting and toasts, prepared by party arts. He was not, however, one of the dinner celebrators. It was "not thought *prudent* that he should attend."[68]

But he attended a meeting of the *reformists* at the Thatched House Tavern on the 20th of the following August, where an inflammatory address and declaration were read and afterwards published.

68 *Rights of Man*, part 2.

Horne Tooke, perhaps the most acute man of the age, was at the meeting; and as it was rumoured, Paine observes,[69] that the great grammarian was the author of the address, he takes the liberty of mentioning the fact, that he wrote it himself. I never heard of the rumour, which was doubtless a fiction formed and asserted by Paine, merely to gratify his egotism. No one could mistake the uncouth and ungrammatical writings of the one for the correct and elegant productions of the other.

"On the 4th of November he assisted, on the eve of the gunpowder plot, at the customary celebration of the 5th, by the revolution society. He was thanked for his *Rights of Man*, and gave for his toast–*The revolution of the world!*"[70]

In February, 1792, he published the second part of his *Rights of Man*. Part first, is full of sedition; part second openly and fearlessly calls on the people to revolt, and unequivocally advocates a subversion of the government.

Never before had the freedom, the protection, and the hospitality of the nation, or of any other nation, been so daringly and outrageously abused. Whatever irregularities or oppressions Mr. Pitt may afterwards have committed, occasioned and probably rendered indispensable by the irregularities and the oppressions of the times, surely he was patient and forbearing with Paine to a fault. Paine was an alien. He was indeed an Englishman

---

69 *Rights of Man*, part 2.

70 Oldys

by birth, but the obligations of birth had been dispensed with by the one party, and alienated by the other, in the treaty of peace of 1783. What government, besides that of England, would have suffered an alien to beard it to set it at defiance—to pronounce it an usurpation in principle and corrupt in practice—to propose its overthrow in language that nobody could mistake—to invite the people to revolution and blood? Would not the government of the United States energetically exert its power to punish offences, committed even by a *citizen*, so intrinsically traitorous? Would the people allow an *alien* thus to interfere in their affairs? I know that the government would promptly and vigourously punish; it ought to do so. I know that the people, were they to relish a dismemberment of the union, a destruction of the national government, if suggested and enforced by a native citizen, would rise indignantly against both, if proposed and urged by an *alien*. On the subject of alienism, there is no nation so tender as the American. Is a man an alien? Does he meddle with politicks? If so, he is told, and with few exceptions he is universally told, that, being an alien, he has no right to speak, much less to write, on our political concerns. Native opposition to alien meddling extends much further. Emigrants, settled with their families and fortunes forever, and naturalized by all the forms of law, are always considered, and by all parties treated, as *foreigners*.[71]

71 On the subject of foreigners, Paine, in the first part of his

Rights of Man, sought to deceive the English people by representations which he knew to be false. "France and America bid all comers welcome, and initiate them into all the rights of citizenship." Two years after this unceremonious assertion, France imprisoned him because he was born in England! As to the constitution and laws of the United States, they do indeed bid all comers welcome, and initiate them, by naturalization, after five or ten years residence,(*) into all the rights of native citizenship, but one or two. But what are constitutions and laws when almost universally opposed by obstinate opinion, unconquerable prejudices, and cherished habits? Birth in the United States would have covered all Paine's faults in his controversy with Deane. LEE's military genius was repressed, even during the revolutionary war, because it was not native. Montgomery's death before Quebec is mentioned only at elections, and then but to operate on the generous feelings of Irishmen in favour of the *republican* party. Gates's conquest of Burgoyne was envied, and is now rarely mentioned, because he was an Englishman. General Hamilton, who was born in one of the English West-India islands, came to the *colonies* when a lad—entered into the revolutionary war with zeal—became, early in the war, one of the aids of Washington—gallantly commanded a regiment at the capture of Cornwallis—fought through the revolution—was a member of the Convention from which our national constitution originated was the first secretary of the treasury, or chancellor of the exchequer, under the national government—he formed the department and brought order out of chaos he was perhaps the ablest writer and most eloquent man in America; even HAMILTON, one of the most ingenuous and disinterested of mankind, was called, considered, and treated as a *foreigner!* His early distinctions are to be ascribed to the circumstances of the times; to a poverty of talents. The late president Adams, who is now in newspaper essays defending or explaining his administration, says, that being a *foreigner*, it could not be supposed that Hamilton could have American feelings, or be well informed on American affairs! And yet he was youth when he came. All that he knew, and he knew as much as man well can know, he learnt during his residence amongst us, which was from the first day of his landing in the colonies. Mr. Gallatin, the present secretary of the treasury, born in Geneva, a gentleman but little if at all inferiour to Hamilton in capacity and acquirements, is, like all the rest, stigmatized as a *foreigner* by *all* parties. He was appointed by Mr. Jefferson, who, great as his other faults are, is, I believe, but undoubtedly in a great measure, exempt from this prejudice. Mr. Madison, on his accession to the presidency, fixed on Mr. Gallatin for his secretary of state, but he was driven from an intended nomination of him to the senate by his own party in that body, who threatened, at all hazards, to negative it if made, *because he was a* FOREIGNER. In this instance the new president was overawed by his party in the senate. He was obliged to nominate Mr. Robert Smith, a *native*; a gentleman, indeed, in manners, but, as may be seen in his diplomatick correspondence, with talents fitting him only for a counting house clerk. The senate readily and unanimously consented to his appointment. Against foreigners by birth and citizens by adoption, universal prejudice has formed an universal conspiracy. The subjoined address, written by me at the suggestion of some of the gentlemen of the meeting by which it was adopted and published, will more fully explain this subject. Its great length may be excused by what may be considered its importance in illustrating our national opinions, national prejudices, national manners, and party management.

At a respectable meeting, consisting of about five hundred Adopted Republican Citizens of the City of New York, held at Lyon's Hotel, Mott Street, on Friday Evening, April 14, 1809.

Mr. Archibald Taylor being unanimously called to the chair, and *Dr. Stephen Dempsey* appointed Secretary.

The subjoined address was unanimously adopted, and ordered to be published.

To the Adopted Republican Citizens of the City New York.

FELLOW CITIZENS,

A long train of disagreeable circumstances have called us together, and induced us to address you upon a subject, which, for years, we have acutely felt and deeply deplored. Some of you, groaning under oppression in your native land, have vol-

Keeping within constitutional bounds—and who

untarily emigrated from it, whilst others, more afflicted by despotism and less favoured by propitious events, find your selves in the condition of involuntary exile. All, however, have chosen as a resting place in the journey through life, this "asylum for the oppressed of all nations." Here, perhaps mistaking the character of human nature, we pleasingly anticipated, from those who avow themselves the friends of freedom, exemption from that religious persecution and civil tyranny, whose inexorable reign had forced us from our native country. Alas! how greatly were we mistaken! how egregiously have we been disappointed! Our constitutions and governments are indeed free, but between these admirable institutions and ourselves a tyranny is intervened, much less tolerable than that from which we fled. *We are denominated* FOREIGNERS *and treated as* SLAVES.

On this odious subject, we beseech you, fellow citizens, to listen to us.

The land in which we live, discovered by an illustrious Spaniard, was settled by our free, enterprising, and hardy countrymen. Oppression in church and state, to which they were too proud and enlightened to submit, forced them, as it has compelled you, to leave their native homes, and to seek, in the wilds of America, freedom and repose. Here, where the panther, and man not less ferocious than the panther, held dominion, they settled, resting their weary limbs and piously thanking God for their deliverance from the intolerance of the church and the despotism of the state; here, our noble and high minded ancestors introducing our principles, our language, our laws, and our habits, laid the foundation of this vast empire; for themselves, for their descendants, and for their countrymen. *This therefore is truly*, and we may emphatically assert, *the land of our fathers*. Why then are we persecuted? Why are invidious distinctions malignantly disseminated and industriously maintained? Why are we branded with the offensive epithet of FOREIGNERS?

Fellow Citizens, we are thirty-three years old as a nation. The moment before the Declaration of Independence was promulgated by Congress and confirmed by the Provincial leg-

ought to transcend them?—he might have written

islatures, every man in the colonies was a subject of the King of England. Then, the Irish, the English, the Scotch, and the native descendants of our countrymen, owed the same allegiance and received the same protection. All, with few exceptions, revolted, and of those exceptions the native descendants of our ancestors were the most numerous. In the memorable war for independence, (freedom was afterwards to be established and maintained) the Europeans, who constituted a full moiety of our efficient force, were distinguished for fidelity to the country, zeal in its cause, wisdom in its councils, and intrepidity in the field. Upon the illustrious Danies of Montgomery, of Gates, and of Mercer, we reflect with proud satisfaction. Irishmen! the gallant MONTGOMERY, who nobly fell in defence of our independence, drew his first breath in the land, exuberant in poets and in orators, whose green fields have for ages been drenched in the blood of her children, for having made generous efforts to obtain national independence and republican freedom. Englishmen! that accomplished soldier, GATES, the conqueror of Burgoyne, the atchiever of a military event most splendid in our history, and upon which in a great measure the success of the revolution depended, was born in that island which gave birth to Shakespeare and to Milton, to Newton and to Locke, to Sydney and to Russel; to many sages and martyrs of freedom, and from which all our correct notions of civil liberty are drawn. Scotchmen! descendants of a learned and gallant ancestry, MERCER, who bravely sealed with his blood the independence of the United States, was the countryman of Bruce and Wallace, of Home and Burns, of Hume and Robertson. All, at the guished but by merit. All, in case of failure in our revolutionary struggles, had committed the same offence, and incurred the same punishment, for all were subjects of the same monarch. Then, animated with a noble ardour in a glorious cause, and united by common danger and common advantages, envious distinctions between citizens of native and foreign birth, the effect of ignorance or the dictate of personal agrandizement, were unknown. Fayette was eulogised—Hamilton caressed—Pułaski lamented, and Steuben revered. Congress, following the sage example of Peter the Great; cherish-

as much and as long as he pleased, unreproached

ing a liberal and enlightened policy; knowing that national population is national strength, and that literature and the sciences constitute the solid foundations of national greatness, invited and encouraged emigration. In one of the many expressive and eloquent appeals to reason and to the passions which were issued to an admiring world by that sagacious and illustrious body, more than native immunities were held forth, as incentives to emigrants. Is the endearing address of Congress to the people of Ireland forgotten? Has faction absorbed —has clamour banished revolutionary opinions, and violence stunned revolutionary feelings? Are we a degenerate race, unworthy of the renown, incapable of appreciating, and unable justly to estimate the virtues of those times? In that address, the people of Ireland were saluted as brethren of the same prin ciples—victims of the same oppression—involved in the same ignominy, and co-inheritors of the same benefits, with which the efforts of Congress might or might not be crowned. They were represented as identified with revolutionary America in consanguinity, in cause, in feeling, and in interest, and they were cordially invited to come and equally partake of the new world. We cheerfully availed ourselves of the invitation; we eame: we have made permanent settlements in the land of our forefathers; we admire and we are attached to our republican institutions; we have complied with the injunctions of the constitutions and the laws, and we will support them, upon equal terms, with our lives and our fortunes. But how are we treated? What has been our reception? Has good faith been observed? Have the promises been performed? Are not we, who are CITIZENS *by all the solemnities and obligations of law*, treated as aliens stigmatised as foreigners_made use of for personal and party purposes, but carefully excluded even from choice in the selection of our rulers? Can any other definition of slavery be given? Can human ingenuity devise offence more galling and complete, more humiliating and degrading? We complain not of the constitutions and the laws: they are liberal in principle and benign in operation. They enjoin an abjuration of former allegiance: have we not with alacrity complied with the injunction? They require an oath of fidelity to the un-

with being a foreigner. There is, however, in ex-

---

ion and to the states: devoted in spirit and in truth to both, we have eagerly taken it. What more is required? What more can be expected? The laws require no more. Shall an under-plot, a counter operation, individual jealousy, and pale-faced cabal, frowned upon by the very elements of the state, subvert the law—put it at defiance trample it under foot? The law places upon the same undis tinguishable level, the citizen of native and the citizen of foreign birth. Are we to be told in this enlightened age that the law is not to govern; that the essence of well-ordered society is not a government of laws, but a government of the worst passions? Go back then to a state of anarchy; tear out the bowels of society; revert to the rude condition of untutored nature, and let the strongest govern. We have never ceased to cherish and to inculcate those opinions which are most consonant to the civil and social state. We have remonstrated against distinctions, at once impolitick and unjust, between native and adopted citizens; but have not our remonstrances and efforts been in vain? No zeal, no exertions, no services, however disinterested, unremitted, or great, have been suffiçient to shield us from an epithet which, while it poisons the social and impairs the enjoyment of political life, must ultimately terminate in the ruin of the republican party in this city. We have been incessantly calumniated for having been born in the land *which gave birth to the fathers of this country*. After long and patient suffering under accumulated abuse, from many of the very party which we have zealously and at great expense of labour and money supported, a line of demarkation is at length drawn, too legible to be mistaken, and too offensive not to rouse your feelings. Fellow citizens, *you are systematically excluded from the republican committee of nomination*, now assembled to *name representatives to govern you*. Look at the ward committees, read over their names, and lo! how entirely, and with what caution and care you have been excluded from a vote in the selection of legislators, by whose acts your lives, your liberty, and your property, will be bound? Is not this the very slavery from which you revolted in your native land? Is it not in kind and degree exactly the despotism from which the colonies, now United States,

treme cases a material difference between an al-

---

revolted when under the dominion of the British king? What greater tyranny can you be under than that which calls upon you to support legislators, in the selection of whom you have no choice? "Representation and taxation," Congress asserted when it severed the ties which had bound the colonies to the parent state, "are inseparable." The maxim was just then; is it not so now? If it at any time stood in need of the force of authority or the persuasions of eloquence, both were lavished upon it in the parliament of England, when England was transporting hither her feets and armies to repress the welcome risings of a free spirit. "My position, said the great Lord Camden in the house of lords, is this; I repeat it; I will maintain it to my last hour. *Taxation and representation are inseparable.* This position is founded on the laws of nature. It is more; it is itself an eternal law of nature. For whatever is a man's own, is absolutely his own. No man has a right to take it from him without his consent. Whoever attempts to do it, attempts an injury; whoever does it, commits a robbery." Alas! has our republick turned upon itself, and in the short period of twenty years (from the adoption of the constitution) abandoned its own principles? To you, fellow citizens, the maxim is now denied: Taxation and representation are no longer inseparable! The same despotism which England attempted to impose upon the United States, is now lorded over you. You will be called upon in the imperious name of the law to contribute your proportion to the maintenance of government: for you, laws will be made, prescribing punishment and awarding death; but remember, that the persons, who view you as their slaves, have assiduously excluded you from the selection of the men to whom power so important and of such magnitude is to be confided. Shall we again name the known and alleged cause of this exclusion? It is said that you are FOREIGNERS! Yes, you who have complied with all the requisites of the constitution and the laws, and are of right and to all intents and purposes *citizens*, are banished, by men calling themselves republicans, from publick confidence! Countrymen of Emmet and of Tone, of Gerald and of Margarot, of Fletcher and of Skirving, what say you to this? If all self respect and national recollec-

ien who has no claim to protection but that which

---

tions be not extinct—if you are not the inglorious descendants of illustrious ancestors—if all remembrance of the tyranny which you yourselves have suffered, and the toils and perils which you have encountered to escape from its deadly grasp, be not removed from the seat memory—if your feelings be not blunted by faction—if your hearts are susceptible of a pang, you will *resist* this systematic effort to reduce you to the condition of slaves. You will be called upon to vote for the republican ticket. *Vote not at all.* Those who for years have ridiculed many of you and calumniated you all, and who have at length capped the climax of their sneers and their insults by excluding you from the committee of domination, will solicit, flatter, and cajole you in behalf of a ticket, which they have kindly nominated for you! Fellow citizens, WITHHOLD YOUR BOTES! Tell them, if you condescend to listen to their importunities for your suffrages, that you will extend your aid to the republican cause when their liberality, equalling the liberality of the laws, will admit you to an equal participation. Resolve to abstain from the polls, and teach your *would-be-masters*, by mildness of demeanour and firmness of resolution, that resisting tyranny wherever you find it, or from whatever quarter it may come, you will be respected.

RESOLUTIONS.

Whereas the just resistance of the colonies, now United States, to the government of England, was founded upon the fact, that the colonies were not represented in the parliament, and that therefore they were not bound by its laws; and whereas our countrymen essentially contributed to the atchievement of our independence; and whereas we have been systematically excluded from the general republican committee, now assembled, and therefore from all choice in the selection of members who are to represent the city of New York in the assembly of the state. Therefore,

Resolved, unanimously, That repelling with just indignation a distinction made between republican citizens of the same state, we will not support a ticket, in the formation of which we have been excluded from any participation.

the common hospitalities of all nations give, and a subject or citizen who of right owes allegiance and enjoys protection . But in either, inflammatory invitations to rebellion are, especially in periods of great agitation, an offence, and the offence is aggravated if committed by an alien who has no interest either in the peace or in the integrity of the state in which he sojourns. Whatever, therefore, party and passion, prejudice and malignity , ignorance and injustice may roundly assert, Paine experienced

---

Resolved, unanimously, That 500 copies of the above address and resolution be printed in hand bills, for the benefit of our fellow republican adopted citizens.

Resolved, unanimously, That the said address and resolutions be published in the *American Citizen.*

ARCHIBALD TAYLOR, Chairman.
S. DEMPSEY, Secretary.

(*) The first naturalization act under the federal government required a previous residence of two years. The second, that of 1798, passed by the *federal party,* then in power, who found that naturalizing operated against them, required *fourteen.* The third and last and present act, passed by the *republican* party in the year 1801, who had just got into power, wanted strength, and knew that eight-tenths of the persons naturalized arrange themselves with the republican party, and generally vote for their masters, requires *five* years previous residence, but it is so clogged with forms, such as giving two years notice of *intention* to become citizens, that the average time of probation may be said to be eight years. Indeed the time of greatest probation, if that mean punishment, is *after* naturalization, for the only right allowed the naturalized, is that of voting for a native. Naturalized citizens are to the Americans what the Helots were to the Grecians. There can be no greater slavery—no greater punishment for human pride and presumption; I might add, for disaffection in one's native land.

from the British government a mildness, a forbearance, which no man, urging amongst us in the boldest language of sedition a dissolution of the union, a destruction of the national government, and a consequent civil war, could expect from the government of the United States. The first part of his *Rights of Man*, not a jot less intemperate and rebellious than the second, was published not only with impunity, but without notice from the government. I do not mention the fact in commendation. Paine ought to have been punished. Alarm, if the government was alarmed, is a poor apology. When did fear beget respect? When did imbecility avert danger?

Parliament had been frequently petitioned for a reform in the representation of the house of commons, and the petitions had been amply and ably discussed by the orators of both parties. These petitions were, however, uniformly and necessarily unsuccessful. I say necessarily, for the ministers and their friends knowing, as I hope, that one innovation would, by an unavoidable succession of innovations, lead to a dissolution of the government, opposed it, and the chiefs of the petitioning party did not agree as to the nature and extent of reform. Fox, the Demosthenes of the Whigs, was vehemently adverse, and in this he was wise, to *universal suffrage*. Grey, Sheridan, Erskine, and the rest, with perhaps one or two exceptions, coincided with him. Their notions of a reform, for they had none of an element that is naturally and necessarily always tumultuous, were judiciously limited. But Paine was against all petitioning. He considered petitioning as a sort of playful skirmishing very unlike that bloody battle which he wished to see fought, and to which he was endeavouring to inspirit the people of England. "I confess I have no idea of petitioning for rights. Whatever the rights of the people are, they have a right to them, and none have a right either to withhold them or to grant them."[72]

If he would not petition, what would he do? Why, revolt—take up arms—plunge the nation into civil war—batter down the government with cannon.

But apart from the criminality of the intention, what shall we say of his reasoning? That, as is usual with him, it is very despicable. What say you, citizens of the United States? If you are wronged, if you are aggrieved, if you but imagine either, do you not petition Congress; do you not petition your state legislatures? Is it not your right and your duty to do so? Would *you* disdain to petition? Would you, without petitioning, without laying your grievances before your legislatures, rashly and ruinously fly to arms? A maxim like Paine's, as foolish as it is wicked, must be abhorred. A doctrine like his—*rebel against all law*—is not nor can it be tolerated by any government or people. If it should be said in his behalf that parliament had often been petitioned in

72 *Rights of Man*, part 2.

vain, and that petitioning had, therefore, become useless; then we perceive the mischievous design; then we perceive the motive, and nothing is necessary or should follow but swift and exemplary punishment.

That his meaning might not be misunderstood, and I see not how it could be, he illustrates it, in another place, by example.

> Much is to be learned from the French constitution. Conquest and tyranny transplanted themselves with William the conqueror from Normandy into England, and the country is yet disfigured with the marks. May the example of all France contribute to regenerate the freedom which a province of it destroyed.[73]

What was the example of France? Revolution: *à la lanterne*! What was her constitution, from which much may be learned? A paper of absurdities; an instrument that lasted nearly a year; a charter, unlike Magna Charta, of which we have wisely taken much into our federal constitution; an unsubstantial production of men trivial in good, but potent in mischief.

Still the government moved not. Even this avowal of his revolutionary mission from France, neither awakened its vigilance nor brought into action its self-preserving powers. Encouraged by lenity, he proceeded.

73 *Rights of Man*, part 1.

> The bill which the present Mr. Pitt brought into parliament some years ago to reform parliament, was on the same erroneous principles. The right of reform is in the nation in its original character, and the constitutional method would be by general convention elected for the purpose. A government on the principles in which constitutional governments, arising out of society, are established, cannot have the right of altering itself.[74]

This is one of the best of his uniformly bad arguments. There never was in any nation, nor can there be, a right like that for which he contends, and which he considers as fundamental and unalienable.

Amongst a people without government, (if there ever were such a people) and over whom government is to be, a convention, *arising out of society* (if such a people can be called society) would be a prerequisite to just government. But where government is established, there never was, I apprehend, a distinct convention constituted for the sole purpose of correcting its abuses: the solecism has been, as yet, too great for the world, and I am pretty certain that it will continue to be so. Such a convention would be a supreme power, rendering the government at once a preposterous and useless existence. Paine might perhaps have allowed, I think

74 *Rights of Man*, part 2. It was probably this passage that suggested the British Convention, which sat in Scotland the following year, of which Gerald and Margarot were members. The convention was a self-created and unauthorised body, organized to overawe Parliament and accelerate revolution.

he does in his *Rights of Man*, that the present government of the United States arose out of society. Now, being established, does it admit of a distinct convention, constituted for the purpose of reforming it? No, it does not, and he knew it, he was very ignorant. The government of the United States—I include all its branches—is its own censor, and it would denominate a convention, even arising out of society, organized to correct its abuses, to overawe and to controul it, a treasonable body, and as such, if not guilty of a base and cowardly desertion of its duty, act against it. Nor is such a convention admissible amongst us for any purpose whatsoever. The people cannot with regard either to the national government or to the governments of the respective states, establish a convention for any one purpose of government. Operative propositions for altering our constitutions cannot come from the people: they must come from the national or from the state legislatures, or they cannot approach us at all. The constitution of the state of New York was altered, I will not say amended, a few years since, by a convention of the state. But did the convention proceed from the people? It did not; it was convened by the state legislature, and if it had not been, there would have been no convention; the people having no right, and they know it, to form one. But even this convention, so called by the state legislature, was not for reforming the abuses of the government; that is a very different and a very inadmissible thing. As to our federal convention, out of which the national government arose, it was not assembled by the national government, for we had none, nor by the people, for they assumed no such power: it was recommended by a competent authority. I say that we had no national government, for that cannot be government which has not enforcing powers. In whatever light Paine's argument—for no doubt he called it an argument—be viewed; whether in respect to abstract principles, as to which it is exceedingly absurd, or in reference to practice, of which there is not nor can there be any example, it was equally weak and mischievous. It abused the ignorant by deceiving them. It was laughed at or despised by the wise.

The second part of the *Rights of Man* is, with unimportant alterations and additions, merely a transcript of the first. Part the second contains chapters

"Of Society and Civilization.

"Of the origin of the present old governments.

"Of the old and new systems of government.

"On Constitutions:" to which a miscellaneous chapter is added.

Whoever recurs to the chapter on "Society and Civilization," in the hope or expectation of finding a regular and able disquisition, will be miserably disappointed. A few loose observations are thrown together without method, and made without either elegance or force. Of the progress from the primitive state to that which is termed the civilized, nothing is said; and as to the diversified nature of society, the infinite complexity of its actions and features, and the principles from which they proceed, there is nothing to recompense the labour of perusal; no originality, no order, no vigour of thought, no gracefulness of expression; nothing to admire, nor anything to condemn, but malice of design, and a gross imposition of a formal chapter on informal nothing.

His chapter "of the origin of the present old governments," consists of two pages! The title is a misnomer, for of the plural he takes no notice. Its wretched contents are confined to the British government, whose origin he ignorantly refers to the Norman conquest. He either knew nothing of the Saxon principles, which form the basis of it, as well as of our own, or, in order to excite the people to tumult and devote the government to subversion, he chose falsely to represent it as one of conquest only. The Norman conquest did not annihilate the ancient liberty of England. It did indeed introduce a new line of kings, and it suspended for a time its freedom. But liberty afterwards shone forth with more than its ancient Saxon splendour. The great charter was succeeded by the treason law of Edward the III. the principal provision of which has been wisely incorporated into our federal constitution. And these and other glorious acts were again followed by those substantial ones of freedom, which were passed at the settlement of William the III. If, therefore, his anomalous thoughts, his worthless remarks, were applicable to England at the period of the Norman conquest, subsequent events had superceded and rendered them inapplicable and impertinent when he wrote them. But his object was not to reason: it was to misrepresent; it was to involve the people in misery, the government in ruin.

On "the old and new systems of governments," he is yet more seditious, but not more argumentative. The *new* differs from the old in the difference, in his opinion, between representative and hereditary functions. If he meant that a representative executive in contradistinction to one that is hereditary, is a branch of government altogether new, what shall we say of his ignorance? Had he no acquaintance with the histories of those nations, ancient and modern, over which executives, no matter by what name called, whether kings or emperours, consuls or dictators, had been *elected?* Was he ignorant of their perpetual turbulence; of the many revolutions which their elections occasioned; of the oceans of blood which were shed, for no purpose but that of capricious and useless change? But these elections were made by a few; by a senate; by a diet; by a cabal; not by the *people*. Indeed! Does then the mere *extension* of a fundamental principle of a government constitute a new principle and a new government? I wish too to know what nation, when his rebellious *Rights of Man* burst upon the world, was in possession of this new government. The United States? Not at all; and yet he alluded to the United States, and to no other nation, for then France had not cut off the head of her monarch, nor overturned her government, nor plundered her churches, nor covered the face of her soil with blood. The constitution of the United States peremptorily denies to the *people*, absolutely withholds from them, the right of electing their president; and it does so undoubtedly upon the presumption, which is the fact, that they are incompetent to a wise choice. If this be not the reason, then the right is wantonly and tyrannically withheld. The president, by the constitution, is to be chosen by electors, an intermediate aristocratical body, thrust in between the president and the people, who may indeed be elected by the people, or be chosen by the state legislatures, as the state legislatures see fit. This was the *principle* when the anarchist wrote, but what is the *practice* to which it has since been reduced by Mr. Jefferson, who is considered by his party as the quintessence of all republicanism; as the very marrow of the *new* system? Considering the constitutional relation of the people to the electors, completely aristocratical as the process of the election is, as too near, he indirectly, but all powerfully, nominates his successor; a caucus of members of Congress is convened at his nod, and managed by him; it echoes his nomination; the people clap their hands and shout for republicanism, and the electors, awed by the popular will, which always obeys the mandate of the president, are forced, by their love of popularity, by considerations of office, if they have any, by present expectations and future prospects, to vote for the successor nominated by the expiring president. Is this *election?* Is this the new system? Is it not as old as intrigue, and is not intrigue as old as politicks? If this be not monarchy in fact, with hypocrisy and abominable delusion added to it, then a right angle is a square.

And yet in this very chapter, contrasting the hereditary and representative systems, Paine says: "but the case is, that the representative system diffuses such a body of knowledge throughout a nation, on the subject of government, as to *explode ignorance and preclude imposition!* The craft of courts cannot be acted on that ground: there is no place for mystery; no where for it to be begun."

How heartily our politicians must laugh at his ignorance, or applaud his imposition!

I hazard nothing in remarking, unless it be hazardous to state the truth, that, however excellent, the system of our government may be in theory, the whole operation of our system of politicks in practice, with the chiefs who lead the two parties, and who by hook or by crook govern the nation, is one of *mystery, craft, and imposition*. In these articles, which abound amongst us, no nation can vie with the United States. That I hold to be impossible. His chapter "on constitutions," is a tedious history of the rise, progress, and final adoption of our national constitution. Upon this he builds an argument which is at war with fact. The constitution, he gravely and didactically remarks, is a law to the government, as the statutes of the government are laws to the people. I grant that it is so in theory, and that it cannot be so in practice. But he affirms that the constitution *cannot* be broken by the government, as in all disputed points, being printed, it can be produced to settle them. Poor innocent man! He makes this *philosophical* assertion in the hope of convincing the people of England, that they would be greatly advantaged by a revolution; by destroying their government, and, if either commotion or usurpation would permit, by making a *paper* constitution, which, being a law to the government as in the United States, the government could not violate.

How many instances have we of a total disregard by Congress of the principles, the spirit, and the letter of the constitution? How often has this law been violated? The chiefs of the two parties do indeed sometimes read it, although, generally speaking, they do not read much; but having different politicks, different expectations, different designs, they expound it differently. To a federalist, it means one thing; to a republican, another, exactly the reverse; and both bend it and break it at pleasure to suit their purposes. Neither party respects it when it is in their way. It has now, in the twenty-second year of its age, been oftener infracted than the English bill of rights has during a period of more than one hundred years. The people of England have another advantage over us. Opposed to all violations of that inestimable act, they have the merit of not being involved in the guilt of its transgression. But when the *federal* majority in Congress, to answer some party purpose, violate it, and they have often done so, the federal party, always following their leaders, commend and support the violation; and when, by ever-fluctuating popular will, power shifts, and the republican majority in Congress tear the paper constitution *to tatters, to very rags*, the republican party, also following their leaders in atrocious acts, and leading them, when, sometimes, they wish not to commit them, ring peals of joy throughout the country. Some advantage has been gained over the opposite party, and as the constitution is always out of the question in party struggles, that is subject enough for triumph. In party marches and counter-marches, skirmishes and battles, the constitution is no impediment in the way of party victory and despotism.

The miscellaneous chapter was peculiarly intended to make the soldiery and the poor eager for a revolution, by holding out to them suitable rewards. It proposes, on the supposition of a new government being established, an augmentation of the pay of the army—a national gift to new married people—a premium to parents for children—a fund for the poor and the aged—for men out of work, and for the education of a million and a half of children. Did we not know that his object was to assort and to organize all the means of national destruction, we might dignify his project with the epithet of chimerical.

He "takes it for granted," in another part of the chapter,[75]

> that an alliance may be formed between England, France, and America, and that the national expenses of France and England may consequently be lessened. The same fleets and armies will no longer be necessary to either, and the reduction may be made *ship for ship* on each side. Though, he adds, I have no direct authority on the part of America, I have good reason to conclude that she is disposed to enter into a consideration of such a measure, *provided* that the governments with which she might ally acted as *national governments*, and not as courts enveloped in intrigue and mystery.

No doubt France would be pleased not only with the reduction but with the destruction of the British fleet. There is not a Jacobin either in Europe or in the United States that does not sigh for the ruin of that force, that proud and triumphant force, which is the safety of the world against the ambition and tyranny of Napoleon. Something there is unaccountably and unutterably silly in the proposition. It contemplates a *national* gov-

75 When the *Rights of Man* reached Lewes, where Paine married Miss Ollive, the women, as with one voice, said: "Od rot im, let im come ear if he dast, an we'll tell im what the rights of women is: we'll toss im in a blanket and ring am out o' Lewes wi' our frying pans."

ernment; a government formed according to the atheistical principles of the desolaters of France, upon the destruction of the old, experienced, solid, and free government of England. If, which God forbid, England should ever have the misfortune to be a republick, still a fleet, with all its present rights and privileges, and even its abuses; all its spirit, all its gallantry, and all its success, would be essential to the maintenance of what I hope will be eternal in duration, her NATIONAL INDEPENDENCE.

But as to the alliance, which America would be "willing to enter into with England, *provided* she had a *national* government," he had not, for sooth, *direct* authority from the United States to make a specifick proposition. No, I think not, nor any indirect authority either, though he wished to make the people of England believe, that, being a man of great consequence, he had some sort of a mission, even from the United States, to revolutionize England, and, if successful, then to propose an alliance with the *national* government. Of all his impostures and vanities, all his presumptions on ignorance of his character, this is the greatest. No direct authority from a government which had found itself obliged to dismiss him from a clerkship for a breach of office!

Wretched as Paine's *Common Sense* is in point of literary merit, his *Rights of Man*, a pandect of anarchy, is still its inferiour. Horne Tooke, it was said, corrected its grammatical errours, but every page of the work refutes the assertion. He could not have sanctioned with his name such sentences as the following, which occur in almost every page of the book.

"He introduced his proposal to the doctor by letter, which is now in the hands of Mr. Beaumarchais in Paris, stating, *that*, as the Americans had dismissed their king, *that* they would want another." *Rights of Man*, part 1.

"In France aristocracy had one feature less in its countenance than what it had in some other countries." *Rights of Man*, part 1,

"He did not, it is true, threaten to go over and conquer America, but only with great dignity proposed, that, if his offer was not accepted, *that* an acknowledgment of about 30,000*l*. might be made to him." Part 1.

"It may therefore be of service to Mr. Burke's doctrine to make this story known, and to in form him, *that*, in case of that natural extinction to which all nobility is subject, *that* kings may be had again from Normandy." Part 1.

"The artificial noble shrinks into a dwarf before the noble of nature, and in the few *instances* in *whom* nature, as by a miracle, has survived in aristocracy, *those men* despise it." Part 1.

"Several other reasons contributed to produce this determination. I wished to know the manner in which a work, written in a style of thinking different to what had been customary in England, would be received before I proceeded further." Part 2.

"The authority of the present assembly is different to what the authority of future assemblies will be." Part 1.

In the few instances in which he was forcible and elegant, it was the force and elegance of nature, irresistibly making their way through an uncultivated and undisciplined mind.

Paine, upon the hypothesis that his motive as to England was not revengeful, which is not probable, and that he had not an understanding with the French revolutionists, which I do not believe, was one of those robustious anarchists who are for tearing every thing up by the roots which they do not like; for prostrating government by violence; for inflicting upon a nation the heaviest calamities, without considering the *end*. They who stir up a nation to revolt with a view to change its form of government, should not only have one to substitute which can and will obtain, but they should be *sure* that it is incomparably better than that which is to be subverted. And herein they always assume an awful responsibility, for what can *assure* them but the fact? A revolution is a positive, a tremendous evil; whereas the object of it is a contingent, and, even if successful, a very problematical good. And when all is destroyed—when the tranquil operations of systematized society are interrupted by violence—when nothing is heard but the frightful howl of commotion—no thing seen but savage man embruing his hands inhuman blood—when ignorance and passion are let loose to tyrannize and to prey, and revolutionary factions, never seeking the common good, stop at no means, however base and cruel, to aggrandize themselves; is it certain that the government, the issue of scenes so unnatural, so shocking, would be the one which was originally intended? Look at France—look at the scenes of confiscation and carnage through which she has passed, if you have a heart stout enough to gaze upon them, and then reflect upon the sort of government in which those scenes of horrour have finally terminated! Would the means be milder in England, the end less deplorable? I think not; both would be much the same. But in case of a revolution, and the final establishment of what is called a representative republick, like ours, for example, of what advantage could it be to England? It would be an errour in fact as well as in argument to consider the relative condition of England and France now, as the relative condition of England and France at the usurpation of Cromwell. If we go a little further back, in order to make ourselves somewhat more familiar with what has been, we may say, that the days of Azincour and Cressy[76] are passed: Shakespeare does, indeed, sometimes remind us of them, else they would be forgotten. Taking circumstances then as

76 The battles of Agincourt (25 October 1415) and Crécy (26 August 1346), during the Hundred Years War, both of which resulted in English victory against the French. —Ed.

they are, I think that if England were a republick like ours, England would be undone: she would be an adjunct of France in a few years; she could not avoid being so. France cannot indeed conquer her, but *universal suffrage* would. The people, in whose hands the votes of the nation would be placed, and to whose blind direction the power of the nation would be confided, feel, but they do not think; they cannot, I mean, think as is necessary to save a nation. War brings distress along with it even upon England, opulent and powerful as she is. Imagine Manchester, Birmingham, Sheffield, &c. and the chief part of the immense population of London, going to the polls of election, pressed by poverty, operated upon by all the arts of demagogues out of power, who want to get in, and suffering, perhaps, the pains of hunger: Need we ask what the consequences would be? New men would come into the government; peace must be made; even a peace which would be the forerunner of national subjugation. France would know that this would be unavoidable; she would know that there could be no escape for England but to a government like that which now preserves her independence, her power, and her grandeur.

I am not drawing from fancy, but from life. What I have said of England in a supposed case applies to us in a real one. It would be foreign from my purpose to inquire into the cause of our late memorable embargo, but it was suspected that, in advising it, Mr. Jefferson was actuated by a strong desire to co-operate with France in the commercial warfare which her tyrant had waged against England. I was of this opinion. I am so still, and there is conclusive circumstantial evidence that the opinion is correct. Suppose, however, that which is not true, that the cause for the embargo was a sufficient one; that the measure was forced upon us by imperious circumstances; that the honour of the country was grossly insulted, and her rights wantonly and flagitiously infringed by England, as was alleged; what would follow? Why, that as the embargo was the most coercive and vindictive measure to which we could resort, not being in a condition to commence offensive war with muskets, cannon, &c. we were called upon by every consideration of duty to support it until it had righted all our wrongs and closed up the breaches which had been made in our honour. But, easy as the people generally are in their circumstances, the embargo occasioned very great distress, and after suffering it a year, and the people, with their *universal suffrage*, came to the polls of the election, the government found that they must either remove the embargo or the people would remove them. No one could mistake the choice that would be made. The embargo was abandoned.

And yet the distress, compared with the distress which war would occasion, was nothing. What then should even we do with our *universal suffrage* in case of war? If the war were at home, as in the revolution; in our harbours, in our streets, upon our farms, we might do, perhaps, well enough with it,[77] for as the bayonet would be at our breasts, safety, not suffrage, not party, nor party triumphs, nor party power and emolument, would be the only consideration. But if it were a war carried on abroad, increasing expenses and occasioning distress at home, *universal suffrage*, managed by our very expert leaders, would speedily bring it to an issue, but whether for the reputation and safety of the country or not, whether with the government with which it was commenced, are problems which I will not attempt to solve.

And pray what in England would be the object of *universal suffrage*? Without it, the wisdom of England, generally speaking, is in parliament; with it, the wisdom of the United States is out of Congress. Virginia, indeed, sends a few able men to Congress, and perhaps the reason is, because *universal suffrage* is there considered anarchial in theory, and not allowed in practice. The honest, the enlightened, the patriotick, and the eloquent Mr. John Randolph, proudly boasts, and well he may, that, in opposition to the wishes of Mr. Jefferson, to whose administration he was opposed, and with the influence and efforts of the government against him, the *freeholders* of his district returned him to Congress. Here

77 It would be curious enough to see an army voting, and the vote would, perhaps, be still more curious. The men would vote as the officers would wish, and the officers would wish as the government desired. Or, it may be, that the officers and the men would turn out the government.

and there, out of Virginia, an able man, as it were by accident, is elected, but the chances are a million to one against him. If in the city of New York, where universal suffrage is in the *full tide of successful experiment*; where those govern who cannot govern themselves, and who ought everywhere to be governed, a *statesman* should ever be elected, it will be by *surprizing* the popular will. Universal suffrage has a mortal aversion from talents. It looks to *itself* for representatives. If in its district shoemakers, for instance, are the most numerous class, every thing being-decided by vote, a shoemaker, a very honest kind of a man no doubt, is transferred from his knife and last to the hall of legislation. No nation can be governed by well meaning but incapable men. England can only be ruined by presumptuous ignorance at the head of her affairs.

Government was at length roused to a sense of what was due to its own dignity, and to the safety and tranquillity of the kingdom. On the 21st of May, 1792, the king issued a proclamation for suppressing "wicked and seditious publications;" alluding to but not naming the *Rights of Man*. On the same day the attorney-general commenced a prosecution against Paine as author of the work. An action had been previously commenced against Jordan the publisher of it, but as he had made concessions which were satisfactory to the government, the prosecution was discontinued.

The king's proclamation was an act of graciousness. The work was clearly seditious in the malice of intention as well as in the criminality of object. As thousands of persons besides the booksellers had industriously published it, the law, if the administrators of it had been vindictively inclined, had full scope for operation. The proclamation notified the kingdom of the diabolical intentions of the author, the tendency of his demoralizing work, and the penalties which all publishers of it incurred of those admirable laws, not that were made for the case, but those ancient and free laws which the United States have adopted for the government of the press. It was therefore preventive, not retributive justice. MACKINTOSH had published, as he now doubtless regrets, his *Vindiciæ Gallicæ*, an elaborate and eloquent defence of the French revolution; of all its excesses, all its robberies and butcheries, in reply to Mr. Burke's *Reflections*. He too considered the British government, no doubt truly, as having abused its constitutional trust, but he was an advocate of a tranquil and constitutional reform; not of a dissolution of the state, not of revolution, not of blood. No legal impediments, therefore, were thrown in the way of the publication of his book, nor any legal animadversions pronounced upon it, for in no nation is the press allowed to go greater lengths than in England. Fox, controverting in parliament in moments of reformation-zeal, some of the maxims of Mr. Burke, quoted Mackintosh's defence in a strain of the finest eulogium. This enlightened friend of enlightened and durable freedom, speaking, however, of the *Rights of Man* in terms of indignant contempt, called it, as it really was, a *libel*[78] on the constitution. The proclamation, view it in whatever light we may, was intended to render unnecessary the operation of the laws, by preventing the commission of offences against them, and to preserve the lives, the liberty, and the property of the subjects, by averting that revolution which was the object of Paine.

Loyal associations now sprung up to counteract the revolutionary efforts of the revolution clubs. Passion met passion until, in the struggle, on the one side for a dissolution of the government, on the other for its existence, the nation became more and more agitated. In this state of things, Paine published, about August, 1792, his "Address to the Addressers." This is a miserable lampoon on the orators in parliament who had spoken on the side of the king's proclamation, as well as on those placemen into whose offices Paine would willingly have crept before he left England, in the year 1774. He states that a prosecution had been commenced against him—declares the incompetency of a jury to decide on a work so recondite and important as the *Rights of Man*—talks quite philosophically of the propriety of taking the *sense of the nation* upon it by *polling each man*—pronounces the laws in relation to the press as fundamentally bad, the administration of them by the courts as notoriously corrupt, and denies that the *Rights of Man* is seditious, for that it

78 Paine's Address to the Addressors.

"contains a plan for augmenting the pay of the soldiers, and meliorating the condition of the poor!" While he was preparing this stuff for the press, he published letters to the chairmen of several of the meetings which were convened to compliment the king on his proclamation. He was now evidently awed by the vigour of the government and the patriotick spirit of the nation. All over England he was carried about in effigy with a *pair of stays* under his arm, and the populace, staymakers and all, alternately laughed and swore at the impudent attempts of a staymaker to destroy their government.

His trial was to come on in the following December. Whilst he foresaw and no doubt dreaded the imprisonment which awaited him, a French deputation announced to him in London, in the preceding September, that the department of Calais had elected him a member of the National Convention. This was doubly grateful; grateful in the escape which it afforded him from a just punishment, without the imputation of cowardice; grateful in the honour which bloody anarchists had conferred upon him by electing him a member of their order. Without delay he proceeded to Dover, where a custom-house officer examined his baggage, and finally let him pass. He had not, however, sailed from Dover for Calais more than twenty minutes, when an order was received from the government to detain him. He states his detention and examination at Dover in a letter to Mr. Dundas, dated Calais, September 15, 1792.

On the 25th of September, he published a letter addressed to the people of France, in which, saluting them as "fellow citizens," as they certainly were, he says:—"I receive with affectionate gratitude the honour which the late National Assembly has conferred upon me by adopting me a citizen of France, and the additional honour of being elected by my *fellow citizens* a member of the National Convention." He is aware that the "moment of any great change, is unavoidably a moment of *terrour and confusion.*" This terrour and confusion, he had, however, endeavoured to excite in England. The world has reason to be thankful that he did not succeed. He encourages the revolutionists of France to persevere by all the arguments which he could draw from his combustible magazine.—A new constitution, he observes, must be formed, in which the "bagatelles of monarchy, royalty, regency, and hereditary succession shall be exposed." Another new constitution has since been formed, in which the tyrant who now governs France has taken to himself all those "*bagatelles!*" This is the natural effect of revolution; of "terrour and confusion. "A mild and wholesome reform of the government would have prevented the confiscations, the proscriptions, and the murders which have been committed; preserved the peace of the world, and left France with much of freedom, of which she has nothing now.

Notwithstanding his escape from England, and his election to the National Convention by his *fel-*

low citizens of France, his trial, as if present, came on at Guildhall, London, December 18, 1792, before Lord Kenyon and a special jury. Mr. Perceval, now chancellor of the exchequer, opened the information. Paine was tried for libellous passages contained in the *Rights of Man*, part second. The Attorney-General, Mr. McDonald,[79] carelessly, and therefore with little ability, opened the case to the jury.

A circumstance had, however, occurred, of which he dexterously and powerfully availed himself. Paine had foolishly written a private letter to the Attorney-General, dated "Paris, 11th November, first year of the republick," which he read to the jury. In this letter he says:

> the time, sir, is becoming too serious to play with court prosecutions and sport with national rights. The *terrible examples* that have taken place *here* upon men who less than a year ago thought themselves as secure as any prosecuting judge, jury, or Attorney-General can now do in England, ought to have some weight with men in your situation.
>
> That the government of England is as great if not the greatest perfection of fraud and corruption that ever took place since governments began, is what you cannot be a stranger to, unless the constant habit of seeing it has blinded your senses.
>
> Is it possible that you or I can believe, or that reason can make any other man believe, that

79 Spelled Macdonald in the original. —Ed.

> the capacity of such a man as Mr. Guelph, or any of his profligate sons, is necessary to the government of a nation?

If the atrocious libel itself, coupled with the situation of France, did not fire the jury with indignation, this insolent letter must have done so. The *terrible examples* of France, which he plainly threatened should be brought home to England, could not but alarm men of feeling and reflection.

In behalf of Paine, Mr. Erskine amused the court with an ingenious and eloquent speech. The Attorney-General rose to reply, but the jury told him that it was unnecessary, and instantly returned a verdict of GUILTY.

As the testimony given by Mr. Chapman upon the trial illustrates the character of Paine, I will here introduce it.

Mr. Chapman, whom Paine calls "an honest man,"[80] was the printer of the second part of the *Rights of Man*. When a few sheets were printed, concluding from the sale of the first part that he could gain something by purchasing the second, he offered Paine a thousand pounds for the copyright. But when he had printed to page 112, finding that it was highly seditious, he declined to have any thing more to do with it, and returned to its author the remainder of his copy. Paine insinuates[81] that the offer to purchase came in fact from the min-

80 Appendix to the *Rights of Man*, part 2.

81 Appendix.

ister through Chapman; that Chapman, contrary to all the rules of printing, had shown the manuscript to Mr. Pitt, and that having ascertained that the work could not be suppressed by purchase, Mr. Pitt had persuaded Chapman to print no more of it. All this accords very well with the vanity of Paine. The reader will now understand Chapman's testimony, which I quote from the London edition, 1793, of the trial.

THOMAS CHAPMAN *sworn.*
Examined by Mr. Solicitor General.

Q. What business are you?
A. A printer, Sir.
Q. Do you know the defendant, Thomas Paine?
A. I do, Sir.
Q. Upon what occasion did you become acquainted with him?
A. Upon the recommendation of Mr. Thomas Christie.
Q. For what purpose was Mr. Paine introduced to you, or you to him?
A. I was introduced by Mr. Christie to Mr. Paine, as a printer, to print some book he had.
Q. You were introduced by Mr. Christie to Mr. Paine to print some book?
A. Yes.
Q. When was that introduction?
A. I cannot exactly remember; it was the beginning of the last year.
Q. The year 1791?
A. I think it was.
Q. Do you remember what book it was that you say Mr. Paine had?

A. It was the first part of the *Rights of Man*.
Q. Are you a publisher as well as a printer?
A. I am not, sir; I am merely a printer.
Q. Did you print the first part of the Rights of Man?
A. I did, sir.
Q. Who was the selling bookseller?
A. Mr. Jordan, of Fleet-street.
Q. Had you any intercourse with Jordan and Paine upon that book?
A. I had, sir.
Q. What was that intercourse relative to?
A. Merely relative to the manner of publishing the book.
Q. Did Jordan in fact publish the book?
A. He did, sir.
Q. Had you any intercourse with Mr. Paine relative to printing this book which I have in my hand? (shewing the book to Mr. Chapman.)
A. The first edition of this book I had, sir; I don't conceive I printed this edition, but the first edition I did the first part of the *Rights of Man* I printed
Q. Is this the first or second part?
A. This is the second part.
Q. Look at that.
A. I printed a part of the second part.
Mr. Erskine.—Q. Do you mean that very book, can you swear to that book?
A. I cannot, sir.
Mr. Solicitor General.—Q. Then this second part of the *Rights of Man*, you say you printed a part of it?
A. A part of it?
Q. Will you inform my lord and the jury what part of it you did print?

A. I printed as far as page 112, signature H. Q. By signature H, you mean that letter H at the bottom of the page?

A. Yes, sir.

Q. Now upon whose employment did you print so much of the second part of the *Rights of Man*?

A. Mr. Paine's employment.

Q. Did you, Mr. Chapman, print the rest of the work, from letter H to the conclusion of it?

A. I had the copy in my possession of it so far as 146.

Q. What do you mean by the copy?

A. The manuscript, sir; I had the manuscript as far as 146.

Q. Did you stop at 112, signature *H*.

A. I stopped at 112, but my people had composed to page 146; which was not printed by me.

Q. Now had you any conversation with Mr. Paine relative to printing the remainder of the work?

A. I had.

Q. And if you had, what was that conversation?

A. When I had finished page 112, or sheet *H*, the proof sheet I came into my hands.

Court. When you printed *G*, you say *I* came into your hands?

A. No, *H*.

Q. And then the proof sheet *I* came into your hands?

A. The proof sheet *I*—upon examining sheet *I*, there was a part which, in my weak judgment, appeared of a dangerous tendency; I, therefore, immediately concluded in my mind not to proceed any further. Accordingly, in determining not to proceed in the work, I wrote a short note to Mr. Paine, about 2 o'clock in the afternoon, determining to send the letter with the copy the following morning. I felt a degree of reluctance and unpleasantness in my own mind, from the circumstance of Mr. Paine's civilities, that I had received, as a gentleman and my employer; and I was fearful I should not have courage in the morning to deliver up his copy; but a circumstance occurred in the course of the day that enabled me to do it with pleasure to myself.

Q. Was Mr. Paine present when that circumstance happened?

A. He was—and as it may exculpate me, in the eyes of the court, from a charge Mr. Paine thought proper to enter, in his appendix, against me as a printer, I should esteem it as a favour of the court if they will suffer me to mention the circumstance.

Court. Certainly.

A. That very day at six o'clock Mr. Paine called upon me.

Q. What day was that?

A. I have a copy of my letter dated 17th of January,[82] so he must have called upon me on the

82 SIR, *January 17, 1792.*

I am much obliged by the favour of your printing, and should have esteemed myself happy in the expectation of your future interest and friendship; but there appear so many observations in the sheet (I) directly personal against the king and government, that I feel myself under the necessity of re questing you will get the remaining sheets printed at another office. Sheet (H) I am willing to finish, but no farther on any account. I beg, therefore, sir, to inclose the remaining part of the copy;

16th; Mr. Paine called upon me, and, which was unusual with him, he was rather intoxicated with liquor; he had been dining with Mr. Johnson, I believe, in St. Paul's Church yard, according to his own account; being intoxicated, he introduced his favourite topic and subject; upon which we unfortunately differed, namely religion, a favourite topic with him when he is intoxicated. I am sorry to mention the circumstance, only as it may justify me in the eyes of the public, as his false insinuation in his Appendix respecting his copy has done me material injury in my profession. The subject of debate ran high, and Mr. Paine proceeded in his argument, till it came at length to personal abuse both to myself and Mrs. Chapman. An observation was made late in the evening (I believe near 10 o'clock) at which Mr. Paine was particularly offended, and rising up, in a great passion, he declared he had not been so personally affronted in the whole course of his life.

Mr. Erskine. The information charges no extrinsic matter.

Lord Kenyon. It appears at present important.

Mr. Erskine. I cannot admit that letter, as I have no reason to believe the existence of it.

Mr. Solicitor General. The circumstances are proper to be explained by him to vindicate himself.

Witness. Mr. Paine rose up in a great passion,

And am, sir,

Your obliged humble servant,

T. CHAPMAN,

T. Paine, Esq.

declaring as I was a dissenter, he had a very bad opinion of dissenters in general, believing them all to be a pack of hypocrites, and he should deal with them accordingly, and desired me to deliver up his accounts the next morning; which I did, and felt a degree of pleasure at the circumstance. I delivered a letter enclosing the whole of his copy—he called upon me immediately, and made many apologies for what he had said, observing it was the effect of the liquor, and hoped I would pass it over, and proceed in the work; but I had determined I would not.

Q. Did you explain to Mr. Paine your reasons why you would not?

A. I did, Sir; my letter told him.

Court. Did you explain the ground why you would not proceed with the work?

A. I did.

Mr. Solicitor General. You have told us that Mr. Paine was your employer to print so far as you did print.

A. Yes.

Q. Did you ever make any offer to any body, to buy the copy of that you call the Second Part of the *Rights of Man*?

A. I did.

Q. To whom?

A. To Mr. Paine

Q. When you made those offers, did Mr. Paine accept, or refuse, or how treat them?

A. I made three separate offers in the different stages of the work: The first, I believe, was 100 guineas; the second, 500: the last, 1000.

Q. To those offers what did Mr. Paine answer?

A. Mr. Paine, to the best of my recollection, an-

> swered, as it was his intention to publish a small edition of the work, he wished to reserve it in his own hands.

Those who personally knew Paine, will fully credit Chapman's very accurate representation of his abuse of Mrs. Chapman, and of his having a "very bad opinion of dissenters in general, believing them all to be a pack of hypocrites;" both being exactly in character, and a *pack of hypocrites* precisely his words upon all occasions, when inveighing, as was his custom, against religion. To the sex, whether animated with liquor, or in his temperate moments depressed with reflection, he paid no sort of deference. He was at all times at war with man and woman, heaven and earth.

The Attorney-General now outlawed him, a measure of which he afterwards felt the inconvenience.

The revolutionary ferment in England increased. The issue of Paine's trial was far from tranquillizing the passions. The seed of rebellion had been sown, and nothing seemed capable of stopping its growth. Projects of parliamentary reform were vehemently pressed upon parliament, as if at a crisis threatening universal commotion, visionary schemes of imaginary good could be either coolly entertained or safely carried into effect. At a period like this, parliamentary reform would have been fatal. Partial success would have invited more desperate efforts at a total overthrow of the government: nothing could have preserved it. The atrocious convention, meditating the murder of Louis, had passed their decree of the 19th of November, 1792, exciting the people of Europe to insurrection against their governments, and promising "assistance and fraternity." Upon the publication of this infamous decree, parliament, which was to have met on the third day of the following January, was convened by proclamation on the 13th of the preceding December. What, under all these circumstances, could have saved the nation from all the horrours of revolution, but war? The remedy was indeed an evil, but it was one infinitely less than that with which it was menaced by the French republick and by Paine; co-operating with the thoughtless or mistaken people of England. Early in January, 1793, Louis was decapitated. On the 23d of the same month, his minister, Chauvelin, resident in London, was ordered by the British government to quit the kingdom, and on the first of the following month, the "French Republick" declared war against Great Britain.

Upon the Trial of Louis the XVI, Paine, who had been employed as a copier of papers to the Committee of Foreign Affairs, and dismissed by Congress for perjury, sat in judgment! He had voted in the convention for the trial of the king, but, upon his trial, he was in favour of imprisoning him during the war, and of transporting him afterwards. His mild nature could not bear the thought of spilling the king's blood! Yes, the man who had endeavoured to raise revolt in England, that the land might be covered with human gore, advanced pretensions to the attributes of humanity! "It has already been proposed," he observes in his speech in the convention, "to abolish the punishment of death, and it is with infinite satisfaction that I recollect the *humane* and excellent oration pronounced by *Robespierre* on the subject, in the constituent assembly." The whole of his speech is hypocritical, fawning, time serving, and pusillanimous. He felt that in the *terrible republick*, whose course and conduct he had recommended to England, there was neither freedom nor safety. If the king was guilty of the charges which murderous and sacrilegious faction had conjured up against him, death was the punishment of his crimes, but as Paine, from the context of his dastardly speech, evidently considered him innocent, imprisonment during the war, and banishment afterwards, proposed by him, were atrocious injustice.

While the trial of the king was going on, the committee of the convention, of which Paine had the *honour* of being a member, were framing the new constitution of 1793. In the short space of two or three years, the Assembly of the Notables, the States-General, and the National Assembly, with its declaration of rights, which Paine had held out to the people of England as worthy of their imitation, had all, with every thing else, been overthrown. All those assemblies were now superceded by a convention, whose business, be sides despatching the king, and sounding some *notes of dreadful preparation*, was to make another constitution. This prodigy of human intellect, or rather, this sediment of ever-renewed intoxication, was presented to the Convention on the 15th of February, 1793. In this disproportioned thing, this dream of well-meaning fanaticks, or deliberate act of cool dilapidators, *universal suffrage* was laid down to perfection. The executive power was vested in an executive council, the members of which were to be elected by the sanguinary rabble of France, whose hands were already clotted with human blood. A power which, if it be any where or at any time usefully practicable, requires the utmost tranquillity and the most unimpassioned judgment, was to be exercised by a national mob in the highest state of frenzy. Is the voice of such men as the convention and its committee were composed of ever to be listened to? They seem to have paid no attention to the state of France. Their system was not at all adapted to the nature and condition of the subject on whom it was to operate. What could be expected but that which followed?

In March, the next month, the new constitution of Condorcet, Paine, and the rest of the committee, was in effect nearly annihilated. The convention, to which supreme and almost exclusive power had been unaccountably left, awed as it was by the Jacobins in and out of it, organized, in March, 1793, the revolutionary tribunal, with its publick accuser and its two assistants. This court, consisting of six judges, or rather of six assassins, having all France within its functions and subject to its power, summarily pronounced sentence without appeal, and sent its victims forthwith to execution. From its terrible operations there was no escape. Suspicion was sufficient cause of death. Nor was a ferocious countenance of any advantage to its possessor, and a mild one, indicating all possible goodness, was fatal.

In the following month, April, 1793, the powers of another engine of horrour, the Committee of Publick Safety, were so amplified as to complete the destruction of the Executive Council. This again was followed in May by a declaration, that the "republick is one and indivisible." In June, 1793, the new constitution of Condorcet, Paine, &c. was formally destroyed, and another new constitution, consisting of a hundred and twenty-four articles, more suited, if possible, to Jacobin tyranny, was as formally adopted by the convention. The Queen was now executed, and this act of unmanly revenge was followed, in October, 1793, by the murder of Brissot and his colleagues. In December, 1793, Paine himself, who had laboured hard to produce a similar state of things in England, was thrown into prison by the committee of safety!

> This even-handed justice
> Commends the ingredients of our poison'd chalice
> To our own lips.

He had just finished, when arrested, the first part of his *Age of Reason*;[83] but considering the work as unsafe in the hands of the *representatives of a free people*, he called on Mr. Barlow; author of the *Columbiad*, in his way to prison, and left it with him.

It has been intimated to me, by a gentleman who has favoured me with his correspondence on the subject of this work, whose name I am not at liberty to mention, that Paine's deistical productions do not form in him a distinctive character, so many able men of different ages and nations having written on the same side of the subject; and therefore, perhaps he would infer, it would be superfluous, if not impertinent, to say one word upon it in writing his life.

With becoming deference I must, however, say, that indistinctiveness of character, or the sameness of his opinions with the opinions of his deistical predecessors, even if granted, could form no solid objection to a liberal notice of his *Age of Reason*. How could I account, in writing his life, for so large a chasm as an omission of it would make?

But his deistical writings do in my judgment help to make out, I do not mean to say that, alone, they constitute, a distinctive character. As a political writer, celebrated as he has been by the illiterate for originality, he was original in nothing but *intention*. In the United States, or rather in the colonies and during the war for independence, he

83 Preface to *Age of Reason*, part 2.

was a very subordinate retailer of the works of the great men of England. As a deistical controversialist, the same observation applies, taking in with some learned men of England, Voltaire, and others of different nations. Here too he had nothing original but *intention*. His *Age of Reason* is an acrimonious attack, not on priestcraft, nor on the abuses of religion, nor on the irregularities of its ministers, but on religion itself. In this he was not original; in this he had been preceded by distinguished statesmen, profound philosophers, and grave historians; by Bolingbroke, by Hume, and by others, to whose works we may turn as curious speculations; as specimens of admirable reasoning, upon premises however false. Nor was he original in his impertinent witticisms, his shocking indecencies, his indecorous scoffs. In these, Voltaire had gone before and surpassed him. A deist—even one indeed who outstrips a deist and sneeringly and contemptuousky views him as a *religious fanatick*; an atheist, if such a being exists, who thinks himself nothing, that he came from nothing, that he is accountable to nothing, and that there is nothing superiour to himself; even he, if he has read Hume on miracles, cannot peruse the wretched scurrility of Paine.

The *intention* of Paine, and the intention only, both in politicks and religion, constitutes a character entirely original. His intention was more completely destructive than that of any other author that perhaps ever lived. While conspiring to subvert all government, he meditated the overthrow of all religion. Whilst planning devastation and blood on Earth, he was hatching rebellion against heaven. With him, the mortal and the immortal parts were to *sink together in the dust*. With him, ruin was to be complete. In this he was original; in this he had a distinctiveness of character. Bolingbroke was no anarchist in government: Hume was for a very solid and durable one; and Voltaire, if he was not a monarchist, affected to adore the Prussian monarch. But in hypocrisy, for Paine was a hypocrite, he was not original.

In the preface[84] to the first part of his *Age of Reason*, he says:—"It has been my intention, for several years, to publish my thoughts upon religion." The *Age of Reason* sufficiently tells us what his thoughts were. In the same preface,[85] he adds:—"Soon after I published the pamphlet, *Common Sense*, in America, I saw the exceeding probability that a *revolution* in the system of government, would be followed by a *revolution* in the system of religion."

All was to be overthrown. The world was to be undone.

The word *system*, affords no refuge even for a quibble in favour of Paine. He was not attacking the Church of England as established by law; he was not assailing this or that church, but the subject of all churches. Those amongst us who may be

84 Page 7, New York, 1795.

85 Page 9.

opposed to the Church of England, can draw from the word *system* no apology for Paine, if they consider to whom the *Age of Reason* is dedicated.

We have no one church established by law in preference to another. All our churches are, thank God, under the protection of the law, but there is no legal pre-eminence given to any one of the numerous sects which flourish amongst us. We, therefore, have no *system*, in the sense which Paine's friends may according to circumstances wish to be understood. And yet it is dedicated to us,—he "puts it under our protection,"—he sent amongst us an edition of several thousand copies, and they were spread from one end of the union to the other with an alacrity which he must have commended. What then was his object *here?* The same as it was every where: licentiousness—confusion—an abolition of the forms of religion—annihilation of religion itself—a letting "loose of reason," as Mr. Jefferson terms it, which, in good English, means madness—a loss of memory—a loss of Judgment—a forgetfulness of obligations to God and man—a state of society more savage, more furious, more criminal, by having been civilized, than the primitive condition of the Choctaws. Surely where the sweets of religion are most sweet, there was no necessity for a work even against a *system* of religion. Every man amongst us can worship God, without pains or disabilities, according to the dictates of his conscience. In no nation is religion more free. In no condition of man, feeling, benevolent, thinking, and good, can a more perfect state of religious freedom exist even here it was to be attacked; even here, all the holds of the state, and the hopes of individuals, were to be destroyed.

Soon after the publication of *Common Sense* in America, and, by fair inference, when he wrote *Common Sense*, he saw that a revolution in government would be followed by a revolution in religion; such a revolution as he advocates; a *destruction of religion*: but he intended this desperate effort as the "last offering he would make to his fellow citizens of all nations."[86] In the mean while the well masked dissimulator pretended to be a pious Christian. This he would denominate *State Craft*, which, he told the people of England in his *Rights of Man*, cannot exist in America!

"For myself," he observes, "I fully and conscientiously believe that it is the will of the Almighty that there should be a diversity of religious opinions amongst us: it affords a larger field for our *Christian* kindness." Here he is a Christian, full of Christian kindness! And yet he had decided in favour of a "revolution in religion," and re solved to unite his efforts to the efforts of congenial men, to effect it, but would reserve the act for one of the last of his life.

"Should Howe be now expelled, I wish, with all the *devotion of a Christian*, that the names of Whig and Tory may never more be mentioned."[87]

86 Preface to the *Age of Reason*, Part First.

87 *Crisis*, Number I.

This he wrote a year after the publication of *Common Sense*. "Soon after I had published *Common Sense*, I saw that a revolution in government would be followed by a revolution in religion." Was he not a hypocrite? Was he not an impostor? The same dissimulation, though not in the same degree, is continued in the *Rights of Man*. He seems to have unmasked himself as he saw the world ripening for his purposes. Even after the French revolutionists had plundered the churches and sent their clergy to the lamp post, he was a Christian, yet not quite so full of "Christian kindness." But he had to deal with the English people, with whom a revolution in government was to precede a revolution in religion. Perdition was to develope itself by degrees.

> Governments thus established, he says, last as long as the power to support them lasts; but that they might avail themselves of every engine in their favour, they united fraud to force, and set up an idol which they called *divine rights*, and which in contradistinction to the founder of the *Christian religion*, twisted itself afterwards into an idol of another shape.[88]

When he wrote this passage, in which he affects to be a disciple of Christ, whose maxims he admires, he had resolved to defer his "last work" no longer; he had decided to write, and probably had commenced, the *Age of Reason*. He tells us so himself in another place.

88 *Rights of Man*, Part I.

> I have mentioned, in the former part of the *Age of Reason*, that it had long been my intention to publish my thoughts upon religion; but that I originally reserved it to a later period in life, intending it to be the last work I should undertake. The circumstances, however, which existed in France, in the *latter end of the year* 1790, DETERMINED ME TO DELAY NO LONGER.[89]

The *Rights of Man*, part first, was published in London in 1791, a year after the "circumstances which existed in France had determined him to delay no longer," his attack on religion! And yet in the *Rights of Man* he passes himself off for a Christian! But as he advanced in composing the work, he cast off the trammels of hypocrisy. The National Assembly of France, that first cause of the national wreck which followed, having displeased him in an article of its declaration of rights, he comments, at the close of his work, undisguisedly and severely upon it.

Article "X. No man ought to be molested on account of his opinions, not even of his religious opinions, *provided* his avowal of them does not *disturb the publick order established by law*."[90]

Paine thinks, and so he expresses himself, that the proviso is an outrage on the rights of man almost as great as any ever committed even by the British government! Society, he is clearly of opinion, has nothing to do with doctrines, whether they

89 Preface to the *Age of Reason*, part 2, page 1, New York, 1796.

90 Declaration of Rights of the National Assembly.

disturb its tranquillity or not!

> It is questioned, he says, by some very good people in France, as well as in other countries, whether the *tenth* article sufficiently guarantees the right it is intended to accord with. Besides which, it takes off from the *divine dignity of religion*, and weakens its operative force upon the mind, to make it a subject of human laws.[91]

Now what is it in the article that takes off from the divine dignity of religion? That which allows all freedom in religious opinions but such disturbs the publick order established by law! According to Paine, therefore, *divine dignity in religion consists in disturbing the publick peace!*

In this he goes, I think, but I am not quite sure, further than Mr. Jefferson. "The legitimate powers of government extend to such acts only as are *injurious to others*. But it does me no injury for my neighbour to say [that] there are twenty Gods or no God.[92] It neither picks my pocket nor breaks my leg."[93]

Mr. Jefferson admits, that the legitimate powers of government extend to such acts as are injurious to others; yet that his neighbour's declaration, that there is no God, may neither pick his pocket nor break his leg. But suppose that the denial of God

---

91 *Rights of Man*, part 1, p. 69, Phil. ed. 1797.

92 Mr. Jefferson writes "lengthy" for long. *Notes*, p. 348, New Appendix.

93 *Notes on Virginia*, p. 235, New York, 1801.

should so harden his neighbour's heart and vitiate his mind as to induce him to break the sage's leg, or to pick his pocket, which I think very likely, it would then follow, from his own doctrine, that as picking pockets and breaking legs are *injurious acts*, they may be legitimately punished. If I am right in thus construing the late president's meaning, he stops short of Paine, who declares, that to *disturb the publick order established by law*, is an essential part of the "divine dignity of religion."

The human mind is apt to run to extremes. From doubting the divinity of the Christian religion, it descends to deism, and it would be surprising if, in sinking, the deist stopped short of atheism. In deism, Paine was, in all probability, a hypocrite. Generally, he expressed detestation of atheism, and yet he has uttered opinions favourable to it. He believes, he asserts in his *Age of Reason*, in one God, but it is probable that he believed in nothing superiour to matter. In conversation with Mrs. Palmer, widow of the deistical haranguer, in the presence of Mr. Carver, of this city, from whom I have the fact, he let out his materialism. Stewart, "the traveller," an insane man, had published a pamphlet, which he called *Opus Maximum*, denying the existence of every thing but matter. Referring to it, Mrs. Palmer remarked:—"Stewart's doctrine, Mr. Paine, may be correct." "It is well enough, replied Paine, to say nothing about it; the *time is not yet come!*" Death then was with him, as well as with the French convention, *eternal sleep*. To this horrid sentence, therefore, this impious declaration, wrapping man in gloom here, robbing him of his brightest hopes of hereafter, Paine wrote nothing in opposition. Robespierre, however, reversed the atheistical decree of the convention. Death, he said, is not eternal sleep. The French people, he caused to be proclaimed, believe in the Supreme Being, and the immortality of the soul. Paine now published the first part of his *Age of Reason*. He too believed, he affirmed, in one God, but, to use his own language, the "*time had not yet come*" for a naked expression of his opinion. As to the scriptures, he confesses that he had not read them. How then, as a reasonable man, could he write against them? He had early thought that governments could not be subverted, that havock could not be commenced, that misery could not be complete, without discarding religion, and this seems to have been cause enough with him, without reading, without reflection, to commence the work.

He suffered eleven months imprisonment in France; from December, 1793, to the 4th of November, 1794. In one place[94] he ascribes his escape from the guillotine to a fever with which he was afflicted; in another, to Providence.[95] The fever was the effect of intemperance. A medical gentleman of great eminence, who rendered him professional service in France, tells me that his body was in

94 Letter to general Washington.

95 Letters written at Washington, addressed to the citizens of the United States.

a state of putrefaction, probably occasioned by drinking brandy, and that, so offensive was the stench which issued from it, he could hardly be approached. It does not, however, appear, that he constantly drank to excess before he left America, in 1787: he was poor. His habitual drunkenness seems to have commenced with the delirium of the French revolution. The practice gained upon him in London. "Reason had been let loose." Wildness naturally followed. A commotion of thoughts is necessarily succeeded by a commotion in action. In France, after he was elected to a seat in the Convention, by whose committee he was immured, his intemperance seems to have increased with the increase of French violence. Some gentlemen have ascribed it to an imputed neglect on the part of general Washington during his imprisonment. Was Paine then so weak? But they overlook dates. The putrescent state of his body while in prison, was brought on by drinking before his imprisonment. His habits were sordid, his thirst for liquor had been great, and to quench it, he had associated with the meanest company in Paris for months before his incarceration.

After his liberation, he found an asylum in the hospitable house of Mr. Monroe,[96] our minister. The near approach of death, for he expected every moment to die, either by the guillotine or by natural dissolution, neither frightened nor dissuaded him from immoderate drinking. Mr. Monroe kept

96 Spelled Munroe in the original. —Ed.

him in his house eighteen months. At first, he drank as he pleased, and therefore to excess. But for his own good, as well as for the reputation of the mission, the minister found it necessary to stint him. Yet what he could not get in the house, he got out of it. A drunkard will have liquor. Intemperance and imprisonment laid waste his mind, such as it had been.

During his imprisonment, an extraordinary revolution happened. The atrocious Robespierre and his accomplices had expiated at the guillotine their proscriptions and massacres. Paine, on his release from his dungeon, was invited to resume his seat in the convention.

As the new faction had triumphed over the old, a new paper constitution was now to be made. Paine and Co.'s constitution of 1793 was in formally abolished a month after it was presented. The two committees of revolution and safety, which had grown out of that constitution, were now to be destroyed.

In April, 1795, a committee of eleven was appointed for the purpose of organizing a fresh constitution, which was reported on the 23d of the following June by Boissy d'Anglas. This was the constitution of elders and youngsters; a council of five hundred, a council of ancients, and an executive directory of five. It formally abolishes the convention; it artfully rejects *universal suffrage*; it establishes electoral assemblies between the people and the government; it permits a citizen of France, if he has paid *direct* taxes, fought a campaign, and possesses several other qualifications, to vote for electors. The directory was to be chosen after Mr. Jefferson's manner; by the legislature, but not, I believe, on the suggestion of the directory itself.

On the 7th of July, the convention granted *permission* to Paine to make a speech against the constitution of Boissy d'Anglas.

This he tremblingly begins with adverting to his imprisonment, and to the fever with which he had been afflicted. He states that he was "proscribed in England for vindicating the French revolution," and that he had been cast into prison in France for doing the same thing. He then commences his objections to the constitution as a Virginia slave would remonstrate against the tyranny and cruelty of his master. On the subject of *universal suffrage*, he is, however, silent. As the operation of that principle in his own constitution had brought upon him eleven months' duresse, he seems not to have been very anxious about it. To the electoral assemblies, intervened between those who were allowed to vote, and the government, he makes no objection. If brandy had not mellowed his understanding, confinement seems to have mitigated his zeal. His objections, fearfully urged, are two. He rejects the usual distinction between direct and indirect taxation, which is in fact a nominal one, and is of opinion, that the citizen who pays any sort of taxes, should be allowed to vote for the electors, who were to choose the council, older and younger. As to the service of a campaign in the army, which was a prerequisite to *citizenship*, where *direct* taxes were not paid, he considers it quite as despotick as any thing even in the British government; because the father who fights for his own liberty, he observes, fights also for the liberty of his children, who he thinks should be suffered to vote for the electors without serving a campaign, and even without paying direct taxes. But in this he is at enmity with himself, his doctrine being clearly, I think, an *hereditary* transmission of right and power. For as the father cannot bind his son to posterity, so he cannot acquire rights for the son, which the son, without any merit of his own, shall exercise with and over posterity. Let the son fight a campaign, as the father did, or pay *direct* taxes, as he did, as the price of voting for electors who are to elect his rulers. The present age is as free as the age which preceded it: *i.e.* to acquire immunities for itself; to pull down that which it finds established, and to build up anew. This is Paine's doctrine in his *Rights of Man*, not mine; a doctrine which he unwittingly combats in his speech against Boissy d'Anglas's constitution. The truth is that every age, whether it will or not, derives benefits from the age which preceded it. In this sense, whatever be the form of government under which we live, there is an hereditary transmission from father to son which is so natural and necessary, that no form of government can destroy it. We are let in to a happy state of society without having contributed an effort to produce it. Resting upon individual rights and exertions, the rights and exertions of the present age, without reference to those of the ages which have preceded it, are born to the condition of the untutored Indian. It is by the civilization of the ages which are passed, that we are civilized; it is by the privileges which they acquired, that we have privileges. For the liberty we enjoy in the United States, we are indebted to our ancestors. We have acquired nothing of it ourselves: not a jot of it is our own. All that we have done, is the effecting of a separation from the parent country: all that we have achieved, is independence. But we have no liberty but that which we have derived from England. We owe it all to our ancestors. The wild parts of the British constitution are, indeed, more wild amongst us, but it may be questioned whether we have the solid portion of it, that which secures life, liberty, and property, in equal perfection. Burr, charged with treason, and tried by the statute of Edward the III. would have had a less vexations if not a more impartial trial in London, than he had in the capital of Virginia. In England, the presses would not have conspired to terrify the presiding judge, by detestable menaces and denunciations, into a violation of the law, in order that the accused, right or wrong, might be hanged. They did not, however, even with us, succeed. The admirable patience and firmness of chief justice Marshall enabled the law to triumph over the machinations of the president, the outrages of the press, and the systematick violence of a party.

No notice was taken by the convention of Paine's speech. Boissy d'Anglas's constitution was adopted in October, 1795, but not without a little depletion of blood. The convention had passed a decree, that, at the first election under the new constitution, two-thirds of its present numbers should be returned. This was to keep out the Jacobins, who with and since the fall of Robespierre, had been driven from the convention. Now as all outs want to get in, and the principal Jacobins could not succeed without forcibly and victoriously resisting the decree, their creatures were organized and a battle was fought near the hall of the convention. After blowing into the air with cannon about two thousand of the insurgents, and striking off the heads, with the national razor, of we know not how many more, the constitution went quietly into operation according to the decree. The convention was now formally destroyed, and as Paine was never afterwards elected, the constitution of Boissy d'Anglas terminated his publick functions in France.

With his speech, he presented to the convention his "Dissertation on the *first* principles of government," an octavo pamphlet of eighteen pages. "This little work," he observes, "I did in tend to have dedicated to the people of Holland, who about the time I began to write it, were determined to accomplish a revolution in their government, rather than to the people of France, who had long before effected that *glorious* object." French principles and force had got into oppressed Holland, and poisoned and overturned every thing. His dissertation is a weak iteration of his *Common Sense* and *Rights of Man*.

His next work was an octavo pamphlet of twenty-two pages, on the English system of finance; a system which the United States have adopted: it was published in April, 1796. In this effusion of malevolence, he predicts, that the *system* "will not continue to the end of Mr. Pitt's life, supposing him to live the usual age of a man." The pamphlet has only served to show his ignorance on financial subjects.

In the following July, he published, in Paris, his Letter to GENERAL WASHINGTON, an octavo pamphlet of sixty-four pages. This is a causeless, ungrateful, virulent, and profligate attack on one of the greatest and best men that ever lived.

The French convention, in December, 1793, passed a decree for the expulsion of all the members of it who were foreigners by birth. Paine coming, as it was thought, within the scope of its operations, was of course expelled. That decree was followed in the same month by one for imprisoning every man in France born in England. Under this decree he was imprisoned.

The cause of the attack on president Washington is, as alleged by Paine, that being a citizen of the United States, the president did not exert his official influence with the French government to obtain his liberation. This is the ground-work of sixty-four pages of impotent invective and malicious slander.

His premises and conclusion are, that in becoming a member of the convention, and a *citizen* of France, he did not forfeit his citizenship in the United States, and that, therefore, remaining a citizen, and being of course entitled to protection as such, official duty and personal gratitude required the interposition of the American executive in his behalf.

His expulsion from the convention seems to favour his position, that he was not considered a citizen of France. His imprisonment for being an Englishman, which immediately succeeded, is *quite* as auspicious to his attack.

It should, however, be remembered, that the convention, when he was expelled from it, was governed by Jacobin violence, stimulated and headed by Robespierre, and that after the execution of Robespierre, the introduction of a new faction, a little more moderate, and violence had for a moment ceased, he was invited to resume his seat in the convention, and that he did resume it.

But Paine says: I have always considered that a foreigner, such as I was in fact with respect to France, might be a member of a convention for forming a constitution without affecting his right of citizenship in the country to which he belongs, but *not a member of a government after a consti-*

tution is formed; and I have *uniformly acted upon this distinction.*"[97]

He was an adopted citizen of France. But as many gentlemen amongst us, who have never crossed the Atlantick, have been complimented, if it be a compliment, with a similar adoption, the mere act of adoption would make nothing against him, if the fraternal process had stopped there.

But he was not only an adopted citizen of France: he went there in consequence of his adoption and election, and he *took the oath of allegiance to the French republick*. Every member of the convention took it as matter of course, and so did Paine. If, therefore, in becoming a citizen of France by adoption, and taking the oath of allegiance, he could alienate his citizenship in the United States, he ceased to be a citizen.

Besides, his own argument is its own refutation. He might, he affirms, be a "member of a convention for making a constitution, without affecting his right of citizenship in the country to which he belongs, but *not a member of a government after a constitution is formed.*"

If then after the constitution was formed, in the making of which he had a hand, he was a member of the government, his citizenship in the United States, according to his own doctrine, was a nullity. In order to take away, therefore, the very pretext for his attack on Washington, all that is necessary is to show, that he was a member of the

97 Letter to General Washington, p. 14

government *after* the constitution was formed.

The constitution of Condorcet and Paine was formed and presented in February, 1793. Here, therefore, his functions ceased. If afterwards he was a member of the government, he admits that he forfeited his right of citizenship in the United States.

Now he was not only a member of the government, when, in December, 1793, ten months after the constitution was formed and presented, he was expelled from it by the decree, but after his imprisonment; and we find him as late as July, 1795, making a speech in the government after his own constitution was destroyed, against *another* constitution.

Again. He was not a member of the convention for forming a constitution only; he was a member to all intents and purposes. He spoke on the trial of the king; he voted on the trial of the king. Was that forming a constitution? He generally assisted in the transaction of publick business.

So much I have said merely to evince how erroneous his arguments are even upon his own premises.

And his premises were assumptions of false facts. No act of his in France, no citizenship; nothing that he could do could alienate his allegiance from the United States.

The article in our national constitution, which he imperfectly quotes, has no reference to situations like his. It applies exclusively to "persons holding any office of profit or trust under the United States." He held no office of profit; certainly none of *trust*.

Neither our national constitution nor our laws allows of self-expatriation. In this regard both are precisely the same as the constitution and laws of England. He who is once a citizen, as Paine was, is always a citizen. He cannot withdraw his allegiance. Our national government can always claim his services. It always owes him protection, and he always owes it obedience.[98]

98 Williams's case, tried before Chief Justice Ellsworth, is the only one that has come before the United States courts. In 1792, Williams was commissioned by the French Consul-General residing in America as a lieutenant on board the *Jupiter*, a French seventy-four [a type of two-decked sailing ship of the line, which nominally carried 74 guns. —Ed.] The *Jupiter* sailed in the autumn of the same year for Rochefort, where Williams was naturalized, renouncing his allegiance to the United States. After his naturalization, he was commissioned by the French Republick a second lieutenant on board the French frigate, the *Caront*. He continued in the commission and service of France until the 27th of February, 1797, when he was seized and arrested for accepting a commission from the French Republick, to commit acts of violence against the king of Great Britain, and his subjects, with whom we were at peace. Williams pleaded in justification his naturalization in France, and his renunciation of his allegiance to the United States. Chief Justice Ellsworth gave the following opinion.

"The common law of this country remains the same as it was before the revolution. The present question is to be decided by two great principles; one is that all the members of the civil community are bound to each other by compact, the other is, that one of the parties to this compact cannot dissolve it by his own act. The compact between our community and its members is, that the community shall protect its members,

But this makes nothing for Paine. Washington was not consequentially bound, nor was it any part of his duty, as executive of the United States, to interfere with the French government for his release from prison. What was he arrested for? For being an *Englishman* by birth. Was not that the fact? Was he not an Englishman? On this point only the principles of the three governments concur. No Frenchman can dispense with his allegiance to his country; and the law is so in the United States, as well as in England. If Paine had been arrested merely because he was a citizen of the United States, then, upon a due representation of the fact to our national executive, it would have been the duty of Washington to have interfered in his behalf. But he was arrested under a decree passed against persons born in England. Paine was born there. Could Washington have said that he was not? Could he have arrogantly insisted on a repeal of the decree?

---

and on the part of the members, that they will at all times be obedient to the laws of the community and faithful in its defence. This compact distinguishes our government from those which are founded in violence or fraud. It necessarily results that a member cannot dissolve this compact, without the consent or default of the community. There has been no consent—no default. Default is not pretended. Express consent is not claimed; but it has been argued that the consent of the community is implied by its policy—its condition—and its acts. In countries so crowded with inhabitants, that the means of subsistence are difficult to be obtained, it is reason and policy to permit emigration; but our policy is different; for our country is but scarcely settled, and we have no inhabitants to spare.

As a matter of right he had no claim upon the interposition of our executive. As a point of expediency, of mercy, or of sympathy, he had no title to it at all.

In the first place he had deliberately embarked in all the horrours of the French revolution. He had written in England for France—he had endeavoured to effect a revolution in England in favour of France—he had been elected a member of the convention, and coolly and thankfully taken his seat—he had been adopted a citizen of and taken the oath of allegiance to France. Was he to be pitied when one of the inevitable consequences of the revolution came upon him? Was the power of the United States to be employed, through the medium of their executive, to extricate him from one of the natural effects of that stupendous violence, tyranny, and rapine, which he had applauded in France, when others were *the subjects of them*, and which he had exerted himself to stir up and bring about in England? He calls his imprisonment despotism, and he accordingly complains of it. What, the free republick of France, whose example he had held up to England, guilty of despotism! But it was the violence of Robespierre! And was not Robespierre's violence an effect of the revolution; of a lawless course, a lawless power? If he did not foresee that such a despotism would grow out of such a revolution, he was unfit to write; and if, writing as he did, he did foresee it, he was unfit to live.

During his imprisonment we had differences with England, which Mr. Jay, honourably to himself and greatly for the interest of his country, happily adjusted. Was this a time for general Washington to use his influence with the rulers of France for the liberation of a man so justly obnoxious to the British government as Paine? Who that knows any thing of the intercourse between nation and nation will say that it was? What would the British government have thought of our professions of friendship; of our desire to be upon good terms with them?

At that period too we also felt the effects of the French revolution; of those anarchial principles which Paine had broached in his *Rights of Man*, and which he had endeavoured to propagate all over Europe. Our government was nearly, though not quite deposed by French revolutionary agents. Our sovereignty had been usurped by a French minister. The President, impartially, ably, and with dignity administering the government, was, in the official communications of that minister to him, grossly insulted. The most opprobrious terms were assiduously culled from the language, as if to try how patiently a good government could brook contumely and insult. Vindicating its conduct upon the principles of the law of nations, that minister said:—"I do not recollect what the worm-eaten writings of Grotius, Pufendorf,[99] or Vattel, say on the subject: *I thank God* I have forgotten what

99 Spelled Puffendorff in the original. —Ed.

these *hired jurisprudists* have written upon the rights of nations at any period when all *were enchained*"*!* France thanked God too, no doubt, with her minister, that she had forgotten both law and justice. Paine had largely contributed to this horrid state of things. What feelings then could WASHINGTON have had for him? Those of friendship? Impossible!

As to gratitude, *Washington* certainly owed him none: he had himself done more than any man living for the independence of his country. But if he ever was in debt to Paine on that score, he discharged it at the end of the war by his strenuous though unsuccessful efforts to procure for him from Congress a provision for life. That the national and two of the state governments did more than adequately reward his revolutionary efforts, is certain. They made him for life independent in his pecuniary circumstances, and that was surely paying him liberally for his trifling revolutionary labour; for writing *Common Sense* and *The Crisis*, two pamphlets, both making not more than two hundred and twenty pages.

The real cause of the attack, if the French rulers had not set him on, was our commercial treaty with England. He lived and died at war with the government by which he had been dismissed from the excise, as well as with the nation which contained his wife.

His total want of principle and disregard of every thing like consistency, are in nothing more manifest than in his calumnies against Washington.

"The victory over the Hessians at Princeton, he observes, by a harassed and wearied party, is attended with such a scene of circumstances and *superiority of generalship*, as will ever give it a place in the first line in the history of great actions." *Crisis*, No. 5.

But in his Parisian assault, Washington is quite a different character. In this, "it *is time*, he says, to speak the *undisguised* language of historical truth."[100] It is no longer necessary, he thinks, to play the hypocrite. He then adds, that "the successful skirmishes at the close of the campaign of 1776,[101] make the brilliant exploits of General Washington's seven campaigns. No wonder we see so much pusillanimity in the president[102] when we see so little enterprize in the general." Letter to Washington, p. 31.

Here are too opposite representations of the same action. In the one, that of the Crisis, there was such "*a superiority of generalship*, as will ever give it a place in the first line in the history of great actions." In the other, that of the Letter to Washington, there was no enterprize, *no generalship at all*, and the GREAT ACTIONS becomes an insignificant *skirmish!*

---

100 Letter to Washington, p. 10. He remarked to Mrs. Palmer: "It is well enough to say nothing about it; the *time is not yet come*." But the *time is now come* to speak, as he calls it, the truth of Washington!

101 Alluding to the ratification of the British treaty.

102 The capture of the Hessians.

"Voltaire has remarked," he tells us,

> that king William never appeared to full advantage but in difficulties and in action. The same remark may be made of General Washington, for the character suits him. There is a natural firmness in some minds which cannot be unlocked by trifles, but which, when unlocked, discovers a cabinet of fortitude; and I reckon it among those kind of publick blessings, which we do not immediately see, that God hath blessed him with uninterrupted health, and given him a mind that can even flourish upon care.[103]

This was written during the war. After he received his compensation money from Congress, he seems to have entertained the same opinion of the virtue, resolution, and philosophy of Washington, to whom he thus dedicates the first part of his *Rights of Man*.

> I present you a small treatise in defence of those principles of freedom which your exemplary virtue hath so eminently contributed to establish. That the *Rights of Man* may become as universal as your benevolence can wish, and that you may enjoy the happiness of seeing the new world regenerate the old, is the *prayer* of sir,

&c.

But Washington is the antipodes of all this in his Parisian letter. "As to you, sir, *treacherous* in

---

103 *Crisis*, No. 1.

private friendship, and a *hypocrite* in publick life, the world will be puzzled to decide, whether you are an *apostate* or an *impostor*; whether you have abandoned good principles, or whether you ever had any!" Letter to Washington, p. 34.[104]

From vilifying Washington, he returned to his abuse of the Christian religion. In October, 1796, he published the second part of the *Age of Reason*. He had now furnished himself with a Bible and Testament, and "I can say, he adds, that I have found them *to be* much worse books than I had conceived."

It appears throughout both the first and second part of the *Age of Reason*, that, as in government, his object was not the maintenance, as a man of letters, if such he considered himself, of a speculative point about which philosophers in their elaborate investigations of abstruse subjects may very harmlessly differ, but the propagation of licentious doctrines amongst the lower orders, with a view to weaken if not to destroy, in practice, that awful fear which restrains them from the commission of sins against God and crimes against man. Admitting that he was not unfaithful to himself in the crude deistical opinions which he rudely dif-

---

104 At the same time he wrote, but never printed, the following epigram, which he gave to me soon after his arrival in New York.

> Take from the mine the hardest, roughest stone,
> It needs no fashion, it is WASHINGTON:
> But if you chisel, let your strokes be rude,
> And on his breast engrave *ingratitude*.

fused, yet as he wrote not for reading and thinking men, could he have had any other object than that of mingling with his wasteful anarchy in the affairs of government, a more detestable anarchy in the more solemn affairs of religion? Our well-being here, without considering the more weighty matter of hereafter, is so inseparable from, so identified with religion, that we have nothing to expect from a relaxation of its high obligations but robberies more vast, ruin more complete, tyranny more intolerable, than the plunderings and butcheries and despotisms, of which France was for so many years the hapless subject. What religion could be substituted of equal excellence with that which sways Christendom, and mollifies the natural ferocity of man? I am putting the divinity of it out of the question, and considering it only in reference to its benign influence upon society. I have associated with deists; I have listened to the dogmas of deism, and although priestly intolerance and persecution, the abuses of the Christian, religion, are principally the alleged causes of their aversion from the one and their attachment to the other, yet I have found them in spirit more intolerant and persecuting, if possible, than anything which distinguishes the sufferings of the Hugonots or the bloody reign of Mary. Elihu Palmer, the deistical spouter, was, in the small circle of his church, more priestly, more fulminating, and looked for more reverence and adoration from his disciples, than the Lauds and Gardiners of England. Without the means, he affected all the haughtiness of Wolsey. Professing to adore reason, he was in a rage if any body reasoned with him. He viewed himself as an oracle, whose sayings no one was to question. Paine was equally a dogmatizer; equally a dealer in authority, which was himself. They who tested every thing but their own opinions, suffered not their own opinions to be tested.

In the year 1797, he published a "Letter to the honourable Thomas Erskine." Williams, of London, a bookseller, had been convicted for publishing the *Age of Reason*, and Erskine had conducted the prosecution for the crown. His speech was sufficiently excellent to excite the rancour of Paine: of the rare eloquence of that gentleman, it is, perhaps, the choicest specimen. The letter repeats, in coarse and indecent language, the ribaldry of his *Age of Reason*.

In January of this year the Society of the Theophilanthropists, calling themselves "adorers of God and lovers of man," a knot of atheists and deists, was commenced in Paris. To these gloomy misanthropists, Paine, the high priest, delivered a discourse, the object of which was to prove the "existence of a '*superiour*' cause, or that which man calls God." It begins with a vapid declamation against atheism; just such a one as a man would write who was anxious for the prevalence of that most execrable of all dogmas. Atheists, he admits, for to the scandal of human nature there have been such persons, reason well upon the maxims which they have assumed, but, explorers of all nature as he thinks they are, they have overlooked a principle, he says, which *he* has discovered, and which, alone, he is positive, introduces us to a knowledge of the existence of God. This he calls a *circumstance*, and that circumstance is *motion*, which, he adds, is *not* a property of matter, and therefore, not being a property of matter, and yet existing, its existence proves the existence of God. This is the amount of *his* discourse; of *his* indubitable proof of the being of God! To evince, therefore, upon this old principle, which he advances as new, that there is no God, as "the fool hath said in his heart," it is only necessary to show, that motion is a property of matter. Was it with this view that he advanced the doctrine? Surely he was not ignorant that we can have no idea of matter without motion, positive or relative, nor of motion without matter. Mirabeau, in his *System of Nature*,[105] founds his atheism upon the dogma, that nature is constantly in brisk motion, decomposing and recomposing; that the "dissolution of one body, which we call death, is but the beginning of life and animation in another," and that matter is never at rest. If of the being of God, of which all existence, all that we see and know and feel are so many demonstrations, we had no better proof than Paine's elaborately obscure, ' weak, and impious discourse, then would our con-

105 Though first published under the name of Jean-Baptiste de Mirabeaud, the author was Paul-Henri Thiry, Baron d'Holbach. —Ed.

dition here be indeed miserable; then should we have no *dread of something hereafter*; no hope of happiness beyond the grave.

In the same year he published a small tract which he entitled *Agrarian Justice*. This is a proposition submitted to all nations, for compelling all land holders to pay a tenth part of the value of their estates, towards constituting a fund out of which every person at the age of twenty one should receive fifteen pounds sterling, and ten pounds when arrived at fifty. Of all the theories of the wretched innovators of the present age, those miserable empericks who have disturbed and desolated the world, this is one of the most visionary, and yet it is probable, that like other fanciful and levelling schemes, it has its advocates. Paine is of opinion, that the exaction would be just, and he grounds it upon the assumption, that no man has a right to appropriate land to himself, God having given it in common to all. "It is the value of the improvement only, he says, and not the earth itself, that is individual property. Every proprietor therefore of cultivated land owes to the community a *ground rent*," of ten per cent, according to his estimate, to be extorted and applied as I have stated.

On a subject like this there is much of folly in going back in argument to that rude or natural state to which society never can revert in practice. But passing over the inutility of the one, and the impracticability of the other, Paine's argument, on the supposition of a state of nature, in which there is no location or appropriation of land, is fundamentally erroneous, and is, besides, at variance with itself. With regard to his contradictions, he affirms, that as the earth cannot become individual property, those who have parcelled it out and possess it, "owe a ground rent to the community." The community then can own it; that is his meaning, else individuals who happen to hold cannot rightfully owe to the community anything for the possession of that to which the community has no title. The community, nation, or government, for in the argument they are one and the same thing, being made up of individuals, how, if individuals cannot locate or appropriate to themselves any portion of the earth, can the aggregate of individuals, the nation, locate and appropriate to itself the whole? If he had said that it necessarily belongs to the sovereignty, he would have found himself in the same dilemma, for the COMMON is then gone; it is no longer a common; it is located; it is the property of the government, and those who wish to cultivate any portion of it for sustenance, must purchase. He would give to all that which he denies to all its parts, and therefore to all.

The rightful acquisition of land is contemporanry with and inseparable from its cultivation, which is antecedent to a community, as civilization, in whatever degree, always precedes government. There is, in the rude state which he has supposed, no community, no government; every thing is in common, and yet there is no common consent, no common rule of action, which means government. In this condition location is essential to cultivation and sustenance; and as no one would bestow labour upon that which he would be unable to secure to himself, and which could not be secured to him; cultivation and acquisition are, in this imaginary state of things, necessarily one and the same rightful act.

This year he also published[106] a *Letter to the People of France, and the French Armies, on the event of the 18th* Fructidor. The 18th Fructidor [September 4, 1797, in Christian language] introduced to Paris a fresh explosion, and Paine's letter was intended to reconcile the armies, &c. to the event. Boissy d'Anglas's constitution of 1795, the constitution of elders and youngsters, and of a directory of five, which lasted until the approach of this Fructidor, had made way for the presidency of Pichegru over the council of five hundred. Pichegru and his associates sought to mitigate the rigours of the revolution by re-opening some of the churches, inviting the return of many of the clergy, and curtailing the proscription list. These comforting measures being deemed a conspiracy against the republick, a *new* revolution happened, in which, to the total disregard of the constitution, Pichegru and his fellow labourers were, without trial, banished.

Paine, who, if he were not a pander of the French government, was a base trembling slave, writes his

106 His *Agrarian Justice*, he states in the preface, was written in the winter of 1795-6.

letter in justification of this "extraordinary measure," as he himself terms it in the very first page, although he admits that the measure, which he is vindicating, was unconstitutional!

And as if to heighten the degree of his own offence and the atrocity of the government, he pronounces upon the constitution which has been violated a most extravagant panegyrick. "A better organized constitution, he says, never was devised by human wisdom. It is, in its organization, free from all the defects to which other forms of government are more or less subject."[107] This is the constitution which destroyed the *universal suffrage* which he and Condorcet had prescribed in theirs. This is the constitution which makes *a campaign* in the army one of the innumerable qualifications of a *citizen*; which places between *the citizen* and his government electoral colleges; which, therefore, does not permit *the citizen* to vote for a member either of the elders or the youngsters; and which, lastly, Paine himself pusillanimously opposed in his speech to the convention, in July, 1795.

His encomiums on this violated constitution, which, in 1795, he opposed as a bad one, and which, in 1797, he declares is the best that "human wisdom ever devised," are regular and systematick, beginning with the council of ancients, proceeding to that of five hundred, and ending with a laboured eulogium on the directory of five. Every branch has

107 Page 1.

his cordial approbation, but with the executive of *five* he is passionately in love.

"In the first place," he remarks, "speaking of the directory of *five*, shall the executive by election be an *individual* or a *plurality*?"[108]

> An individual by election [as in the United States] "is *almost as bad*, he continues, as the HEREDITARY SYSTEM, except that there is always a better chance of not having an ideot. But he will never be any thing more than a chief of a party, and none but those of that party will have access to him.[109]

This is the reverse of the language which, in his *Rights of Man*, he spoke to the people of England. There, the constitution of the United States was the paragon of all constitutions: it was the *new* system in contradistinction to the old. There, the election of the president was sumptuously described as embracing all excellence. But compared with Boissy d'Anglas's constitution, in which the executive was not elected by the people, nor by the electoral colleges, but by the legislative body, that excellence becomes "almost as bad as the hereditary system!" The only 'exception,' in Paine's opinion, to the equal baseness of the two is, that, by election, there is a better "*chance* of not having an idiot!"

---

108 There was no question about a new constitution. He is only endeavouring to show that that which is, is right.

109 Page 6. In the latter remark he is undoubtedly correct. It is so in the United States

Preferring a *plural* executive to an individual, the next question is, he observes, "what shall be the number of that plurality?"

"Three are *too few*, either for the variety or the quantity of business. The constitution has adopted *five*, and experience has shown that this number of directors is sufficient for all the purposes, and therefore a greater number would only be an unnecessary expense."[110]

The number which France had hit upon, and which, I agree with him, is *quite sufficient*, he seems to think designed by *nature* for all governments, although human wisdom, in no part of the world, except in France, has as yet adopted it. *Nature*, he says, has given us exactly five senses, and the same number of fingers and toes, pointing out to us, by this kindness, the propriety of an executive directory of five, precisely as in France.[111] If one sense, he continues, had been sufficient, she would have given us no more: an individual executive, he therefore infers, is unnatural and unphilosophical, "individuality being exploded by nature." Surely tyranny never had a more fawning parasite, freedom a more decided enemy.

The efficacy of *paper* constitutions, as described by him in the *Rights of Man*, was, in the proceeding against Pichegru and his friends, not only disproved by the fact, but the fact itself, which was very agreeable to him, gave the lie to his former

110 Page 6–7.

111 Page 7.

doctrines. During the ascendancy of the two committees of revolution and safety, there was a form of trial; a mockery indeed and an outrage, but under the *paper* constitution of Boissy d'Anglas, which it was supposed had terminated summary proceedings and instant executions, Pichegru and his colleagues were banished from the council of five hundred without even the ceremony of a trial. Where now was the cogency and omnipotence of a paper constitution? Party and injustice had laid it aside, and Paine panegyrizes the act! *Suspicion* was sufficient even with him to authorise a dispensation with all constitutional obligations. There was no evidence of guilt: none was produced; none was sought for. Nor was guilt, in his estimation, necessary; presumption, ill-grounded presumption was enough.

> The obstinacy with which the conspiracy, he says, persevered in its repeated attacks upon the directory, *in framing laws in favour of emigrants and refractory priests*, admitted of no other direct *interpretation* than that something was rotten in the council of five hundred. The evidence of *circumstances* became every day too visible not to be seen.[112]

I feel great difficulty in repressing the indignation which rises from reviewing the nefarious publications and conduct of this man. Robespierre, he says, was a tyrant. Why? Because he sent men to

112 Page 14.

their account on suspicion. Speaking of his own case, when in prison, he remarks, that owing to the prevalence of this doctrine of suspicion, "there was no time when I could think my life worth twenty-four hours."[113] What difference was there between Robespierre and himself? *Suspicion* was enough with Robespierre; *suspicion* was enough with Paine. Robespierre called out conspiracy, and off went a head; Paine, when he himself was not the subject of the same despotism and cruelty, echoed the cry, and Pichegru and his associates were banished. Pichegru, he asserts, was guilty of a conspiracy against the state. In what was he a conspirator? Paine tells us—"in framing laws in favour of emigrants and refractory priests." This was the conspiracy! Admitting that the framing of such laws was treason, where is the proof; what is it? The "evidence, Paine answers, of *circumstances*." Without accusation, then, without trial, *circumstances*, susceptible of a thousand interpretations, authorised the banishment of Pichegru, and the destruction of the paper constitution!

Pichegru and his banished associates were legislators. If, wishing to relax the rigours and the proscriptions, and to lessen the miseries of the revolution, they had "*framed* laws favouring emigrants and refractory priests;" had they not, as legislators, a right to do so? It did not follow, because such acts were framed, that the acts would become laws. If, as members, they had no voice in legisla-

113 Letters to the citizens of the United States.

tion, they were puppets; and if they erred in opinion, is errour of opinion criminal in a legislator? And banish them too without trial! Is this republicanism? Is this freedom?

In the early stages of the revolution, the armed force, at the beck of the dominant party, overawed the legislative body. Boissy d'Anglas's constitution had guarded against this dreadful evil, as far as a *paper* constitution could do so. The armed force was not to approach nearer to Paris than twelve leagues. But the party in the government to which Paine was attached, and of which he was an infamous tool, meditating the overthrow of Pichegru and his friends, ordered the armed force within the constitutional limits, as instruments of their designs. This indication of a bloody purpose excited alarm. Paine justifies the march of the troops; Paine vindicates this atrocious violence committed on the paper constitution, "*Conspiracy*," he observes, "is quick of suspicion, and the fear which the *faction* in the council of five hundred manifested upon this occasion, could not have suggested itself to innocent men. Neither would innocent men have expostulated with the directory upon the case." "The leaders of the *faction* conceived that the troops were *marching against them*, and the conduct they adopted in consequence of it, was sufficient to *justify the measure*, even if it had been so. From what other motive than the consciousness of their own designs could they have fear?"[114] The murderous sayings of Jeffreys to Sydney are inferiour in atrocity to this. Paine infers guilt from a meritorious act. The constitution is outraged by the march of the troops. The faction, as he indecorously denominates a part of the legislative body, express fear in behalf of the constitution. This fear, so natural, so commendable, so patriotick, he construes into guilt, and this guilt, he profligately asserts, was "sufficient to justify the marching of the troops against the legislators!" Can there be baseness, can there be despotism greater than this?

His letter to the army was his last work in France. Wearied with the republick, though obstinately bent on maintaining his principles against his feelings, he now sighed to return to the United States, "whose election of the chief magistrate is almost as bad as the hereditary system." He knew not indeed what to do with himself. He could not return to England, where he had been wisely outlawed, and he was aware that he was odious in the United States. Washington justly considered him an anarchist in government, and an infidel in religion. He had no country in the world, and it may truly be said that he had not a friend. Was ever man so wretched? Was ever enormous sinner so justly punished? He must, however, return to the United States, for he was poor; the plunderers of France having plundered only for themselves. He still retained his farm at New Rochelle, and he was

114 Page 15 .

sensible, that greatly increased in value, it would abundantly supply all his wants.

But how to get to the United States with safety, was the question. The ocean, bearing proudly upon its swelling bosom the gallant force of England, was impassable to him. He now felt the force of the prosecution at which he had laughed. By it he was limited to the Bastille of France, and compelled to endure all its horrours. He had made arrangements, he says, to return with Mr. Monroe, and that it was fortunate he did not, as the vessel in which that minister returned was "boarded by a British frigate on her passage, and every part of her searched, down even to her hold, for Thomas Paine."115 Immediately after he went to Havre, in order to embark, but as several British frigates were cruising off the port, he returned to Paris. "I then," he states,

> wrote to Mr. Jefferson, that if the fate of the election should put him in the chair of the presidency, and he should have occasion to send a frigate to France, he would give me an opportunity of returning by it, which he did. But I declined coming by the Maryland, the vessel that was offered me, and waited for the frigate that was to bring the new minister, Chancellor Livingston, to France, but that frigate was ordered round to the Mediterranean; and as at that time the war was over, and the British cruisers [were] called in, I could come any way. I then

115 Letter 4 to the people of the United States.

> agreed to come with commodore Barney, in a vessel he had engaged. I was again fortunate I did not, for the vessel sunk at sea, and the people were preserved in a boat.[116]

He continued in France from the year 1797, the date of his letter to the French army, to the year 1802, associating, during that time, with the lowest company, and indulging, to still greater excess his thirst for liquor. He became so filthy in his person, so mean in dress, and so notorious a sot, that all men of decency in Paris avoided him.

On the 30th of October, 1802, he arrived at Baltimore, under the protection of President Jefferson. The subjoined is an extract of Mr. Jefferson's answer to Paine's request for permission to return to the United States in a publick vessel.

> You expressed a wish in your letter to return to America by a national ship; Mr. Dawson, who brings over the treaty, and who will present you with this letter, is charged with orders to the captain of the *Maryland* to receive and accommodate you back, if you can be ready to depart at such a short warning. You will in general find us returned to sentiments worthy of former times; in these it will be your glory to have steadily laboured, and with as much effect as any man living. That you may live long to continue your useful labours, and reap the reward in the thankfulness of nations, is my sincere prayer. Accept the assurances of my high

116 *Ibid.*

esteem, and affectionate attachment.
THOMAS JEFFERSON.

Paine was followed from Paris, with the consent of her husband, in whose house he had lived, by Margaret Brazier Bonneville, and her three sons; Lewis, Benjamin, and Thomas; Mr. Bonneville having himself proposed to emigrate to America. Madame Bonneville arrived at Norfolk a few days after Paine's arrival at Baltimore.

From Baltimore he went to Washington, in order to make his compliments to President Jefferson: he was soon after followed by Madame Bonneville and her sons. His reception at Washington was cold and forbidding. Even Mr. Jefferson received him with politick circumspection; and such of the members of Congress as suffered him to approach them, did so from motives of curiosity. *Policy* dictated this course. If Paine had been *popular*, no matter how despicable or how wicked, he would have been courted, but as he was not, he was shunned. The leaders of the party in power were apprehensive that he would write for it, and they were sure that if he did, he would injure it; hence he was contemptuously neglected by them. His figure was indeed much against him: it was that of a little old man, broken down by intemperance, and utterly disregardful of personal cleanliness. His intemperance he could not conceal, nor had he, to all appearance, a wish to conceal it. He was daily drunk with his favourite brandy, and everybody saw or heard of his intoxication.

Fearful as the leaders of the party were that he would injure their *popular* prospects by publishing, his pen could not be restrained. Sufficiently intrenched with popularity to trample upon the constitution, to sanction political anarchy, or to countenance irreligion, Mr. Jefferson had expressed a wish that he would "continue his useful labours," and, in this instance grateful, he had resolved not to disappoint his expectations. Encouraged, therefore, by the president, urged by his inordinate vanity, and cheered with his bottle, he commenced at Washington the publication of half a dozen letters, addressed "to the citizens of the United States." These, except his letter to Samuel Adams, are party, rude, malignant effusions. In one of them he remarks, with equal coarseness, impudence, and vanity:—"The scribblers who know me not, and who fill their papers with paragraphs about me, besides their want of talents, *drink too many slings and drams in a morning* to have any chance with me."[117] This he published at Washington, where it was notorious that he was in the constant practice of drinking *slings and drams*, not only in the morning, but all the day through.

His letter to Samuel Adams was in reply to a cool and cautious one which that gentleman, respected for the services he had rendered his country, and interesting from the loss of his sight, had

117 Letter 4.

written to him on the subject of the Christian religion. "When," he observes,

> I heard that you had turned your mind to a defence of infidelity, I felt myself much astonished and more grieved, that you had attempted a measure so injurious to the feelings and so repugnant to the interest of the citizens of the United States. Will you excite among them the spirit of angry controversy? I am told that some of the newspapers have announced your intention to publish an additional pamphlet on the principles of your Age of Reason. Do you think that your pen, or the pen of any other man, can unchristianize the mass of our citizens? We ought to think ourselves happy in the enjoyment of opinion, without the danger of persecution by civil or ecclesiastical law.

Paine's answer was returned through the medium of the newspapers! In this he counterfeits a friendship for Mr. Adams, which he was incapable of feeling for any human being. Rejoicing in the opportunity which the letter had given him, to propagate his deistical doctrines, his answer is full of vulgar sayings and impertinent sneers. He assigns some reasons for publishing, sooner than he had originally intended, his *Age of Reason*, which, that his disciples in the United States might be countenanced and encouraged, he vindicates. Speaking of the causes which induced him to publish the *Age of Reason* when he did, he observes:—"In the first place, I saw my life in continual danger. My friends were falling as fast as the guillotine could cut their heads off; and as I every day expected the same fate, I resolved to begin my work."

Paine's memory was uncommonly good, but his great want of veracity often got the better of it.

If the reasons which he here assigns for writing the *Age of Reason* when he did be true, those which he had assigned before are false, The period of which he speaks was the year 1793. It was then that his friends were losing their heads in Paris as fast as the *national razor* could cut them off; it was then that he every day expected the same fate. His election to the national assembly was announced to him in London, on the 13th of September, 1792. On the 15th of the same month, he wrote his letter at Calais, addressed to Mr. Dundas. In January, 1793, the king was decapitated. In the summer of the same year, Robespierre cut off heads in gross and without ceremony. In December, 1793, Paine himself was imprisoned. Having witnessed all these catastrophes, but his own, which he anticipated, "I resolved, he adds, to begin my work." Let us compare this with what follows.

In his preface to the *Age of Reason*, part second, is the subjoined passage, which, in another place, and for another purpose, I have quoted.

> I have already mentioned, in the former part of the *Age of Reason*, that it had long been my in-

> tention to publish my thoughts upon religion, but that I had originally reserved it to a late period of life, intending it to be the last work I should undertake. Some circumstances, however, which existed in France in the latter end of the year NINETY, *determined me to delay it no longer*. The just and humane principles of the revolution, which philosophy had diffused, had been departed from.

Here, he had "*determined*," in the year 1790, to delay the work no longer, because the humane principles of the revolution, even then, had been departed from.

But in his letter to Mr. Adams, it was not, he says, until the year 1793, that "I resolved to begin my work," and he assigns very different reasons for it. These are, because the heads of his friends were struck off, and because he himself every day expected the same fate. No two accounts of the same fact could be more contradictory and opposite. The first in date is probably true, being first written. The last, which is not true, was written in the hope of inducing Mr. Adams to believe, that he had something of humanity about him.

Having paid his compliments to Mr. Jefferson, and gratified him by "continuing his useful labours," he left Washington for New York, accompanied with Madame Bonneville and her sons:[118]

118 Passing through Baltimore, he was accosted by the Reverend Mr. Hargrove, minister of a new sect called the New Jerusalemites. "You are Mr. Paine," said Mr. Hargrove. "Yes." "My

he arrived, as I have mentioned in the preface. He found his farm at New Rochelle greatly increased in value, notwithstanding the consumable part of the mansion had, in the year 1790, been accidentally destroyed by fire. "Even in my worldly concerns, he observes, I have been blessed. The little property I left in America has been encreasing in the value of its capital more than eight hundred dollars every year for the fourteen years and more, that I have been absent from it."[119] In another place he remarks:—"My property in this country is now worth six thousand pounds sterling, which put in the funds will bring me 400 *l.* sterling a year."[120] Yet with all this property, meanness and avarice would not permit him to remain at Lovett's hotel more than eight or ten days. During his stay, he was visited by the labouring class of emigrants from England, Ireland, and Scotland, who had there admired his *Rights of Man*. With these he drank grog in the tap room, morning, noon and night. Admired and praised by them, he strutted about, or rather staggered about, shewing himself to all and shaking hands with all. One day-labourer would say; "drink with me Mr.

name is Hargrove, sir, I am minister of the New Jerusalem Church here. We, sir, explain the scripture in its true meaning. The key has been lost above four thousand years, and we have found it." "Then," said Paine, drily, "it must have been very rusty."

119 Letter 4 to the citizens of the United States.

120 Letter to Thomas Clio Rickman, of London. See the London ed. 1804, of his letters to the citizens of the United States.

Paine;" another, "drink with me," and he very condescendingly gratified them all. The leaders of the party to which he had attached himself, paid him no attention: he was studiously avoided by them. But two or three persons of any thing like distinction *publickly* visited him, and seeing his vulgarity and love of liquor, their visit was short. He complained of inattention without perceiving the cause. While at Lovett's, he fell over a high stair-case in a paroxysm of intoxication. Being much hurt, it was given out that his fall was occasioned by an apoplectick fit!

In making his arrangements for a permanent residence amongst us, he contemplated the abandonment of Madame Bonneville, whom her husband had placed under his protection, and who was now among strangers! Besides his estate at New Rochelle, he had a small house and a few barren acres at Bordentown, New Jersey. This little property, which he afterwards sold for seven hundred and fifty dollars, he proposed to give to her, and to settle her upon it as a school mistress, but she resolutely and successfully resisted his unfeeling project. He represented her as the wife of his friend, a *republican* printer in Paris, with whom he had boarded, and who, disliking the new order of things under the First Consul, was every day expected to emigrate to the United States. Many thought well of that kindness in which his friend's wife and children had found refuge, but his treatment of her soon dissipated the delusion, and convinced all who knew him, that to his fatal promises, made to her husband in Paris, he was now adding inhumanity.[121]

From Lovett's he went to the house of Mr. Carver, farrier, in Cedar Street, whom I have already mentioned; an honest, faithful, industrious man, who gratuitously accommodated him for a few weeks. At Carver's he finally concluded to live on his farm, as soon as he could remove Mr. Purdy, the occupant, from it; to take the two children with him, and to leave Madame Bonneville in the city, to provide for herself as well as she could.

But before his departure for New Rochelle, the persons who had paid him attention at Lovett's, angry at the neglect of the higher orders, were anxious to testify their esteem for him by giving him a publick dinner, if a sufficient number could be prevailed with to be present. The intended honour was mentioned to Paine, who highly approved of it, and manifested great solicitude for its accomplishment. After many consultations on the sort of dinner which could be given, and the sort of persons who on such an occasion would probably attend in open day at Lovett's, the pro-

121 The elder Bonneville, about fourteen, returned to his father in Paris, in the year 1805. He detested Paine, and lad as he was, would scarcely speak to him. Ah! he would often say, Paine is not so well known in the United States as in Paris. He has broken up the tranquillity of my father's house! Paine did not pay his passage to France. The boy returned in a French ship, in which his mother procured him a passage gratis. Benjamin and Thomas remained with Paine.

posed place of feasting, a subscription was set on foot, and the city canvassed for names. Two or three weeks of diligent search and importunity obtained between sixty and seventy. The dinner was therefore given, and Paine conducted from the table as mellow as he wished to be.[122]

---

122 Paine, as he himself observes, had a taste and talent for poetry. The following effusion of fancy, addressed to Mrs. Smyth, lady of Sir Robert, which he wrote in Paris, he repeated to me, from memory, soon after his arrival in New York. He thus introduced the lines himself. "Mr. Paine corresponded with a lady, and dated his letters from *The Castle in Air*, while she addressed hers from *The Little Corner of the World*. For reasons which he knew not,(*) their intercourse was suddenly suspended, and for sometime he believed his fair friend in obscurity and distress. Many years afterwards, however, he met her unexpectedly at Paris, in the most affluent circumstances, and married to Sir Robert."

FROM THE CASTLE IN AIR,
TO THE
LITTLE CORNER OF THE WORLD,

In the region of clouds where the whirlwinds arise,
　　My castle of fancy was built;
The turrets reflected the blue of the skies,
　　And the windows with sun-beams were gilt.

The rainbow sometimes in its beautiful state,
　　Enamell'd the mansion around,
And the figures that fancy in clouds can create
　　Supplied me with gardens and ground.

I had grottos and fountains, and orange tree groves,
　　I had all that enchantment has told;
I had sweet shady walks for the Gods and their Loves,
　　I had mountains of coral and gold,

From Mr. Carver's, he went in June, 1803, to New Rochelle, and boarded on his farm with Purdy, leaving Madame Bonneville in the city. Unprotected and distressed, she followed him, after the lapse of six or seven weeks, and lived with him and her

---

But a storm that I felt not, had risen and roll'd,
 While wrapp'd in a slumber I lay;
And when I look'd out in the morning, behold!
 My castle was carried away.

It pass'd over rivers, and vallies, and groves,
 The world, it was all in my view—
I thought of my friends, of their fatas, of their loves,
 And often, full often, of you.

At length it came over a beautiful scene,
 That nature in silence had made:
The place was but small—but 'twas sweetly serene,
 And chequer'd with sunshine and shade.

I gaz'd and I envied with painful good will,
 And grew tired of my seat in the air:
When all of a sudden my castle stood still,
 As if some attraction was there.

Like a lark from the sky it came futtering down,
 And plac'd me exactly in view
When who should I meet, in this charming retreat,
 This corner of calmness—but you.

Delighted to find you in honour and ease,
 I felt no more sorrow nor pain,
And the wind coming fair, I ascended the breeze,
 And went back with my castle again.

(*) No one but himself could mistake them. A delicate female could not bear his company.

children at Purdy's until the fall of the year, when they all returned to New York. Purdy's family, who were very poor; Paine, Madame Bonneville, and her children, all ate together. Paine had a small room to himself. His furniture were a miserable straw bed, on which he slept, a small deal table, a chair, a Bible, and a jug of spiritous liquors. He preferred brandy, but being too dear in the country for his penurious spirit, he drank New England Rum. Sometimes the young Bonnevilles went to school at New Rochelle, but, generally, they rambled in the fields, unheeded and almost unnoticed. Although Tom was Paine's favourite, both were always dirty and shabbily dressed, frequently without shoes and stockings. In the winter, he lived in Dover street, a sort of rendezvous for sailors.

In the spring of 1804, he returned to his farm at New Rochelle, Purdy having left it, taking with him the two Bonnevilles, and leaving their mother in the city. Not chusing to live upon the farm himself, he hired one Christopher Derrick,[123] an old man, to work it for him. While Derrick was husbanding the farm, Paine and the two young Bonnevilles boarded, sometimes with Mr. Wilburn, in Gold Street, in the city, but principally with Mr. Andrew A. Dean, at New Rochelle. Mrs. Dean, with whom I have conversed, tells me that he was daily drunk at their house, and that, in his few sober moments, he was always quarrelling with her and disturbing the peace of the family. She represents him as

123 Spelled Derick in the original. —Ed.

deliberately and disgustingly filthy; as chusing to perform the offices of nature in his bed! It is not surprising, therefore, that she importuned her husband to turn him out of the house, but owing to Mr. Dean's, predilection for his political writings, her importunities were, for several weeks, unavailing. Constant domestick disquiet very naturally ensued, which was increased by Paine's peevishness and violence. One day he run after Miss Dean, a girl of fifteen, with a chair whip in his hand, to whip her, and would have done so, but for the interposition of her mother. Enraged, Mrs. Dean, to use her own language, "flew at him." Paine retreated up stairs into his private room, and was swiftly pursued by his antagonist. The little drunken old man owed his safety to the bolts of his door. In the fall of the year, Mrs. Dean prevailed with her husband to keep him in the house no longer. The two Bonnevilles were quite neglected.[124]

124 In July, he wrote, for Mr. Carver, the following obscene and impious lines on the birth of Jesus Christ. If any thing could add to their impiety, it would be the disgusting immorality and the perpetual turbulence of the man who wrote them. They are *printed from Paine's hand-writing*. The life of their author is the most powerful antidote to their infidelity. A man more honest, temperate, social, and just, could not, in all probability, have written them. The reader, when perusing the lines, should carry along with him the ideas, that while writing them, Paine was, in all likelihood, drunk, and that he had undoubtedly been exciting husband against wife, destroying family peace, wrangling with all his neighbours, cheating, in his dealings, all whom he could cheat, and living a life distinguished by seduction, by oppression, by beastly intoxication, and by every species of imposition and injustice.

From Dean's, he went to live on his farm. Here

Commentary on the Eastern Wise-Men travelling to Bethlehem, guided by a star, to see the Little Jesus in the manger. —Mat., ch. 2.

Three pedlars trav'ling to a fair,
To see the fun and what was there,
And sell their merchandise.
They stopt upon the road to chat,
Refresh, and ask of this and that,
That they might be more wise.

And pray, the Landlord said to them,
Where go ye sirs? To Bethlehem,
The Citizens replied.
Ye are merchants, sirs, to them said he;
We are, replied the pedlars three,
And eastern-men beside.

And pray what have ye in your sacks,
If worth the while, I will go snacks?
To them quoth major domo.
We've buttons, buckles, spectacles,
And every thing a merchant sells,
Replied the trav'ling trio.

These things are very well, said he,
For beaux, and those who cannot see
Much further than their knuckles;
But Bethlehem fairs' for boys and girls
Who never think of spettacles,
And cannot buy your buckles.

I have a pack of toys, quoth he,
A trav'ling merchant left with ine,
Who could not pay his score;
And youshall have them, on condition
You sell them at a cheap commission,
And make the money sure.

There's one of us will stay in pawn,
Until the other two return,
    If you suspect our faith, said they.
The Landlord thought this was a plan
To leave upon [his] hands, the man,
    And therefore he said, nay.

They truck'd, however, for the pack
Which one of them took on his back,
    And off the merchants travell'd:
And here the tale the Apostles told,
Of wise- men and their gifts of gold,
    Will fully be unravell'd.

The star in the east that shin'd so bright
As might be seen both day and night,
    If you will credit them;
It was no other than a sign
To a public house, where pedlars dine,
    In East-street, Bethlehem.

The wise-men were those pedlars three,
As you and all the world may see,
    By reading to the end;
For commentators have mistook
In paraphrasing of a book
    They did not understand.

Our Travellers coming to the house,
Scarce fit to entertain a mouse,
    Inquired to have a room,
The Landlord said he was not able
To give them any but the stable,
    So many folks were come.
And pray who have you there, said they,
And how much money must we pay,
    For we have none to spare?

with whom he had wrangled, and to whom he had been a tyrant, from the moment of their engagement. Derrick left him with revengeful thoughts.

Being now alone, except the company of the two Bonnevilles, of whom he took but little notice, fond

---

Why, there's one Joscph, and a wench,
Who are to go before the bench,
    About a love affair.

Some how or other, in a manger
A child, expos'd to every danger,
    Was found as it was sleeping;
The girl, she swears that she's a maid,
So swears the man, and I'm afraid
    On me will fall the keeping:

Now, if you'll set yourselves about
To find this knotty story out
    I'll pay whate'er it may be.
So in the trav'ling pedlars went
To pay their birth-day compliment,
    And talk about the baby.

They first unpack'd their pack of toys,
Some for show and some for noise,
    But mostly for the latter;
One gave a rattle, one a whistle,
And one a trumpet made of gristle,
    To introduce the matter.

One squeak'd away, the other blew,
The third play'd on the rattle too,
    To keep the bantling easy,
And hence the story comes to us
Of which some people make such fuss
    About the eastern magi.

as he was of Tom, he engaged an old black woman of the name of *Betty*, to do his housework. Betty lived with him but three weeks. She seems to have been as intemperate as himself. Like her master, she was every day intoxicated. Paine would accuse her of stealing his New England rum, and Betty would retort by calling him an old drunkard. Often, Mrs. Dean informs me, would they both lie prostrate on the same floor; dead-drunk, sprawling and swearing and threatening to fight, but incapable of approaching each other to combat. Nothing but inability prevented a battle.

In the meanwhile Madame Bonneville was boarding in the city of New York on the faith of Paine, who, in November, was brought up on a warrant before the justices of the justices' court for the amount of her board. The subjoined minute is copied from the records of the court.

November 20, 1804.
James Wilburn vs Thomas Paine
Warrant, 50 dols. Paulding, Marshal.

Plaintiff, by Peter Paulding, demands 35 dols. for boarding Mrs. Bonneville, at defendant's request.

Defendant pleads non-assumpsit.

Adjourned till 11 o'clock to-morrow.

November 21.
Same vs Same
On adjournment, &c.

Parties appear.
John Fellows, witness for plaintiff.
Nonsuit.

The court was crouded to gaze at Paine, who exhibited no signs either of fear or shame. He denied the debt with incomparable assurance and intrepidity; and as the plaintiff had neglected to subpoena Madame Bonneville, to prove that he had promised *her* to pay her board, the scandalous old man obtained a non-suit. He afterwards, however, paid Mr. Wilburn's demand. Probably a menace of a publick exposure in the gazettes forced him, in this instance, to do justice.

He now returned to his farm at New Rochelle, taking with him Madame Bonneville and her sons. On his arrival, he hired *Rachel Gidney*, a black woman, to cook for him. Rachel made out to stay with him about two months. But as he never thought of paying for services, or for meat, or for anything else, Rachel had to sue him for five dollars, the amount of her wages. She got out a warrant, on which he was apprehended, and Mr. Shute, one of his neighbours and political admirers, was his bail. The wages were finally obtained, but he thought it hard that he should be sued in a country for which he had done *so much!*[125]

125 During Rachel's stay, Mr. Carver, an uneducated man, but a respectable citizen, made him a visit, which he describes to me in the following communication.

"To MR. CHEETHAM.

"SIR,

"As you are about writing the life of Thomas Paine, if you think the following remarks are worth noticing, you are at liberty to publish them in the work.

"During the time that Mr. Paine resided at his own place, at New Rochelle, I frequently paid him a visit, and possessing a slight acquaintance with a minister of the gospel in this city, who was friendly to Paine's political works, but had not had an opportunity of seeing Mr. Paine, although it was his wish to see him, I informed the gentleman that in a few days I was going to see Mr. Paine, and if he thought proper to ride with me in my chair, he should be exceedingly welcome: he willingly agreed to my proposition, and in a few days after we set off for New Rochelle. At our arrival we found the old gentleman, living in a small room like a hermit, and I believe the whole of the furniture in the room, including a cot-bed, was not worth five dollars: Mr. Paine, however, had the politeness to invite us to breakfast, but I believe of all the scenes that my companion had witnessed, this was one of the most novel: Mr. Paine's breakfast cloth, being composed of old newspapers: after the breakfast furniture was placed on the table, the black woman that was a servant to Paine, asked him if she was to put fresh tea in the pot, his answer was in the affirmative, the reason why the servant made this enquiry was, that Paine's general method was to re-dry the tea leaves, before the fire, and have them put in the tea-pot again, the next time he drank tea: this custom I had often seen when I was at New Rochelle, but nowhere else in my lifetime. Our tea at that time was common bohea, and coarse brown sugar, and part of a rye loaf of bread, and about a quarter of a pound of butter: the black woman brought in a plate of buckwheat pancakes, which Mr. Paine undertook to butter; he kept turning them over and over with his snuffy fingers, so that it astonished my companion, and prevented him from partaking of them; but the country air having created an appetite with me, I ate heartily of them. After breakfast, the reverend gentleman and myself took a walk into the fields; he accosted me thus: Mr. Carver, I think you

the ill-usage he had received from Paine, and who like him was revengeful, atrociously conspired, the neighbours say and believe, against his life. On Christmas Eve, 1804, he borrowed a musket, and, just after dark, went out with it from Mr. Dean's, with whom he had lived since his dismission by Paine. Mrs. Dean, who has mentioned to me the circumstances, asked him where he was going with the musket? Derrick replied, only to fire a Christmas-eve salute. He proceeded towards Paine's, who lived hard by, and who, having a lighted candle in his room, was sitting near the exposed window. In this situation a musket was fired at him, the contents of which, striking the bottom of the window frame, where he sat, dropped down between the inner plaster and weather-boards of the wooden house, to the foundation. In a few minutes after the report of the musket, Derrick returned to Dean's. He was apprehended, and tried for the offence, but acquitted. Since Paine's death, he has often said, Mrs. Dean tells me,[126] that he was sorry

---

are a strange man, or you could not have eat those pancakes, after the old man's turning them over and over with his snuffy fingers; besides neither his hands or face appear to have been washed for twelve months. Why sir, said I to him, I thought you professed to be a Christian, and the book or scripture so called, that you believe in, says, 'that which goeth into the man, does not defile the man.'

"I am, sir, your's respectfully,

"WILLIAM CARVER."

126 My interviews with Mrs. Dean have been in the city, where she was ona visit to her friends. I have since conversed with Mr. Dean, who corroborates all that has been communicated to me

the musket did not do execution, but without mentioning that he fired it at Paine.

In February, 1805, he removed from New Rochelle to the city, where he boarded with Mr. Carver six or eight weeks. The two Bonnevilles he left at school at New Rochelle. Madame Bonneville was stationed in a miserable garret in Liberty Street. From Carver's he returned on the 13th of May, to his farm at New Rochelle. In August he again visited the city, and lived with Mr. Carver' a few weeks. He proposed to continue at Carver's, but owing to illness in the family, he could not be accommodated. He therefore went back to his farm at New Rochelle, and took the two Bonnevilles from school to wait on him. Here he remained until the approach of winter, when he came to the city, and lived at Glen's, an obscure house, in Water-street, until March, 1806.

During the summer of 1805, the pestilential fever raged in the city of New York, which became nearly evacuated by its inhabitants. The garret-residence of Madame Bonneville, who was in effect abandoned by Paine, was the focus of the pestilence. Unable to get out of town, she would in all probability have perished of hunger, but for the pecuniary aid which Mr. Carver liberally and humanely afforded her. Paine was acquainted with her condition, but had he no feeling.

At the latter end of March, 1806, he returned to New Rochelle. Unwilling to be at any expense on his

---

by his wife. Mr. Dean is a sensible man, and a judicious observer. He is one of the justices of the peace for the county.

farm, and unable, from the bad character which he had, to procure a servant to attend him, he boarded with the two Bonnevilles, at the Bull's Head, New Rochelle, a small tavern kept by Mr. Jones, a Welshman. He continued at the Bull's-head until about the 20th of May, when the Welshman actually turned him out. His increased inebriation and filth were so offensive to Mr. Jones, that he could not keep him in his house any longer; and as Paine knew not where to go, (no one in the neighbourhood being willing to take him in the Welshman was obliged to drive him from his habitation.

He now, Mrs. Dean informs me, returned to their house, and begged to be admitted for a short time.[127] Mrs. Dean made a stout resistance, but at her husband's solicitation, and on Paine's promise that he would not stay long, he was permitted to enter the house. He brought with him a gallon of New England rum, and in the evening got so drunk that he fell from his chair, broke his nose, and sprinkled the room with his blood. At the end of the week, Mrs. Dean insisted that he should leave the house. And where, said the wretched old man, shall I go? Nobody will take me in! Go where you will, she replied, you shall not stay here. He went to Mr. Daniel Pelton's, one of his political friends, in the neighbourhood, but Mrs. Pelton refused him admission, having accommodated him one night before, and found him exceedingly offensive. Repelled from house to

127 He had not paid a farthing for his former board at Mr. Dean's, nor had he when he died.

house, he finally went back to the Welshman's, who gave him shelter on obtaining his promise that he would not stay longer than a day. This was on the 29th of May. On the first of June, Mr. Carver went to Jones's for him, and brought him to his house in the city. He remained until early in the following November at Carver's, where he was cleaned, and treated with the greatest kindness. While at Carver's, he sold his farm at New Rochelle, at fifty dollars an acre, to Mr. Shute, who had been his bail in the suit of Rachel. The subjoined correspondence will elucidate his character, and account for his conduct while at Carver's. Paine's letter, with its bad orthography, its pointing, and its capitals, is printed, literally, from his own hand-writing. I have already said that Mr. Carver is an unlettered man.

No. I.

New York, Nov. 21, 1806.

CITIZEN FRIEND,

I take this opportunity to inform you, that I am in want of money, and should take it as a favour if you would settle your account; you must consider that I have a large family, and nothing to support them with but my labour. I have made a calculation of my expenditures on your account, the last time that you was at my house, and find that they amount to one hundred and fifty of sixty dollars; your stay was twenty-two weeks, and Mrs. Palmer twelve weeks board on your account. I expect, therefore, you will have the goodness to pay me; for you must recollect you was with me almost the whole of the winter before last, for which you only gave me four guineas. If I, like yourself, had an independent fortune, I should not then require one cent of you; but real necessity, and justice to my family, thus prompts me to urge payment from you.

Your's, in friendship,
WILLIAM CARVER.

MR. THOMAS PAINE.

No. II.

MR. CARVER,

I received your letter of the 21st inst. and as there are several mistakes in it I sit down to correct them. You say to me in your letter—"You must recollect you was with me almost the whole of the winter before last, for which you only gave me four guineas." This is a misstatement in every part of it. I paid you four dollars per week for the time I was at your house and I told you 80 when I gave you the money which was in the shop. I had lodged and boarded at Mr. Glen's in Water Street before I came to your house. I paid him five dollars per week, but I had a good room with a fire place and liquor found for dinner and supper. At your house I had not the same convenience of a room and I found my own liquor which I bought of John Fellows, so that you were paid to the full worth of what I had.—As I paid by the week it does not signify how long or short the time was, but certainly it was not "*almost the whole of the winter.*" I had burnt out my wood at Mr. Glen's, and did not chuse to buy a new stock because I wanted to go to New Rochelle to get Purdy of the farm, I therefore came to your house in the mean time. How does it happen that those who receive do not remember so well as those who pay.

You say in your letter—"You have made a calculation of your expences on my account the last time I was at your house and find that they amount to one hundred and fifty or sixty dollars, that I was 22 weeks and Mrs. Palmer twelve weeks on my account."—I know not how you calculate nor who helps you, but I know what the price of boarding is. The [time] I was at your house consists of two parts. First, from the time I came from New Rochelle till I was taken ill and from thence till I came away Nov 3d I know not exactly the time I came from New Rochelle but I can know by writing to Mr. Shute. I know it was some short time before the eclipse which was the 16 June. The time I was taken ill I can know by refering to my will which is in the hands of a friend.

You seem not to know any thing about the price of boarding. John Fellows took board and lodging for me and Mrs. Palmer at Winships Coerlear's hook Winship ask seven dollars per week for me and her. The room I was to have was a handsome spacious room, and Mrs. Palmer was to have her room. At your house I found my own bedding and the room I had was no other than a closet to the front room, and Mrs. Palmer had none, nor a fire to come to when the weather grew cold. As to myself I suffered a great deal from the cold. There ought to have been a fire in the parlour.

The things which Mrs. Palmer did for me were those which belonged to the house to do, making the bed and sweeping the room; and when it happened Mrs. Palmer was not there, which often happened, I had a great deal of trouble to get it done; the black woman said she should not do anything but what Mrs. Carver told her to do, and I had sometimes to call John from his work to do the servant woman's work and your wife knew it. Sometimes the room became so dirty that people that came to see me took notice of it and wondered I staid in such a place.

I am at a loss to understand you when you say 'I have made a calculation of my expenditures *on your account* and find they amount to one hundred and fifty or sixty dollars.' 2: Why did you not send me the particulars of that expenditure that I might know if those particulars were true or false?—The expence, however, that you were at on my account was the addition of one more to your family than had before I came and no more, except for the time Mrs. Palmer was there, which *was not twelve weeks*, and your wife often called her down to cut out and make things for herself and the children. I had tea with brown sugar and everything else in common with the fare of the kitchen, so that unless I eat more than any body else I was of no more expense than any body else. What liquor I had I sent out for myself, on what ground then is your calculation founded. I suppose the case is that you have been a good deal cheated and your wife and son try to make you believe that the expence has been incurred upon my account.

I had written thus far on the Sunday evening when Mr. Butler called to see me and I read it to him and also your letter and I did the same to John Fellows who came afterwards. Any body seeing your letter and knowing nothing further would suppose that I kept you out of a great deal of property and would not settle the account. Whereas the case is that I told you the last time you came for money, and I gave you ten dollars, that I did not chuse to pay any more till the account was settled, you ought therefore to have come for that purpose instead of writing the letter you did which contains no account at all.

I did not like the treatment I received at your house. In no case was it friendly and in many cases not civil, especially from your wife. She did not send me my tea or coffee till every body else was served, and many times it was not fit to drink.

As to yourself you ought not to have left me the night I was struck with the appoplexy. I find you came up in the night and opened the little cupboard and took my watch—Did you take any thing else?

I shall desire John Fellows and Mr. Morton to call on you and settle the account and then I desire that all communication between you and me may cease.

Butler called on me last evening, Tuesday, and told me of your goings on at Mustin's[128] on the sunday night. I did not think, carver, you were such an unprincipled false hearted man as I find you to be; but I am glad I have found it out time enough to dispossess you of all trust

128 A tavern in Little George Street. Paine gave his letter to Walter Morton, who took it to Mustin's and read it in the tap-room.

I reposed in you when I made my will,[129] and, of every thing else to which your name is there mentioned.

THOMAS PAINE.
New York, Nov. 25, '06.

No. III.

Mr. Thomas Paine,

I received your letter dated the 25th ult. in answer to mine dated Nov. 21, and after minutely examining its contents, I found that you had taken the pitiful ground of subterfuge and lying for your defence. You say that you paid me four dollars per week for your board and lodging, during the time that you were with me, prior to the first of June last; which was the day that I went by your order to bring you to York, from New Rochelle. It is fortunate for me, that I have a living evidence that saw you give me four guineas and no more, in my shop, at your departure at that time; but you said you would have given me more, but that you had no more with you at present. You say, also, that you found your own liquors during the time you boarded with me; but you should have said, "I found only a small part of the liquor I drank during my stay with you; this part I purchased

129 He afterwards "dispossessed" John Fellows, to whom he had bequeathed something. I know not how many wills he made, for he "dispossessed" his friends as often as he quarrelled with them, which was continually.

of John Fellows, which was a demijohn of brandy containing four gallons, and this did not serve me three weeks." This can be proved, and I mean not to say anything that I cannot prove; for I hold truth as a precious jewel. It is a well known fact, that you drank one quart of brandy per day, at my expence, during the different times you have boarded with me, the demijohn above-mentioned excepted, and the last fourteen weeks you were sick. Is not this a supply of liquor for dinner and supper? As for what you paid Mr. Glen or any other person, that is nothing to me. I am not paid, and found you room and firing besides. You say as you paid by the week it matters not how long mý stay was. I accede to your remark, that the time of your stay at my house would have been of no matter, if I had been paid by the week, but the matter is otherwise. I have not been paid at all, or at least, a very small part; prove that I have if you can, and then I shall be viewed by my fellow citizens in that contemptible light that they will view you in, after the publication of this my letter to you.[130] You ask me the question, "How is it that those who receive, do not remember as well as those that pay?" My answer is, I do remember, and shall give you credit for every farthing I have received, and no more. I will ask you what consolation you derive to your mind in departing from truth, and endeavouring to evade paying a just and lawful debt. I shall pass over a great part of your letter with silent contempt, and oppose your false remarks with plain truths. As the public will see your letter as well as mine, they

130 This is the first time the letter has been published.

will be able to judge your conduct and mine for themselves. You say that I seem not to know any thing about the price of boarding in the city; but I know the price is from three dollars to five, and from that to ten; with additional charge if the boarder should be sick for three months or upwards. I shall show you how I calculate my expenditures, by the bill that will be rendered to you, and I believe it will be an important lesson to those that may undertake to board you here after. I have no person to help me to calculate or write, but fortunately took the advice of a friend, and got him to keep an account of all the times you stayed with me. You assert that your being at my house only added one more to the family; I shall prove that it added to the number of three. You know very well when you came, I told you I must hire a servant girl if you staid with me. This I did for five months, at five dollars per month and her board. This I should not have done, unless you had given me ground to believe you would have paid me. After your departure she was discharged. Now, sir, how will you go to prove that yourself, and Mrs. Palmer and the servant girl are one? In order to do this, you must write a new system of mathematics. You complain that I left your room the night that you pretend you were seized with the apoplexy; but I had often seen you in those fits before, and particularly after drinking a large portion of ardent spirits, those fits have frequently subjected you to falling. You remember you had one of them at Lovett's Hotel, and fell from the top of the stairs to the bottom. You likewise know I have frequently had to lift you from the floor to the bed. You must also remember that you and myself went to spend the evening at a certain gentleman's house, whose peculiar situation in life, forbids me to make mention of his name; but I had to go to apologize for your conduct; you had two of those falling fits in Broadway, before I could get you home.

You tell me that I came up stairs in the night and opened the cupboard, and took your watch: this is one more of your lies;. for I took it during the time your room was full of different descriptions of persons, called from a porter house and the street, at the eleventh hour of the night to carry you upstairs. After you had fallen over the banisters, and the cupboard door was open, and the watch lay exposed; I told you the next morning I put your watch in my desk, and you said I had done right. Why did not you complain before? I believe that I should do the same again or any other person in my situation; for had the watch been lost you would have thought that I, or some one of my family had got it. I believe it will not be in your power to make one of my fellow citizens believe, that at this period of life, I should turn rogue for an old silver watch.

You go on and say, 'did you take any thing else?' Have you assumed the character of a father confessor as well as a son of Bacchus? Did you lose any thing? Why do you not speak out? You have been so long accustomed to lying, one more will not choak you. Now, sir, I have to in form you I lost a silver spoon that was taken to your room, and never returned. Did you take that away with you? If not, I can prove that you took something else of my property without my consent. You likewise gave a French boy that you imported to this country, or was imported on your account, a nice pocket bottle that was neither yours nor mine; it being the property of a friend, and has since been called for; I lent the bottle to you, at the time you was sick with what you call apoplexy, but what myself and others know to be nothing more than falling drunken fits. * I believe you have broken up the domestic tranquillity of several families with whom you have resided; and I can speak by experience as to my own.—I remember you undertook to fall out with my former wife, and one of the foolish epithets you attempted to stigmatize her with, was, that she originally was only in the character of a servant. Was this a judicious remark of the Author of the *Rights of Man*?' I well remember the reply she made you, which was that you had not much to boast of on that ground, as yourself had been a servant to the British government. And now again you try to break up our tranquillity, by insinuating that my wife and son had deprived me of my property. I call this pitiful employment for a man that calls himself a philanthropist.—When you tell me that Mrs. Palmer did the work belonging to my family, you know the assertion to be false; which can be proved by her and others that resided in the house. You have written well on just and righteous principles, and dealt them out to others; but totally deny them in practice yourself; and for my part I believe you never possessed them. An old acquaintance of your's and mine called on me a few days ago, I asked him if he had been to see you? His answer was, he had not, neither did he want to see you.[131] He said he believed that you had a good head, but a very bad heart. I believe he gave a true description of your character in a few words: it has been my opinion for some time past, and many more of those you think are your friends, that all you have written has been to acquire fame and not the love of principle; and one reason that led us to think as we do, is, that all your works are stuffed with egotism. You say farther, that you were not treated friendly during your stay with me, and hardly civilly. Have you lost all principle of gratitude, as well as those of justice and honesty, or did you never possess one virtue?

From the first time I saw you in this country, to the last time of your departure from my house, my conscience bears me testimony that I treated you as a friend and a brother, without any hope of extra-rewards, only the payment of my just demand. I often told many of my friends, had you come to this country without one cent of property, then as long as I had one shilling, you should have a part. I declare when I first saw you here, I knew nothing of your possessions, or that you were worth four hundred per year, sterling. I sir, am not like yourself. I do not bow down to a little paltry gold, at the sacrifice of just principles. I, sir, am poor, with an independent mind, which perhaps renders me more comfort, than your independent fortune

131 Admiral Landais, a French gentleman, who knew Paine in France, and who was in the naval service of the United States, during the revolution.

renders you. You tell me further, that I shall be excluded from any thing, and every thing, contained in your will. All this I totally disregard. I believe if it was in your power you further, and say you would prevent my obtaining the just and lawful debt that you contracted with me; for when a man is vile enough to deny a debt, he is not honest enough to pay without being compelled. I have lived fifty years on the bounty and good providence of my Creator, and I do not doubt the goodness of his will concerning me. I likewise have to inform you, that I totally disregard the powers of your mind and pen; for, should you, by your conduct, permit this letter to appear in public, in vain may you attempt to print or publish any thing afterwards. Do look back to my past conduct respecting you, and try if you cannot raise one grain of gratitude in your heart, towards me, for all the kind acts of benevolence I bestowed on you. I showed your letter, at the time I received it, to an intelligent friend; he said it was a characteristic of the vileness of your natural disposition, and enough to damn the reputation of any man. You tell me that I should have come to you, and not written the letter. I did so three times; and the last you gave me the ten dollars, and told me you were going to have a stove in a separate room, and then you would pay me. One month had passed and I wanted the money, but still found you with the family that you reside with; and delicacy prevented me to ask you for pay of board and lodging; you never told me to fetch the account, as you say you did. When I called the last time but one, you told me to come on the Sunday following, and you would pay or settle with me; I

came according to order, but found you particularly engaged with the French woman and her two boys; * * * * * * * * * * * *
* * * * * * * * * * * * * * *
* * * * * * * * * * * * * * *
* * * * * * * * * * * * * * *
* * * * * * * * * * * * * * *

I know that the poor black woman, at New Rochelle, that you hired as a servant, and I believe paid every attention to you in her power, had to sue you for her wages, before you would pay her, and Mr. Shute had to become security for you.

A respectable gentleman,[132] from New Rochelle, called to see me a few days past, and said that every body was tired of you there, and no one would undertake to board and lodge you. I thought this was the case, as I found you at a tavern[133] in a most miserable situation. You appeared as if you had not been shaved for a fortnight, and as to a shirt, it could not be said that you had one on; it was only the remains of one, and this likewise appeared not to have been off your back for a fortnight and was nearly the colour of tanned leather, and you had the most disagree able smell possible; just like that of our poor beggars in England. Do you not recollect the pains I took to clean you? That I got a tub of warm water and soap, and washed you from head to foot, and this I had to do three times before I could get you clean. I likewise shaved you and cut your nails, that were like birds claws. I remember a remark that I made to you at that

132 Mr. Shute, who was afterwards a justice of the county.

133 Jones's, the Welshman.

time, which was, that you put me in mind of Nebuchadnezzar, who is said to be in this situation. Many of your toe nails exceeded half an inch in length, and others had grown round your toes, and nearly as far under as they extended on the top. Have you forgotten the pains I took with you, when you lay sick, wallowing in your own filth? I remember that I got Mr. Hooton, (a friend of mine, and whom I believe to be one of the best hearted men in the world) to assist me in removing and cleaning you. He told me he wondered how I could do it; for his part he would not like to do the same again for ten dollars. I told him you were a fellow being, and that it was our duty to assist each other in distress. Have you forgotten my care of you during the winter you staid with me? How I put you in bed every night, with a warm brick to your feet, and treated you like an infant one month old? Have you forgotten likewise how you destroyed my bed and bedding by fire;[134] and also a great coat that was worth ten dollars. I have shown the remnant of the coat to a tailor, who says that cloth of that quality could not be bought for six dollars per yard. You never said that you were sorry for the misfortune, or said that you would recompense me for it. I could say a great deal more, but I shall tire your and the public's

134 One day in winter, just after dinner, when he had drank rather more than his usual portion of brandy, he overheated the brick which, wrapped up in cloth, he was in the habit of putting to his feet when he lay down. The brick communicated fire to the bed. The smell of fire led Mr. Carver to his room, the door of which he broke open, and dragged Paine out of it. Mr. Carver tells me that five minutes longer would have terminated his existence.

patience; after all this and ten times as much more, you say you were not treated friendly or civilly. Have I not reason to exclaim, and say, O the ingratitude of your obdurate heart.

You complain of the room you were in, but you know it was the only one I had to spare—it is plenty large enough for one person to sleep in. Your physician and many others requested you to remove to a more airy situation, but I believe the only reason why you would not comply with the request was, that you expected to have more to pay, and not to be so well attended; you might think nobody would keep a fire, as I did, in the kitchen, till 11 or 12 o'clock at night, to warm things for your comfort, or take you out of bed two or three times a day, by a blanket, as I and my apprentice did for a month; for my part I did so till it brought on a pain in my side, that prevented me from sleeping after I got to bed myself.

I remember during one of your stays at my house you were sued in the justices court, by & poor man, for the board and lodging of the French woman, to the amount of about thirty dollars, but as the man had no proof, and only depended on your word, he was non-suited, and a cost of forty-two shillings thrown upon him. This highly gratified your unfeeling heart. I believe you had promised payment, as you said you would give the French woman the money to go and pay it with. * You complain that you suffered with the cold, and that there ought to have been a fire in the parlour. But the fact is that I expended so much money on your account, and received so little, that I could not

> go to any further expence, and if I had, I should not have got you away. A friend of your's[135] that knew my situation told you that you ought to buy a load of wood to burn in the parlour; your answer was, that you should not stay above a week or two, and did not want to have the wood to remove; this certainly would have been a hard case for you, to have left me a few sticks of wood.
>
> Now, sir, I think I have drawn a complete portrait of your character; yet to enter upon every minutia would be to give a history of your life, and to develope the fallacious mask of hypocrisy and deception, under which you have acted in your political as well as moral capacity of life. There may be many grammatical errours in this letter. To you I have no apologies to make; but I hope the candid and impartial public will not view them "with a critick's eye."
>
> WILLIAM CARVER.
>
> Thomas Paine, New York, Dec. 2, 1806.

Mr. Carver's description of Paine's filthiness, which was notorious, is very unequal to the reality. Fancy cannot picture an object so offensive to sense. No father could have been more kind and attentive to his degraded and lost child. Such services as Mr. Carver's may be gratefully remembered, but they cannot be compensated with money. Paine had not, however, in his heart, a place for gratitude; and as to the golden rule of justice, he disregarded it in practice. To have set Mr. and

135 Mr. John Fellows.

Mrs. Carver at variance, and destroyed their peace forever, by accusing the latter, in conjunction with her son, of fraud, would have been much more pleasing to him, than the observance of equity between man and man. If to the infamy of his conduct, in this particular, any thing could be added, it would be, that the charge of *cheating*, which he brings against Mrs. Carver and her son, was advanced to cover his own injustice.[136]

---

136 While at Carver's, drinking his quart of brandy a day, and suffering Madame Bonneville to procure a livelihood as she could, or to perish of want, he wrote the following impiety.

THE STRANGE Story OF KORAH, DATHAN, AND ABIRAM, NUMBERS, CHAPTER XVI. ACCOUNTED FOR

Old ballads sing of Chevy Chase;
Beneath whose rueful shade,
Full many a valiant man was slain,
And many a widow made.

But I will tell of one much worse,
That happ'd in days of yore,
All in the barren wilderness,
Beside the Jordan shore.

Where Moses led the people forth,
Call'd chosen tribes of God,
And fed them forty years with quail,
And rul'd them with a rod.

A dreadful fray once rose among
These self-named tribes of I AM,
Where Korah fell, and by his side,
Fell Dathan and Abiram.

Soon after the date of Mr. Carver's rejoinder,

An earthquake swallowed thousands up,
    And fire came down like stones,
Which slew their sons snd daughters all,
    Their wives and little ones.

"Twas all about old Aaron's tithes,
    This murderous quarrel rose,
For tithes are worldly things of old,
    That lead from words to blows.

A Jew of Venice(*) has explain'd
    In language of his nation,
The manner how this fray began,
    Of which here is translation.

There was a widow, old and poor,
    Who scarce herself could keep,
Her stock of goods was very small,
    Her flock one single sheep.

And when the time of shearing came,
    She counted much her gains,
For now, said she, I shall be bless'd,
    With plenty for my pains.

When Aaron heard the sheep was shear'd
    And gave a good increase.
He straight-way sent his tithing man,
And took away the fleece.

At this the weeping widow went
    To Korah, to complain,
And Korah he to Aaron went,
    In order to explain.

But Aaron said, in such a case
    There can be no forbearing
The law ordains that thou shalt give

his demand was paid by Paine, through Mr. John

The first fleece of thy shearing.

When lambing time was come about,
This sheep became a dam,
And bless'd the widow's mournful heart,
By bringing forth a lamb.

When Aaron heard the sheep had young,
He staid till it was grown
And then he sent his tithing man,
And took it for his own.

Again the weeping widow went
To Korah, with her grief,
But Aaron said, in such a case,
There can be no relief.

For in the holy law ‘`tis writ,
That whilst thou keep'st the stock,
Thou shalt present unto the Lord,
The firstling of thy flock.

The widow then, in deep distress,
And having nought to eat,
Against her will she kill'd the sheep,
To feed upon the meat.

When Aaron heard the sheep was kill'd,
He sent and took a limb,
Which, by the holy law, he said,
Pertained unto him.

For in the holy law ‘tis writ,
That when thou kilst a beast,
Thou shalt a shoulder and a breast,
Present unto the priest.

The widow then, worn out with grief,

Fellows and Mr. Walter Morton.

From Mr. Carver's, he went to live with the ingenious Mr. Jarvis, portrait-painter, in Church street. Mr. Jarvis, unmarried, kept what is called *Bachelor's Hall*. Here he lived five months. Whether his correspondence with Mr. Carver had tended to reform his conduct or not, I do not know, but Mr. Jarvis tells me that it was better at his house than common fame had previously represented it. His temper was by nature sour, and age, with the buffets he had met with in journeying through life, had made him exceedingly peevish: yet, Mr. Jarvis says, he was perfectly manageable by art, patiently and assiduously applied. He was easily put into a passion; he was easily calmed. He did not constant-

---

Sat down to mourn and weep,
And in a fit of passion said,
The devil take the sheep.

Then Aaron took the whole away,
And said the laws record,
That all and each devoted thing,
Belongs unto the Lord.

The widow went among her kin:
The tribes of Israel rose,
And all the widows, old and young,
Pull'd Aaron by the nose.

But Moses call'd an earthquake up,
And fire from out the sky,
And all the consolation is
The Bible tells a lie!!!

(*) In commentaries which Paine had been reading.

ly drink to excess, yet he frequently got excessively tipsey. Once Mr. Jarvis knew him to abstain from liquor two weeks. He had fits of intoxication, and when these came on, he would sit up at night, tippling until he fell off his chair. Disposed to listen to his conversation, Mr. Jarvis sat with him one night from twelve to three, doing all he politely could to keep him sober. At three he left him at his bottle. At four he returned to the room and found him drunk on the floor. Mr. Jarvis wished to raise him up, but Paine desired to lie still. I have the vertigo, the vertigo, said he. Yes, said Mr. Jarvis, taking up the bottle and looking at its diminished contents, you have it deep—deep! In this posture and plight he talked about the immortality of the soul. My corporeal functions have ceased, he said, and yet my mind is strong. My body is inert, but my intellect is vigorous. Is not this proof of the immortality of the soul? I am glad, said Mr. Jarvis, that you believe in the immortality of the soul, and in a future state. That, said Paine, is a wrong term. We have strong testimony, I have strong hope of a future state, but I know nothing about it. As the soul, said Mr. Jarvis, will live hereafter, will it be conscious that it has lived now? To live hereafter, said Paine, and not be conscious that I have lived now, would not be identity; it would amount to nothing.[137]

One day, sitting with a volume of his works on a table before him, containing his *Age of Reason*, the

137 He once said to Mr. Carver, that if he lived hereafter, he should be conscious that he had written *Common Sense*, &c.

servant girl took it up to read. Mr. Jarvis said she should not open it for the world, and took it from her. Why, said Paine, rising up angrily? Because she is a good girl now: she has the fear of God, and will do nothing wrong. She cannot reason as you can, and if she reads your *Age of Reason*, and divests herself of those restraints which now govern her conduct, she may cheat me; she may rob me; she may be undone. Pshaw, pshaw, said Paine, walking testily across the room with his hands behind him, why should any body believe in Jesus Christ? Come here, said Mr. Jarvis, to the window; look there, pointing to a congregation of people of colour, coming out of their church; do you see that black man? Three years ago he was a great reprobate; he was guilty of all sorts of offences. He had not been brought up as my servant has; he was egregiously immoral; he had no religious awe, and was not disposed to make use of the little reason which he possessed. He has since been converted. He is now a regular attendant on his church. You see that he is dressed well and has a goodly appearance. All in his neighbourhood now shake hands with him and are his friends: formerly he was avoided by them all as a pestilence. Paine had no answer to make, but pish, and pshaw, and I had not thought that you were such a man. He saw, to use the words of Mr. Jarvis, the fact, and it was unanswerable.

On another occasion he very seriously advised Mr. Jarvis to get married, observing that the marriage institution is an excellent one. And why did not you get married?[138] Why, I thought, said Paine, that I had talents, and that if I married, I should not be able to make a present of my works to the world, for its benefit!

As to his person, his disposition, Mr. Jarvis observes, was to nastiness. He would eat his breakfast, if he could, without washing himself; but Mr. Jarvis would not allow him to do so. He would pleasantly say, take the coffee away; give Mr. Paine a little time; he is a gentleman; he wants to wash himself: bring him some soap and water. Treating him in this way, and paying great attention to him, he was able to keep him tolerably clean.

No one could recommend matrimony with greater force than Paine. By habit he was to tally indifferent to his person. Cleanliness, with out which there can be no comfort, he entirely disregarded. In his old age, when the affection ate attentions of a wife are inestimable, he had no house, no home; no one to help or to comfort him. But recommending marriage to others, it

138 On his arrival at New York, I rode out with him to General Gates's, where we dined, *en famille*. Wishing to talk a little with Paine, and to hear his conversation, Mrs. Gates continued after the cloth was drawn. After a while she said: "I always threatened, if ever I saw you, to ask you a question, Mr. Paine." "Well, Madam," said Paine, "what is it." Why, I've heard a great deal about your being married in England; were you ever married?" "I never answer," said Paine, in a very surly manner, "impertinent questions." The general, with much of the frankness, and all the language of a soldier, turned the conversation.

was profligate in him to deny, as Mr. Jarvis understood him, his own marriage. If he could not satisfactorily reflect upon his connubial state, and upon his conduct towards his wife, he might have avoided a falsehood.

Principally from his penurious disposition, and, in some regard, from the impertinent anonymous letters which were addressed to him, he refused, while at Mr. Carver's, to take his letters from the post-office. If Carver would pay the postage, he would receive and read them with pleasure, but if not, he never troubled himself about them. Several anonymous letters were left for him at Mr. Jarvis's, while he lived there, desiring his opinion, whether, in baptism, immersion was better than sprinkling, or sprinkling better than immersion? Advise them, said Mr. Jarvis, to use *soap and water*. Paine did not perceive the point.

He usually took a nap after dinner, and would not be disturbed let who would call to see him.[139] One afternoon, a very old lady, dressed in a large scarlet cloak, knocked at the door, and inquired for Thomas Paine. Mr. Jarvis told her he was asleep. I am very sorry, she said, for that, for I want to see him very particularly. Thinking it a pity to make an old woman call twice, Mr. Jarvis took her into Paine's bed-room and waked him. He rose upon one elbow, and then with an expression of eye that staggered the old woman back a step or two, he asked—"What do you want?" "Is

139 Like this in the original. —Ed.

your name Paine?" "Yes." "Well then, I come from Almighty God, to tell you, that if you do not repent of your sins and believe in our blessed Saviour Jesus Christ, you will be damned, and"—"Poh, poh, it is not true. You were not sent with any such impertinent message. Jarvis, make her go away. Pshaw, he would not send such a foolish ugly old woman as you about with his messages. Go away. Go back—Shut the door." The old lady raised both her hands, kept them so, and without saying another word, walked away in mute astonishment.

From Mr. Jarvis's he went, in April, 1807, to Broome Street, an out-part of the city, where he boarded with Mr. Hitt, a baker. I have several times called on Hitt, who has tried to elude me, evidently in the hope of concealing facts; and when, at last, I saw and interrogated him, his communications were reluctant and scanty. The little information which I extorted from him, corroborates, however, that which had been incidentally mentioned to me by two or three gentlemen who sometimes visited Paine when he resided at Hitt's. Both enable me to say, that having less care taken of him than at Mr. Jarvis's, he relapsed into much of his former nastiness. He ate with Hitt's family, and had a small chamber to sit in, adjoining which was a closet, just large enough to hold his bed. In this chamber he received his night-visitors, and would sometimes, but not often, permit them to taste his rum. Hitt tells me that he was not always drunk, but admits that he frequently was. He thinks that he did not drink more than three quarts of rum a week, while he lived with him, which was about ten months; but allowing that he had no wish to extenuate, none to suppress the truth, he could have had but a very imperfect knowledge, his business calling him much from home, of the quantity of liquor which Paine consumed. From breakfast, he retired, Hitt says, to his room, where he remained until dinner. After dinner he would go to bed and sleep till tea-time. From tea, he again retired to his room and drank grog until late at night, when, if able, he would crawl into bed, but if not, which was most probable, he would fall off his chair and sleep himself sober on the floor. Not more than four or five persons visited him, and one or two of these, gentlemen with whom I am in daily habits of intercourse, did so from curiosity; to learn whether he was dead or alive. Some editors complimented him with their gazettes. These served him at once for a carpet and a table-cover. His room was full of dirt and confusion. Hitt says that he had expected he would have hired a servant boy to attend him, but that he did not. Why did he leave you? Because, said Hitt, I wanted to raise the price of his board. How much had he paid you? Five dollars a week. How much did you want? Seven. What did he offer to give? Six. Immediately after Paine left, I rode past Hitt in the country, and asked, him how came Paine to leave you? Why, said he, "the dirty, drunken, cross old devil, I would not let him stay any longer." This was no doubt true. He was somehow apprized, when I called on him for information, that I was writing Paine's life, and, being one of his disciples, he has very reprehensibly endeavoured to suppress the truth.

While at Hitt's, Paine corresponded with President Jefferson. In every thing he was slovenly; and he was regardless of all the principles and rules of honour. He laid the president's letters open upon his table, where every body who entered his room could read them. The substance of one of them got into our gazettes. It related to our differences with England, in regard to which, Mr. Jefferson had, much to the satisfaction of Paine, very improperly given an unfavourable opinion. Paine wrote paragraphs on the same side of the question, for one of our Jacobin gazettes. In his newspaper essays, he was completely a Frenchman. In one of them he joyfully anticipates the arrival of a hostile French force in the city of New York, and hopes that they will "trim the jackets of the *Tory* merchants!"[140]

At the same time Madame Bonneville, utterly neglected by Paine, was somehow procuring subsistence in the city. Her son, Ben, was with

140 He was always an advocate either of democratick anarchy or of imperial despotism: there was no medium with him. They talk, he said to a friend of mine, of the tyranny of the emperour of France, "I know Bonaparte; I have lived under his government, and *he allows as much freedom as I wish, or as any body ought to have.*" With Napoleon's invasion of Spain, he was enraptured, and, of course, wished him success! Could such a man be a friend of freedom?

her. Tom was at New Rochelle, frequently at Mr. Dean's, and sometimes at Joshua Fowler's. He was maintained on the credit, but not, I believe, at the request of Paine. His board is not yet paid for. The persons who took the abandoned child in, for he was in effect abandoned, have presented to his executors claims for his maintenance.

I have already mentioned his letter, which, soon after his arrival in the United States in 1802, he wrote to Thomas Clio Rickman,[141] of London. In this he states, that his property was worth 6000 *l.* sterling, which, put into the funds, would yield him 400 *l.* sterling a year. Still, however, he was not satisfied. Avarice had either mastered his former professions of disinterestedness, or those professions were deceitful. "In a great affair, where the happiness of man is at stake, I love, he said, to work for nothing; and so fully am I under the influence of this principle, that I should lose the spirit, the pleasure, and the pride of it, were I conscious that I looked for reward."[142]

But, in January, 1808, while at Hitt's, he presented a memorial to Congress for compensation for accompanying Col. Laurens in his mission to Paris, in the year 1781.[143] This was a "great affair, where the happiness of man was at stake," and yet he looked

141 Preface to the London edition, 1804, of his Letters to the citizens of the United States.

142 Letter 4 to the citizens of the United States. He has similar remarks in his *Rights of Man*.

143 See his memorial in the Appendix.

for "reward "! And he tells Congress, that unless they compensate him, the *story will not tell well in history*. Had his claim been a substantial one, neither his wealth, of which he had boasted, nor his former professions of disinterested patriotism, to which his memorial gave the lie, would have prevented Congress from adequately compensating his services. But he had no claim, as I have elsewhere shown, and as Congress, in effect, resolved.

There is a passage in his memorial that merits a more particular, though it shall receive but a very brief notice.

In the second part of his *Rights of Man*, doing every thing in his power to excite the people of England to revolt against their government, he compares the constitution of England with the constitution of the United States: describes the former, if he allows that there is a constitution in England, as every thing that is absurd and pernicious, and represents the latter, the constitution of the United States, as containing all possible excellence. But, in his memorial to Congress, he expresses a very different opinion. Speaking of the services which he had rendered the United States, he says:

> The country has been benefited by them, and I make myself happy in the knowledge of it. It is, however, proper to me to add, that the mere independence of America, were it to have been followed by a system of government, *modelled after the corrupt system of the English government*, it would not have interested me with the unabated

> ardour it did. It was to bring for ward and establish the representative system of government, that was the leading principle with me.[144]

The middle sentence is ill expressed, and ungrammatical, but its meaning will be understood. He was an enemy to our government, because it is *modelled after the corrupt system of the English.* The one, in his estimation, is quite as bad as the other, for that of the English he thought excessively vicious. Where now were his *old* and *new* systems of government? The *new* was that of the United States, which he had recommended to England, but which in his opinion, when revolution was not his object, was precisely the same as the constitution of England!

He published, while at Hitt's, but I know not when he wrote, his "Examination of the passages in the New Testament, quoted from the Old and called Prophecies concerning Jesus Christ, to which is prefixed, an Essay on Dream, showing by what operation of the mind a dream is produced in sleep, and applying the same to the account of dreams in the New Testament; with an Appendix, containing my private thoughts of a future state, and remarks on the contradictory doctrine in the books of Matthew and Mark;" an octavo pamphlet of 65 pages.

The metaphysical part of this impious work is very wretched. The whole is indeed the feeblest of

144 See his memorial in the Appendik.

his productions. It has been very ably and satisfactorily answered by Mr. Colvin, of Baltimore.

From Hitt's, he removed early in February, 1808, to No. 63 Partition Street, where he boarded. This was a small tavern, where a sixpenny show was daily exhibited. Here he had no care taken of him: he was left entirely to himself, and I hardly, therefore, need to add, that, drunk every day, he was neither washed nor shaved, nor shirted for weeks. He was so completely and notoriously nasty, that he might well contend with the showman for the most numerous audience of curious spectators. One of my friends, actuated by feelings of humanity, paid him a visit, and, in language sufficiently delicate, proposed to accompany him to the baths, to wash him, but to no purpose. His crust of filth seemed to give him comfort. As an inducement, my friend told him, that washing in the baths would cost him nothing; meaning that he would pay the expense himself, but Paine said that neither his beard nor his appearance gave him any uneasiness. He was truly an object of compassion, for great as his offences were, he was a human being. He had here one of his *apoplexies*, from which it was supposed he could not have recovered.

In the same month, (February 14, 1808) he presented a letter to the committee of Congress, to which his memorial had been referred. In this he grossly misrepresents his conduct, and that of Congress, in reference to his controversy with Silas

Deane.[145] The object of the letter was to induce the committee to report in favour of rewarding what he had been pleased to term services rendered in Laurens's mission to France, and he seems to have thought, that he could accomplish his object by a no very dexterous statement of many very palpable falsehoods.

On the 28th of the same month, the committee having made no report, he addressed a letter to the speaker of the house of representatives.[146] In this he says:

> It will be convenient to me to know what Congress will decide on, because it will determine me whether, after so many years of generous services, and that in the most perilous times, and after seventy years of age, I shall *continue in this country* or offer my services to some other country! It will not be to England, unless there should be a revolution.

This is degenerating into a poor Hessian soldier, who fights for any country or cause for pay. His continuance in the country depended on a grant of money by Congress upon a fraudulent claim! Where were his 6000 *l.* sterling; his 400 *l.* sterling a year? Surely he was above want. What then shall we say of his justice, his avarice, his attachment to the "promised land?" He was ready, in his seventieth year, to offer his services to "some other country,"

145 See the Appendix.

146 See Appendix.

for reward, but "not to England, unless there should be a revolution!" No, indeed, whatever might have been his desire, England was prohibited to him.

Receiving no answer from the speaker, he again addressed him on the 7th of the following March.[147] In his letter he speaks of the committee, who had not yet reported, with great contempt. "If, he adds, my memorial was referred to the committee of claims, for the purpose of losing it, it is unmanly policy. After so many years of service, *my heart grows cold towards America!*"

His heart grows cold towards America, because America will not gratify his avarice.

In the postscript, he says, "I repeat my request, that you would call on the committee of claims to bring in their report, and that Congress would decide upon it."

The speaker, Mr. Varnum, answered his letter, and, after observing that the committee had been much employed, very sarcastically begged him to have a little *Christian* patience! Hang him, said Paine, why does he talk to me about *Christian* patience?

One or two of his disciples took him away from the tavern in Partition Street, as it were by force, in July, 1808, and prevailed with Mr. Ryder, at Greenwich, near the State Prison, to board him. I have found Mr. Ryder, who is a cartman, sensible and communicative. He lives in a small comfortable house, and he and his family make a very or-

147 Appendix.

derly and decent appearance. Mr. Staley, he says, called on him, and asked him if he would board Thomas Paine, at seven dollars a week? I inquired, said Mr. Ryder, if he were the man they called old Tom Paine? Mr. Staley answered yes. Why, I don't know; I'll try him for a week. He accordingly came, dirty enough, and when he had been three days, I told Mr. Staley, said Mr. Ryder, that he must take him away, for he was such a cross, drunken, morose old man, that I could do nothing with him. Mr. Staley asked me if another dollar a week would do me? (meaning, tempt him to keep Paine.) I told him it might; so he staid. When the first month was out, Paine gave me twenty-eight dollars. I then told him it was eight dollars a week, according to Mr. Staley's promise. Then, said Paine, Staley may pay the extra-dollar himself, for I won't; seven are enough: why you'd take all my money from me and make me a poor man. Eight were afterwards paid. He lived at Ryder's until the 4th of May, 1809, about eleven months; during which time, except the last ten weeks, he got drunk regularly twice a day; by dinner time, when he went to bed, and at night, after he awoke to tea. As to his person, said Mr. Ryder, we had to wash him like a child, and with much the same coaxing, for he hated soap and water. I soon found that I could not keep and attend him for eight dollars a week, and told Walter Morton that they must take him away unless he would pay more, for I had to wait on him all night, and many weeks together I never had my clothes off: a little more was allowed. And he was so peevish that one could hardly live with him. He once threatened to beat my woman, (Mrs. Ryder) but I came home at the time and prevented the violence. He would often talk about death, and wished to die. Sometimes, though rarely, he was good humoured, but his language was generally rude, and his conduct insulting and tyrannical. Frequently he would have boiled milk and bread after tea, for supper, of which he would eat two or three spoonsful, and invariably throw the rest into the fire-place. He would have the best of meat cooked for him, eat a little of it, and always throw away the rest. Why did he do so? Why, said Mr. Ryder, smiling, that he might have the worth of the money which he paid for his board! Here, as elsewhere, he chose to perform all the functions of nature in bed. When censured for it by Mrs. Ryder, he would say, "I pay you money enough, and you shall labour for it."

In January 1809, he began to be so feeble and infirm as to be incapable of doing any thing for himself. Mr. Ryder found that Paine must either leave his house, or he himself must abandon his cart and horse, in order to attend him. He mentioned this to Walter Morton, one of Paine's executors, and it was agreed that he should be paid twenty dollars a week for constant attendance on him. In February, he began to drink milk punch, which, until he left Mr. Ryder's in May, was his diet. Often Mr. Ryder found him in tears, but he cannot say whether they were the effect of bodily pain or of reflection. He was very anxious to die, but still more anxious about his body after death.[148] He wished to be interred in the cemetery of the Quakers. Staley laughed at him, and told him, that as his body was nothing but matter, it was of no moment what became of it. Paine thought differently. Nothing, on this subject, could mitigate his apprehensions, or lighten the gloominess of his mind. He desired Mr. Ryder to go to Mr. Willet Hicks, a highly respectable Quaker gentleman, whose country seat is in the neighbourhood, and to say that he wished to see him. I have seen Mr. Hicks, who tells me that he called on Paine on the 19th of March, according to his desire. After the customary salutations, Paine said, that as he was "going to leave one place, it was necessary to provide another. I am now in my seventy-third year, and do not expect to live long: I wish to be buried in your burying ground. I could be buried in the Episcopal church, but they are so arrogant; or in the Presbyterian,

148 His language in the *Rights of Man*, part 1, p. 53, Phil. 1797, very ill accords with his conduct in the moments of his dissolution. "It may perhaps be said, he there remarks, that it signifies nothing to a man what is done to him after he is dead; but it signifies much to the living." "He was, however, full of solicitude about the disposition of his body after death. He seemed to be afraid that it would have no resting-place; that it would be exposed to offence, or be given to the winds. I know not whether this be a weakness, for death-bed thoughts are no doubt very different from those of vigorous health. The soul, when about to depart, has perhaps a natural and necessary concern for the body.

but they are so hypocritical!"[149] He added that his father was a Quaker, and though he did not think well of any Christian sect, he thought better of the Quakers than of any other.[150] Mr. Hicks laid his request before the committee who have the superintendance of the Quaker cemetery and funerals, eight in number, of which he himself was one, but the committee did not comply with his desire to be interred in their burying ground. This decision, which was communicated with great delicacy, affected him deeply.

Mr. Hicks was so kind as to give me the following in his own hand-writing.

"In some serious conversation I had with him a short time before his death, he said his sentiments respecting the Christian religion were now precisely the same as they were when he wrote the *Age of Reason.*"

Mr. David Gelston, collector of the customs of the port of New York, made him a visit early in April. He mentioned to Paine that he had a letter for him from Mr. Monroe, who was our minister in France when he was liberated from imprisonment in Paris. Confined to his bed, Paine desired that it might be read, and Dr. Manley read it. It

149 Mr. Hicks does not exactly remember the epithet which he applied to the Presbyterians, but it was one of reproach, and as hypocritical is that which he used to apply to them, I have supplied the omission of Mr. Hicks with the term. The positive assertion, that he could be interred in the cemetery of either, was nothing but assertion. He had made no application.

150 I have this remark from Mr. Ryder.

appears, that besides hospitably and gratuitously keeping him in his house near a year and a half after his release from prison, which he had in a great measure procured, Mr. Monroe had generously lent him considerable sums of money. The letter, which Dr. Manley tells me was equally elegant and polite, stated that Mr. Monroe did not know, nor did he with regard to himself care, whether Paine was able immediately to refund the money or not; all that Mr. Monroe desired was, that he would so acknowledge the debt, as that, at some future day, his children might have the benefit of it. Paine listened attentively to the letter, but made no reply. No acknowledgment could be got from him! Not a word did he speak either then or afterwards respecting it!

Madame Bonneville lived at Greenwich, in the neighbourhood, where she taught French to a few scholars: Ben was with her. Sometimes she made Paine a visit, though but seldom. He always treated her rudely, and she never manifested any affection. Tom was sent from New Rochelle, the people there being tired of keeping him, as had hitherto been the case, for nothing. From Greenwich he was removed to Bergen, a small village in New Jersey, where he was placed in a boarding-school. Ben. remained with his mother, to whom Paine now and then sent some money.

Symptoms of his dissolution were now so evident, and he was so sensible of them himself, that, on the 4th of May, he was removed from Mr. Ryder's to a small house owned by a Mr. Holbron, in Columbia Street, in the neighbourhood. The house was rented by Madame Bonneville, for Paine, who occupied the whole of it. The *lady* did not, however, consent to do so until a nurse had been engaged, being unwilling to pay the necessary attention to him herself. This nurse was Mrs. Hedden, a pious elderly matron, with whom I have conversed on the subject. She was aware, she says, of Paine's bad temper; determined, however, to take all the care of him she could, but not to bear ill treatment. During the first three or four days his conduct was tolerable, although he always quarrelled with Madame Bonneville when she went into his room. About the fifth day his language was offensive to Mrs. Hedden, who told him she would instantly leave the house. Sensible of her value as a nurse, and that in all probability no other person would attend him, he made her satisfactory concessions, and was afterwards civil. For the first week he drank much milk punch, which was his sustenance, but he then became too feeble to take scarcely any thing. He suffered, she says, much bodily pain. He would long and frequently call out "O Lord help me! O Lord help me! O Christ help me! O Christ help me!" as observed by Dr. Manley, in the letter which follows. She then said, that if he would throw himself on the mercy of Jesus Christ, he would find relief. He made no reply.

About two weeks before his death, he was visited by the Rev. Mr. Milledollar, a Presbyterian minister of great eloquence, and the Rev. Mr. Cunningham. The latter gentleman said—"Mr. Paine, we visit you as friends and neighbours. You have now a full view of death: you cannot live long, and *whosoever does not believe in Jesus Christ will assuredly be damned*." "Let me," said Paine, "have none of your Popish stuff. Get away with you—good morning—good morning." The Rev. Mr. Milledollar attempted to address him, but he was interrupted with the same language. When they were gone, he said to Mrs. Hedden, "don't let 'em come here again: they trouble me." They soon renewed their visit, but Mrs. Hedden told them that they could not be admitted, and that she thought the attempt useless, for that if God did not change his mind, she was sure no human power could. They retired.

After suffering very violent pain, which he said was in no particular place, but all over him, Mrs. Hedden would read the Bible to him for hours, and he would attentively listen. Did he, I inquired, ask you to read it? No. Did he ask you to stop? No. I read and he said nothing. He was very feeble; quite, to all appearance, exhausted. Poor man, how I felt for him! How I wished that he was a Christian! He would be a day without speaking a word, except asking "is no body in t'e room—who's there?" He never mentioned Tom Bonneville, who was at Bergen; but every now and then, seeing Ben, he inquired—"Does he go to school?" Madame Bonneville did not often go

into his room. She wished that he was dead, *
* * * * * * * * * * * * * * *
* * * * perhaps that he might be rid of the pain with which he was tortured, and which he impatiently bore. She was soon gratified. On the 8th day of June, 1809, about nine in the morning, he placidly, and almost without a struggle died, as he had lived, an enemy to the Christian religion.[151] He was born in January, 1737—aged seventy-two years and five months.

Dr. Manley's letter, which follows, will be read with interest.

Bloomingdale, New York, Sept. 27, 1809.

SIR,

Having lived in the neighbourhood of Mr. Paine, and, in his last moments, attended him as his physician, I should esteem myself much obliged, if you would be so kind as to communicate to me in writing, to be incorporated into his life, which I am preparing for the press, your observations on his temper and habits, the cause and nature of his disease, the kind of persons by whom he was visited during his illness, their general conversation with him respecting his deistical works, his own remarks, opinions, and behaviour, when on his death-bed, and; gener-

151 According to our gazettes, Mrs. Paine died at Lewes, in England, in the year 1808. From her womanhood she was intelligent and pious. She bore with more than ordinary fortitude her connubial misfortunes. She left this world with an excellent character. She had much of that supreme happiness which is derived from unaffected sympathy with unavoidable distress.

ally, such information as in your judgment may interest the publick.

I am, sir, your most obedient,
Humble servant,
JAMES CHEETHAM

DR. MANLEY.

***

New York, October 2, 1809.

SIR,

Your note of the 27th ult. has been duly rescceived, and I hasten in conformity to your wishes therein expressed to communicate the information I possess respecting its subject. Though my opportunity has been great, you will no doubt observe my knowledge to be very limited; the reason of which will be obvious to those who are in the least acquainted with the character of the man. Such as it may be, I assure you it is much at your service, and if any part of it afford matter for serious speculation to any portion of the publick, I shall feel a pleasure in having communicated it.

I was called upon by accident to visit Mr. Paine, on the 25th February last, and found him indisposed with fever, and very apprehensive of an attack of apoplexy, as he stated that he had that disease before, and at this time felt a great degree of vertigo, and was unable to help himself as he had hitherto done, on account of an intense pain above the eyes. On inquiry of the attendants, I was told, that, three or four days previous, he had concluded to dispense with his usual quantity of accustomed stimulus, and that he had, on that day, resumed it. To the want of his usual drink, they attributed his illness; and it is highly probable, that the usual quantity operating upon a state of system more easily excited, from the above privation, was the cause of the symptoms of which he then complained.

After having done and directed what I thought necessary, I left him, with a promise that I would make him a visit next day, when I expected to see his friends, and state to them his situation. Accordingly I called and saw two of his particular friends, (one of whom is an executor to his estate) related to them his situation, and was requested to pay him particular attention. From that time I considered him as under my care, visited him frequently, and prescribed for symptoms as they occurred, endeavouring by every mean in my power to alleviate his distress, and conduce to his comfort, which I assure you was no easy service.

In the course of a fortnight from the commencement of my attendance, I observed that his feet were oedematous, and his abdomen beginning to be distended with water, which, with several other circumstances equally unequivocal, indicated dropsy, and that of the worst description, as I soon found it pervaded every part of his body, which was sufficiently depending to admit the lodgement of water, and such as I had every reason to believe must terminate fatally to persons under his circumstances. About this time he became very sore, the water which he passed when in bed excoriating the parts to which it applied; and this kind of ulceration, which was sometimes very extensive, continued in a greater or less degree till the time of his death, producing infinite pain from the constant application of the cause which at first induced it. And here let me be permitted to observe, (lest blame might attach to those whose business it was to pay particular attention to his cleanliness of person) that it was absolutely impossible to effect that purpose. Cleanliness appeared to make no part of his comfort; he seemed to have a singular aversion to soap and water; he would never ask to be washed, and when he was he would always make objections; and it was not unusual to wash and to dress him clean, very much against his inclination. In this deplorable state, with confirmed dropsy, attended with frequent cough, vomiting and hiccough, he continued growing from bad to worse, till the morning of the 8th of June, when he died. Though I may remark, that during the last three weeks of his life, his situation was such, that his decease was confidently expected every day, his ulcers having assumed a gangrenous appearance, being excessively foetid, and discoloured blisters having taken place on the soles of his feet, without any ostensible cause, which baffled the usual attempts to arrest their progress: and when we consider his former habits, his advanced age, the feebleness of his constitution, his constant practice of using ardent spirits, *ad libitum*, till the commencement of his last illness, so far from wondering that he died so soon, we are constrained to ask, how did he live so long?

Concerning his conduct during his disease, I have not much to remark, though the little I hare may be somewhat interesting.

Mr. Paine professed to be above the fear of death, and a great part of his conversation was principally directed to give the impression, that he was perfectly willing to leave this world, and yet some parts of his conduct are with difficulty reconcileable with this belief. In the first stages of his illness, he was satisfied to be left alone during the day, but he required some person to be with him at night, urging as his reason, that he was afraid, that he should die when unattended, and at this period, his deportment and his principle seemed to be consistent; so much so, that a stranger would judge from some of the remarks he would make, that he was an infidel. I recollect being with him at night, watching; he was very apprehensive of a speedy dissolution, and suffered great distress of body, and perhaps of mind, (for he was waiting the event of an application to the society of Friends, for permission that his corpse might be deposited in their grave ground, and had reason to believe that the request might be refused) when he remarked in these words. "I think I can say what they make Jesus Christ to say—My God, my God, why hast thou forsaken me?" He went on to observe on the want of that respect which he conceived he merited, when I observed to him, that I thought that his corpse should be matter of least concern to him; that those whom he would leave behind him would see that he was properly interred; and further, that it would be of little consequence to *me* where I was deposited, provided I was buried: upon which he answered, that he had nothing else to talk about, and that he would as leave talk of his death as of anything, but that he was not so indifferent about his corpse as I appeared to be. During the latter part of his life, though his conversation was equivocal, his conduct was singular; he would not be left alone night or day; he not only required to have some person with him, but he must see that he or she was there, and would not allow his curtain to be closed at any time; and if, as it would sometimes unavoidably happen, he was left alone, he would scream and holla, until some person came to him: when relief from pain would admit, he seemed thoughtful and contemplative, his eyes being generally closed, and his hands folded upon his breast, although he never slept without the assistance of an anodyne. There was something remarkable in his conduct about this period, (which comprises about two weeks immediately preceding his death) particularly when we reflect, that Thomas Paine was author of the *Age of Reason*. He would call out during his paroxysms of distress, without intermission, "O Lord help me, God help me, Jesus Christ help me, O Lord help me," &c. repeating the same expressions without any the least variation, in a tone of voice that would alarm the house. It was this conduct which induced me to think that he had abandoned his former opinions, and I was more inclined to that belief, when I understood from his nurse, (who is a very serious, and, I believe, pious woman), that he would occasionally inquire, when he saw her engaged with a book, what she was reading, and being answered, and at the same time asked whether she should read aloud,[152] he assented, and would appear to give particular attention.

I took occasion during the night of the 5th and 6th of June, to test the strength of his opinions respecting revelation. I purposely made him a

152 The book he usually read was Mr. Hobart's *Companion for the Altar*.

very late visit; it was a time which seemed to sort exactly with my errand; it was midnight, he was in great distress, constantly exclaiming in the words above mentioned, when, after a considerable preface, I addressed him in the following manner, the nurse being present.

"Mr. Paine, your opinions, by a large portion of the community, have been treated with deference: you have never been in the habit of mixing in your conversation, words of course: you have never indulged in the practice of profane swearing: you must be sensible that we are acquainted with your religious opinions as they are given to the world. What must we think of your present conduct? Why do you call upon Jesus Christ to help you? Do you believe that he can help you? Do you believe in the divinity of Jesus Christ? Come now, answer me honestly; I want an answer as from the lips of a dying man, for I verily believe that you will not live twenty four hours." I waited some time at the end of every question; he did not answer, but ceased to exclaim in the above manner. Again I addressed him. "Mr. Paine, you have not answered my questions; will you answer them? Allow me to ask again—Do you believe? or let me qualify the question—do you wish to believe that Jesus Christ is the son of God?" After a pause of some minutes, he answered, "I have no wish to believe on that subject." I then left him, and know not whether he afterwards spoke to any person, on any subject, though he lived, as I before observed, till the morning of the 8th.

Such conduct, under usual circumstances, I conceive absolutely unaccountable, though with diffidence I would remark, not so much so in the present instance: for though the first necessary and general result of conviction be a sincere wish to atone for evil committed, yet it may be a question worthy of able consideration, whether excessive pride of opinion, consummate vanity, and inordinate self-love, might not prevent or retard that otherwise natural consequence?

For my own part, I believe, that had not Thomas Paine been such a distinguished infidel, he would have left less equivocal evidences of a change of opinion.

Concerning the persons who visited Mr. Paine in his distress as his personal friends, I know very little, though I may observe, that their number was small, and of that number, there were not wanting those who endeavoured to support him in his *deistical* opinions, and to encourage him to die "like a man," to "hold fast his integrity," lest Christians, or, as they were pleased to term them, *hypocrites*, might take advantage of his weakness, and furnish themselves with a weapon, by which they might hope to destroy their glorious system of morals.

Numbers visited him from motives of benevolence and Christian charity, endeavouring to effect a change of mind in respect to his *religious* sentiments. The labour of such was apparently lost, and they pretty generally received such treatment from him, as none but good men would risk a second time, though some of these persons called frequently.

De mortuis nil nisi bonum,[153] is a maxim to which, under certain limitations, I do willingly subscribe, but in its unqualified extent I have always viewed it as a highly erroneous rule of

153 Latin: Of the dead, [say] nothing but good. —Ed.

conduct, and although it might have originated in a heart overflowing with benevolence, yet it must be allowed that it paid no compliment to its judgement.—Youthful indiscretions and the infirmities of nature may very properly require its application, but it must be recollected, that there are vices of riper years, and practices, deduced from depraved principle, which the benefit of society requires should not be buried with the bones of their abettors. I make this observation (otherwise unnecessary) lest my remarks may be attributed to unworthy motives:—The task of animadverting on the disposition and habits of persons deceased, must always be disagreeable, because there are no characters without their faults; but in the present case it is peculiarly so, since the utmost partiality will have infinitely less to applaud, than indifference itself will find to condemn, but as they may be supposed largely to depend upon education, and to be influenced much by habits of thinking, in the instance of Mr. Paine they may appear to require special attention.

His disposition was singularly unfortunate, inasmuch as it required great correction, and admitted of none—his anger was easily kindled, and I doubt not that his resentments were lasting. His vanity and self-love were so excessive, that to differ from him in opinion was, in his estimation, to be deficient in common understanding; and his opposition to the doctrine of Christianity was so rancorous, that in the early part of his illness, he would treat its professors with rudeness.

I have had no opportunity of judging of the humanity of his disposition, but I may remark, that he considered himself under no obligation to those who administered to him in his illness, and acted accordingly: he was penurious to an extreme; would sometimes dispense with a comfort rather than purchase it; and as he set a higher value on money than it really merited, he thought such obligations completely cancelled by payment of that which he could not withhold. In the latter part of his life, he had his companions, though he seemed unfitted for sociability; and perhaps the reason why he affected company rather inferior to himself in point of understanding and acquirement, might be found in the peculiarities of his temper, which required acquiescence in his opinions to recommend to his attention.

In fine, if Mr. Paine had amiable qualities, I have been singularly unfortunate in never having had any evidence of them; and though you may conceive the above remarks too severe, I can as sure you, sir, that they are the result of my serious convictions; for during the whole course of his illness, his petulence, vanity, and self-will were so excessive, that I have been constrained frequently to remark, that he of all others should, from motives of policy, have been induced to keep terms with Christians, as his temper was such as to preclude the possibility of his enjoying the sincerity of friendship, and none but they (and the best of them too) could possess charity sufficient to cover its manifold imperfections.

Your's, with due consideration,

JAMES R. MANLEY.

MR. CHEETHAM.

At nine o'clock of the morning of the 9th of June, the day after his decease, he was taken from his house at Greenwich, attended by seven persons, to New Rochelle, where he was interred on his farm. A stone has been placed at the head of his grave, according to the directions of his will, with the following inscription: "Thomas Paine, author of *Common Sense*: died June 8, 1809, aged seventy-two years and five months."

Exclusive of Mr. Hicks, the Rev. Mr. Milledollar, the Rev. Mr. Cunningham, and one or two other gentlemen, who visited him from humane and Christian motives, he was abandoned on his deathbed, except by a few obscure and illiterate men, his former bottle companions, who attended him, merely, it should seem, to urge him to persevere to the end in his deistical opinions. What his admissions would have been during those compunctious visitings of nature which he experienced, had it not been for the whips and spurs of those persons, we cannot positively say. That he manifested symptoms of repentance, something like an inward willingness to believe in Jesus Christ, and yet an outward pride of obstinacy in denying that willingness in words, is certain from the testimony of Dr. Manley and Mrs. Hedden. But we have no evidence of his conversion. His seemingly attentive listening to Mrs. Hedden, when reading the bible, if not the effect of debility and a wish for repose, is an indication rather of a mitigation of his fury against it, than of his conversion to it. It was a passive act: there was nothing in it either active or certain. It was after this that Dr. Manley interrogated him. He paused. Possibly for a moment he doubted. But there is nothing equivocal in his answer. He had "no wish to believe on that subject." In something less than forty- eight hours after he died. During this time he had no conversation with any one respecting the Christian religion. The language of action is sincere. His fear of being alone is evidence against his conversion. The last moments of Locke and Addison were sweetly tranquil.

His association with low and disreputable persons, is attributable to his attachment to ardent spirits, and his love of personal distinction. Neither the one nor the other could be gratified in respectable company. He looked for adoration with as much constancy as he did for brandy. Since over poor ignorant men he could tyrannize as much as he pleased, and yet be looked up to by them with a sort of reverential awe, he chose them for his associates. He who could not listen with admiration and assent to all he would say, and with a kind of pleasure bear to be called blockhead and fool, and other names of insult and reproach, was no companion for him. And as the monarch of such men he was not content with limited powers. Nothing short of absolute despotism would do for him. Peter, of Russia, got drunk, and, with his own hand, committed murder for his amusement. Paine, reeling amidst his unlettered subjects, was equally a barbarian in manners, though not quite so atrocious in acts.

Of his moral character, nothing, perhaps, can be added to the facts which have already been stated. His conduct towards his wife were sufficient to blast the memory of a man even in all other respects virtuous; but Paine had no good qualities. Incapable of friendship, he was vain, envious, malignant; in France cowardly, and everywhere tyrannical. In his private dealings he was unjust, never thinking of paying for what he had contracted, and always cherishing deadly resentments against those who by law compelled him to do justice. To those who had been kind to him he was more than ungrateful, for to ingratitude, as in the case of Mr. Monroe, he added mean and detestable fraud. He was guilty of the worst species of seduction; the alienation of a wife and children from a husband and a father. Filthy and drunken, he was a compound of all the vices.

His system of government was simple, and therefore despotick. Universal suffrage—annual elections—a legislature consisting of one assembly, and a plural executive, like the executive directory of France, elected by universal suffrage, were its elements. It is not certain that judges, according to his scheme, were to be elected by universal suffrage, but it is that they were to be dependent on the popular will. His one-eyed legislature was to have supreme power, and by the very nature of its constitution the people would controul it.

Evidence of universal suffrage and annual elections we have in his French constitution of 1793, as well as in all his writings, except his letter to the people and armies of France, on the subject of the constitution of Boissy d'Anglas. His predilection for a plural executive is manifest in that work, as well as in others.

In one of his letters to the citizens of the United States, written at Washington, he says, referring to the constitution of the United States:—"Many were shocked at the idea of placing, what is called executive power, in the hands of a *single individual*." "The executive part of the federal government was made for a man, and those who consented, against their judgment, to place executive power in the hands of a *single individual*, reposed more on the supposed moderation of the person they had in view, than on the wisdom of the measure itself."[154]

When our constitution was formed, Paine was in Europe, and had he indeed been here, he could have known but little of what took place in the convention, every member being either sworn or put upon his honour not to divulge its proceedings. Our knowledge of the motions, speeches, and opinions of the members, which is very limited, is principally derived from Mr. Luther Martin's report to the legislature of Maryland, of which state he was a delegate. But minute and elaborate as it is, there is in it nothing that I recollect to authorize even a conjecture, that there was a single member favourable to a *plural* executive. The only contest, as far as we understand it, which on this subject arose was,

154 Letter 2.

and it was one of vehemence, whether the executive should in fact be a monarch with the title of President? Paine's intimation, that a *plural* executive was warmly agitated and reluctantly yielded, is in all probability one of his bold presumptions on assumed ignorance. Such an executive, besides its absurdity, is in its nature a tyranny. We are convinced that it is so by theory, and we know that it is so in fact. Unavoidably factious, it cannot but break up a nation into as many parties as it has members. Always distracted, it must always be feeble.

His attachment to a legislature consisting of one body, is indicated in the Rights of Man. "The objection," he says,

> against a single house is, that it is always in a condition of committing itself too soon. But it should be remembered, that when there is a constitution which defines the power and establishes the principles within which a legislature shall act, there is already a more effectual check provided, and more powerfully operating, than any other check can be.[155]

That which he considers as most powerfully checking precipitancy of action, has no efficacy. The declaration of rights of the French National Assembly, which was in truth a constitution, had no coercive effect on the convention. This "Single House," always passionate, as every single house must be, never had time for cool deliberation. It

155 *Rights of Man*, part 2, works, vol. 2, p. 184, Phil. 1797.

conceived in a passion; it executed in a rage. Nor had it any thing to restrain it, for how is it possible for a written constitution to assuage the most furious of the passions? A constitution, in such a government as Paine was in favor of, would be not the least of absurdities. Under the influence of universal suffrage and annual elections, nothing could be attended to in a single bodied legislature, but party strifes, victories, proscriptions, and oppression. Party-voters would be gratified, or party-representatives would be dismissed! The tyranny of an absolute monarch must fall infinitely short of the tyranny of such a government.

Formerly, Pennsylvania was at once oppressed and disgraced by a similar anarchy. Of this, Paine[156]

---

156 "In 1776, and 1777 there had been great disputes in Congress and the several states concerning a proper constitution for the several states to adopt for their government. A convention in Pennsylvania had adopted a government in one representive assembly, and Dr. Franklin was president of that convention. The Doctor when he went to France, in 1776, carried with him the printed copy of that constitution, and if plan of government of Mr. Franklin. In truth it was not Franklin's, but Timothy Matlock, James Cannon, Thomas Young, and *Thomas Paine*, were the authors of it. Mr. Turgot, the Duke de La Rochefoucault, Mr. Condorcet, and many others, became enamoured with the constitution of Mr. Franklin, and in my opinion the two last owed their final and fatal catastrophe to this blind love." President Adams's Letter to S. Perley, written June 19, 1809; see the American Citizen of September 2, 1809.

The conclusion of Mr. Adams is no doubt correct, Condorcet became an advocate of a single representative assembly. He was gratified. The convention was established, and it is to the uncontrouled fury and tyranny of the convention that his death is attributable. May not Paine's constitution of Penn-

was in all probability the author. Mr. Adams has rescued the memory of Franklin from the infamy of the act. But even in Pennsylvania, full of democratick faction and anarchy as that state always. is, the single representative assembly, perpetually despotick, became universally odious. Yet the constitution was so constructed as to require a *Senate*, but the unorganized senate was if possible more odd than the organized assembly. Section 15, of that constitution says:—"To the end that laws, before they are enacted, be more *maturely considered*, and the inconvenience of *hasty determinations* as much as possible prevented, all bills of a publick nature shall be printed *for the consideration of the people*."

Here the *people* stood in the place of a *Senate!* Bills were to be printed for their information and decision! Bills therefore could not become laws until this cool, sensible, and dignified senate had decided! This senate of all that was eloquent, magnanimous, and wise, could negative, or the appeal to it were a mockery; it could affirm, or it were useless. But it could do neither with out *mature deliberation!* Where—how was it to deliberate? In the senate house? No, but in taverns. Orderly? The whole system and process was disorder. What could be expected in such meetings but a tumult of the passions? Conflicting demagogues assembled the multitude in ale houses—harangued them—tore the state to pieces in an ardent pursuit of per-

---

sylvania have been the cause of the tyranny of Robespierre?

sonal aggrandizement—oppressed as they were victorious, and committed injustice as they were powerful. Such was Paine's constitution of Pennsylvania. It did not however last long. In 1790, it was superceded by the present constitution of that state. But it has left behind it the most deleterious effects. There is yet a party there, powerful in numbers, in favour of going back to it; a party avowedly opposed to the independence of judges, to trial by jury, and to every attribute of legitimate polity, to which we have been accustomed to look, and on which alone we can rely, as efficient guards of life, liberty, and property.

THE END

APPENDIX I

From the Journals of Congress

FIRST SESSION; TENTH CONGRESS

In the House of Representatives of the United States, 4th February, 1808.

r. CLINTON presented a representation of Thomas Paine, stating various services performed by him for the United States, during the revolutionary war with Great Britain; and praying that Congress will take the same into consideration, and grant him such compensation therefore, as to their wisdom and justice shall seem meet. The said representation was read and referred to the committee of claims.

[No report made during this session.]

***

SECOND SESSION; TENTH CONGRESS.

December 15th, 1809.

On motion of Mr. Johnson,

Ordered, That the letter and representation of Thomas Paine, presented on the 4th of February last, be referred to the committee of claims.

On the 1st of February, 1809, the committee of claims made a report, which was read and ordered to lie on the table.

[Not further acted on during this session.]

***

ELEVENTH CONGRESS; FIRST SESSION.

31st May, 1809.

On motion of Mr. Lyon,

Ordered, That the representation of Thomas Paine, of the city of New York, presented on the 4th of February, 1808, be referred to the committee of claims.

[Congress adjourned without any report being made by the committee on the subject.]

Report of the committee of claims on a letter and representation of Thomas Paine, referred the fifteenth December last.

February 1, 1809. Read, and ordered to lie on the table.

REPORT . . .

The memorialist states, that in the beginning of February, 1781, he sailed from Boston in the frigate *Alliance*, with colonel Laurens, who was appointed by Congress to negociate a loan with the French government, for the benefit of the United States; that he aided in effecting the important object of this mission, and thus voluntarily rendered an essential service to the country, for which he has received no compensation. This memorial was presented to Congress at their last session, unaccompanied with any evidence in support of the statement of facts. The committee of claims, to whom it was then referred, endeavoured to procure, from proper sources, such in formation as would guide them in making an equitable decision upon the case. The journals of Congress, under the former confederation, were diligently examined, but nothing was therein found, tending to shew that Mr. Paine was, in any manner, connected with the mission of colonel Laurens. It appears that on the 18th day of October, 1783, two resolutions were adopted in favour of major Jackson: one for defraying certain expenses incident to the mission; the other allowing him fourteen hundred and fifty dollars, as a full compensation for his services, while acting as secretary to colonel Laurens. A letter from the vice-president, in answer to one addressed to him, by the chairman of the committee of claims, is herewith presented. It will be observed, that the statement of this gentleman is from information, and not from his own knowledge. That Mr. Paine embarked with colonel Laurens from the United States for France, may be admitted; but it does not appear that he was employed by the government, or even solicited by any officer thereof, to aid in the accomplishment of the object of the mission, with which colonel Laurens was intrusted, or that he took any part whatever after his arrival in France in forwarding the negotiation; your committee are, therefore, of opinion, that the memorialist has not established the fact of his having rendered the service for which he asks to be compensated. On the 26th of August, 1785, Congress, by a resolution, declared that Thomas Paine was entitled to a liberal gratification from the United States for his unsolicited and continued labours in explaining and inforcing the principles of the late revolution; and on the 3d of October following, the board of treasury were directed to take order for paying Mr. Paine three thousand dollars for the considerations mentioned in the above resolution. This sum it appears Mr. Paine received on the 11th of October, 1785. That Mr. Paine rendered great and eminent services to the United States during their struggle for liberty and independence, cannot be doubted by any person acquainted with his labors in the cause, and attached to the, principles of the contest. Whether he has been generously requited by his country for his meritorious exertions, is a question not submitted to your committee, or within their province to decide.

The following resolution is offered to the House;

Resolved, That Thomas Paine have leave to withdraw his memorial and the papers accompanying the same.

APPENDIX II

Correspondence

NEW YORK, *January* 21, 1808.

To the honourable the representatives of the United States.

he purport of this address is to state a claim I feel myself entitled to make on the United States, leaving it to their representatives in Congress to decide on its worth and its merits. The case is as follows:

Towards the latter end of the year 1780, the continental money had become so depreciated, a paper dollar not being more than a cent, that it seemed next to impossible to continue the war.

As the United States were then in alliance with France, it became necessary to make France acquainted with our real situation. I therefore drew up a letter to Count Vergennes, stating undisguisedly the true case, concluding with the request whether France could not either as a subsidy or a loan, supply the United States with a million sterling, and continue that supply annually during the war.

I shewed the letter to M. Marbois, secretary to the French minister. His remark upon it was, that a million sent out of the nation exhausted it more than ten millions spent in it. I then shewed it to Ralph Isard, member of Congress for South Carolina. He borrowed the letter of me and said, we will endeavor to do something about it in Congress.

Accordingly, Congress appointed col. John Laurens, then aid to general Washington, to go to France and make representation of our situation for the purpose of obtaining assistance. Col. Laurens wished to decline the mission, and that Congress would appoint Colonel Hamilton, which Congress did not choose to do.

Colonel Laurens then came to state the case to me. He said he was enough acquainted with the military difficulties of the army, but that he was not enough acquainted with political affairs, nor with the resources of the country; but, said he, if you will go with me, I will accept, which I agreed to do, and did do.

We sailed from Boston in the *Alliance* frigate, captain Barry, the beginning of February, 1781, and arrived at L'Orient the beginning of March. The aid obtained from France was six million livres as a present, and ten millions as a loan borrowed in Holland on the security of France. We sailed from Brest in the French *Resolve* frigate the first of June, and arrived at Boston the 25th August, bringing with us two millions and a half in silver, and convoying a ship and a brig laden with clothing and military stores. The money was transported in sixteen ox teams to the national bank at Philadelphia, which enabled the army to move to York Town to attack, in conjunction with the French army under Rochambeau, the British army under Cornwallis. As I never had a cent for this service, I feel myself entitled, as the country is now in a state of prosperity, to state the case to Congress.

As to my political works, beginning with the pamphlet *Common Sense*, published the beginning of January, 1776, which awakened America to a declaration of independence, as the president and vice-president both know, as they were works done from principle I cannot dishonour that principle by asking any reward for them. The country has been benefitted by them, and I make myself happy in the knowledge of it. It is, however, proper to me to add, that the mere independence of America, were it to have been followed by a system of government modelled after the corrupt system of the English government, it would not have interested me with the unabated ardour it did. It was to bring forward and establish the representative system of government, as the work itself will shew, that was the leading principle with me in writing that work and all my other works during the progress of the revolution: And I followed the same principle in writing the *Rights of Man* in England.

There is a resolve of the old Congress, while they sat at New York, of a grant to me of three thousand dollars—the resolve is put in handsome language, but it has relation to a matter which it does not express. Elbridge Gerry was chairman of the committee who brought in the resolve. If Congress should judge proper to refer this me morial to a committee, I will inform that committee of the particulars of it.

I have also to state to Congress, that the author ity of the old Congress was become so reduced towards the latter end of the war, as to be unable to hold the states together. Congress could do no more than recommend, of which the states frequently took no notice, and when they did, it was never uniformly.

After the failure of the five per cent. duty, recommended by Congress to pay the interest of a loan to be borrowed in Holland, I wrote to Chancellor Livingston, then Minister for Foreign Affairs, and Robert Morris, Minister of Finance, and proposed a method for getting over the whole difficulty at once, which was by adding a continental legislature to Congress, who should be empowered to make laws for the Union, instead of recommending them. As the method proposed met with their full approbation, I held myself in reserve to take the subject up whenever a direct occasion occurred.

In a conversation afterwards with governor Clinton, of New York, now vice-president, it was judged, that for the purpose of my goingfully into the subject, and to prevent any misconstruction of my motive or object, it would be best that I received nothing from Congress, but leave it to the states individually to make me what acknowledgment they pleased.

The state of New York made me a present of a farm, which, since my return to America, I have found it necessary to sell:[1] and the state of Pennsylvania voted me five hundred pounds, their currency. But none of the states to the eastward of New York, nor to the south of Philadelphia ever made me the least acknowledgment. They had received benefits from me, which they accepted, and there the matter ended. This story will not tell well in history. All the civilized world knows I have been of great service to the United States, and have generously given away talents that would have made me a fortune.

I much question if an instance is to be found in ancient or modern times of a man who had no personal interest in the cause he took up, that of

1 To Mr. Shute, in 1806, but as Mr. Shute died shortly after, and his widow found it to be an inconvenience, Paine, at her solicitation, took it back.

independence and the establishment of the representative system of government, and who sought neither place nor office after it was established, that persevered in the same undeviating principles as I have done for more than thirty years, and that in spite of difficulties, dangers and inconveniencies, of which I have had my share.

THOMAS PAINE.

***

NEW YORK, Feb. 14, 1808.

Citizen Representatives,

In my memorial to Congress of the 21st of January, I spoke of a resolve of the old Congress of three thousand dollars to me, and said that the resolve had relation to a matter it did not express; that Elbridge Gerry was chairman of the committee that brought in that resolve, and that if Congress referred the memorial to a committee, I would write to that committee and inform them of the particulars of it. It has relation to my conduct in the affair of Silas Deane and Beaumarchais. The case is as follows. When I was appointed secretary to the Committee for Foreign Affairs, all the papers of the Secret Committee, none of which had been seen by Congress, came into my hands. I saw by the correspondence of that committee with persons in Europe, particularly with Arthur Lee, that the stores which Silas Deane and Beaumarchais pretended they had purchased were a present from the court of France, and came out of the king's arsenals. But as this was prior to the alliance, and while the English ambassador (Stormont) was at Paris, the court of France wished it not to be known, and therefore proposed that "a small quantity of tobacco or some other produce should be sent to the Cape (Cape Française) to give it the air of a mercantile transaction, repeating over and over again that it was for a cover only, and not for payment, as the whole remittance was gratuitous." See Arthur Lee's letters to the secret committee. See also B. Franklin's.

Knowing these things, and seeing that the public were deceived and imposed upon by the pretensions of Deane, I took the subject up, and published three pieces in Dunlap's Philadelphia paper, headed with the title of "Common Sense to the Public on Mr. Deane's affairs." John Jay was then president of Congress, Mr. Laurens having resigned in disgust.

After the third piece appeared, I received an order, dated Congress, and signed John Jay, that "Thomas Paine do attend at the bar of this house immediately," which I did.

Mr. Jay took up a newspaper and said, "Here is Mr. Dunlap's paper of December 29. In it is a piece entitled "Common Sense to the Public on Mr. Deane's affairs," I am directed by Congress to ask you if you are the author." Yes, sir, I am the author of that piece. Mr. Jay put the same question on the other two pieces and received the same answer. He then said, you may withdraw.

As soon as I was gone, John Pen, of North Carolina, moved that "Thomas Paine be discharged from the office of secretary to the committee for foreign affairs," and prating Gouverneur Morris seconded the motion, but it was lost when put to the vote, the states being equally divided. I then wrote to Congress requesting a hearing, and Mr. Laurens made a motion for that purpose which was negatived. The next day I sent in my resignation, saying, that "as I cannot consistently with my character as a freeman submit to be censured unheard, therefore, to preserve that character and maintain that right, I think it my duty to resign the office of Secretary to the Committee for Foreign Affairs, and I do hereby resign the same."

After this I lived as well as I could, hiring myself as a clerk to Owen Biddle of Philadelphia, till the legislature of Pennsylvania appointed me clerk of the General Assembly. But I still went on with my publications on Deane's affairs, till the fraud became so obvious that Congress were ashamed of supporting him, and he absconded. He went from Philadelphia to Virginia and took shipping for France, and got over to England where he died. Doctor Cutting told me he took poison. Gouverneur Morris by way of making apology for his conduct in that affair, said to me after my return from France with Colonel Laurens, well! we were all duped, and I among the rest. As the salary I had as Secretary to the Committee of Foreign Affairs was but small, being only 800 dollars a year, and as that had been fretted down by the depreciation to less than a fifth of its nominal value, I wrote to Congress then sitting at New York, (it was after the war) to make up the depreciation of my salary, and also for some incidental expences I had been at. This letter was referred to a committee of which Elbridge Gerry was chairman, Mr. Gerry then came to me and said that the committee had consulted on the subject, and they intended to bring in a handsome report, but that they thought it best not to take any notice of your letter or make any reference to Deane's affair or your salary. They will indemnify you, said he without it. The case is, there are some motions on the journals of Congress, for censuring you with respect to Deane's affair, which cannot now be recalled, because they have been printed. Therefore, will bring in a report that will supersede them without mentioning the pur port of your letter.

This, citizen representatives, is an explanation of the resolve of the old Congress. It was an indemnity to me for some injustice done me, for Congress had acted dishonorably to me. However, I prevented Deane's fraudulent demand being paid, and so far the country is obliged to me, but I became the victim of my integrity.

I preferred stating this explanation to the committee rather than to make it public in my memorial to Congress.

THOMAS PAINE.

***

NEW YORK, PARTITION STREET,
NO. 63, FEB. 28, 1808.

SIR,

I addressed a memorial to Congress dated January 21, which was presented by George Clinton, junior, and referred to the committee of claims. As soon as I knew to what committee it was referred, I wrote to that committee and informed them of the particulars respecting a vote of the old Congress of 3000 dollars to me, as I mentioned I would do in my memorial, since which I have heard nothing of the memorial or of any proceedings upon it.

It will be convenient to me to know what Congress will decide on, because it will determine me, whether, after so many years of generous services, and that in the most perilous times, and after seventy years of age, I shall continue in this country, or offer my services to some other country. It will not be to England, unless there should be a revolution.

My request to you is, that you will call on the committee of claims to bring in their report, and that Congress would decide upon it. I shall then know what to do.

Yours in friendship,
THOMAS PAINE.

The Honourable Speaker
of the House of Representatives.

***

NEW YORK, MARCH 7, 1808.

SIR,

I wrote you a week ago, prior to the date of this letter, respecting my memorial to Congress, but I have not yet seen any account of any proceedings upon it.

I know not who the committee of claims are, but if they are men of younger standing than "*the times that tried men's souls*," and consequently too young to know what the condition of the country was at the time I published Common Sense, for I do not believe independence would have been declared had it not been for the effect of that work, they are not capable of judging of the whole of the services of Thomas Paine. The president and vice-president can give you in formation on those subjects, so also can Mr. Smilie, who was a member of the Pennsylvania legislature at the times I am speaking of. He knows the inconveniencies I was often put to, for the old Congress treated me with ingratitude. They seemed to be disgusted at my popularity, and acted towards me as a rival instead of a friend.

The explanation I sent to the committee respecting a resolve of the old Congress while they sat at New York should be known to Congress, but it seems to me that the committee keep every thing to themselves and do nothing. If my memorial was referred to the commitee of claims, for the purpose of losing it, it is unmanly policy. After so many years of service my heart grows cold towards America.

Yours in friendship,
THOMAS PAINE.

The honourable the Speaker
of the house of representatives.

P. S. I repeat my request that you would call on the committee of claims to bring in their report, and that Congress would decide upon it.

***

SENATE CHAMBER, MARCH 23, 1808.

SIR,

From the information I received at the time, I have reason to believe that Mr. Paine accompanied colonel Laurens on his mission to France in the course of our revolutionary war, for the purpose of negotiating a loan, and that he acted as his secretary on that occasion; but although I have no doubt of the truth of this fact, I cannot assert it from my own actual knowledge.

I am with great respect,

Your most obedient servant,

GEORGE CLINTON.

David Holmes, Esquire.

Appendix III

Last Will and Testament

he People of the State of New York, by the Grace of God, Free and Independent, to all to whom these presents shall come or may concern,

Send greeting:

Know ye, That the annexed is a true copy of the will of THOMAS PAINE, deceased, as recorded in the office of our surrogate, in and for the city and county of New York. In testimony whereof, we have caused the seal of office of our said surrogate to be hereunto affixed.—Witness, Silvanus Miller, Esq. surrogate of said county, at the city of New York, the twelfth day of July, in the year of our Lord one thousand eight hundred and nine,

and of our Independence the thirty-fourth.
SILVANUS MILLER

***

The last will and testament of me, the subscriber, THOMAS PAINE, reposing confidence in my Creator God, and in no other being, for I know of no other, nor believe in any other, I Thomas Paine, of the state of New York, author of the work entitled *Common Sense*, written in Philadelphia, in 1775, and published in that city the beginning of January, 1776, which awaked America to a Declaration of Independence, on the fourth of July following, which was as fast as the work could spread through such an extensive country; author also of the several numbers of the American *Crisis*, "thirteen in all," published occasionally during the progress of the revolutionary war—the last is on the peace; author also of the *Rights of Man*, parts the first and second, written and published in London, in 1791 and 92; author also of a work on religion, *Age of Reason*, part the first and second. "N. B. I have a third part by me in manuscript and an answer to the Bishop of Llandaff;" author also of a work, lately published, entitled *Examination of the passages in the New Testament quoted from the Old, and called Prophecies concerning Jesus Christ*, and shewing there are no prophecies of any such person; author also of several other work s not here enumerated, *Dissertations on First Prin-*

ciples of Government—Decline and Fall of the English System of Finance—Agrarian Justice, &c. &c. make this my last will and testament, that is to say: I give and bequeath to my executors herein after appointed, Walter Morton and Thomas Addis Emmet, thirty shares I hold in the New York Phoenix Insurance Company which cost me 1470 dollars, they are worth now upwards of 1500 dollars and all my moveable effects and also the money that may be in my trunk or elsewhere at the time of my decease paying thereout the expences of my funeral, IN TRUST as to the said shares, moveables and money for Margaret Brazier Bonneville, wife of Nicholas Bonneville, of Paris, for her own sole and separate use, and at her own disposal, notwithstanding her coverture. As to my farm in New Rochelle, I give, devise, and bequeath the same to my said executors Walter Morton and Thomas Addis Emmet and to the survivor of them, his heirs and assigns forever, IN TRUST, nevertheless, to sell and dispose of the north side thereof, now in the occupation of Andrew A. Dean, beginning at the west end of the orchard and running in a line with the land sold to Coles, to the end of the farm, and to apply the money arising from such sale as hereinafter directed. I give to my friends Walter Morton, of the New York Phoenix Insurance Company, and Thomas Addis Emmet, counsellor at law, late of Ireland, two hundred dollars each, and one hundred dollars to Mrs. Palmer, widow of Elihu Palmer, late of New York, to be paid out the money arişing from said sale, and I give the remainder of the money arising from that sale, one half thereof to Clio Rickman, of High or Upper Mary-la-Bonne Street, London, and the other half to Nicholas Bonneville, of Paris, husband of Margaret B. Bonneville aforesaid: and as to the south part of the said farm, containing upwards of one hundred acres, in trust to rent out the same or otherwise put it to profit, as shall be found most adviseable, and to pay the rents and profits thereof to the said Margaret B. Bonneville, in trust for her children, Benjamin Bonneville and Thomas Bonneville, their education and maintenance, until they come to the age of twenty-one years, in order that she may bring them well up, give them good and useful learning, and instruct them in their duty to God, and the practice of morality, the rent of the land or the interest of the money for which it may be sold, as herein after mentioned, to be employed in their education. And after the youngest of the said children shall have arrived at the age of twenty-one years, in further trust to convey the same to the said children share and share alike in fee simple. But if it shall be thought adviseable by my executors and executrix, or the survivor or survivors of them, at any time before the youngest of the said children shall come of age, to sell and dispose of the said south side of the said farm, in that case I hereby authorise and empower my said executors to sell and dispose of the same, and I direct that the money arising from such sale be put into stock, either in the United States bank stock or New York Phoenix insurance company stock, the interest or dividends thereof to be applied as is already directed for the education and maintenance of the said children; and the principal to be transferred to the said children or the survivor of them on his or their coming of age. I know not if the society of people called Quakers admit a person to be buried in their burying ground, who does not belong to their society, but if they do, or will admit me, I would prefer being buried there; my father belonged to that profession, and I was partly brought up in it. But if it is not consistent with their rules to do this, I desire to be buried on my farm at New Rochelle. The place where I am to be buried, to be a square of twelve feet, to be enclosed with rows of trees, and a stone or post and rail fence, with a head stone with my name and age engraved upon it, author of *Common Sense*. I nominate, constitúte, and appoint Walter Morton,[1] of the New York Phoenix In surance Company, and Thomas Addis Emmet,[2]

1 A Scotchman by birth. He is a clerk in the Phenix company; was a steady companion of Paine before his illness, but paid him no visit for a week before his decease.

2 The respectability of Mr. Emmet's family is better known in Europe than in the United States. He was one of those gentlemen who considered his country as oppressed, and was willing to make great sacrifices to redeem her freedom. He was involved in the general charge of corresponding with the French Directory, with the view of introducing into his country a powerful French force, but, much as I have read on this subject, I have seen nothing to convince me, that the accusation, with regard to him, is not groundless. I have the honour

counsellor at law, late of Ireland, and Margaret B. Bonneville, executors and executrix to this my last will and testament, requesting them the said Walter Morton and Thomas Addis Emmet, that they will give what assistance they conveniently can to Mrs. Bonneville, and see that the children be well brought up. Thus placing confidence in their friendship, I herewith take my final leave of them and of the world. I have lived an honest and useful life to mankind; my time has been spent in doing good; and I die in perfect composure and resig-

---

of being personally acquainted with Mr. Emmet. His former and present opinions of the French government respecting his country, are correct. France would not invade Ireland to liberate her from oppression, but to oppress her more. That he is a friend of freedom is true, but surely this ought not to be considered as an offence in England, the birth-place of the most illustrious advocates of liberty that the world has known. He was, however, arrested in Dublin in March, 1799, and, without trial, imprisoned in Fort George, Scotland, the following April. Here he continued until June, 1802, when, without trial, he was liberated at Cuxhaven, whence he passed to Holland, and thence, in February, 1803, to Paris. He sailed from Bordeaux in September, 1804, and arrived in New York the following month, where he was admitted to the bar in the February term of 1805, and now wholly devotes his time to his laborious profession. Perhaps it were invidious to say that he occupies the first professional standing in the state. He is universally respected, as he deserves to be, and has as much as he can attend to of the first professional business. He is now in the 45th year of his age, has an amiable wife, and mine promising children. Why Paine appointed him an executor I know not, except from his known integrity, for those who pay no regard to that virtue in their actions, must respect it when making a will. Unless professionally, Mr. Emmet, I believe, had no intercourse with Paine.

nation to the will of my Creator God. Dated this eighteenth day of January, in the year one thousand eight hundred and nine, and I have also signed my name to the other sheet of this will in testimony of its being a part thereof.

THOMAS PAINE. (L.s.]

Signed, sealed, published and declared by the testator, in our presence, who at his request, and in the presence of each other, have set our names as witnesses thereto, the words "published and declared" first interlined.

WM. KEESE,
JAMES ANGEVINE,
CORNELIUS RYDER.

Appendix IV

Works by Thomas Paine

Title	Pag.	Format
Introduction to the Pennsylvania Magazine, January 24, 1775	1	8vo.
To the Publisher on the utility of Magazines, no place, no date, Philadelphia, 1775 (supposed)	5	do.
"Useful and entertaining hints on the internal riches of the colonies", *Pennsylvania Magazine*, Phil. 1775.	6	do.

"Reflections on the death of Lord Clive", *Pennsylvania Magazine*, (not seen)		
"New Anecdotes of Alexander the Great", *Penn. Mag.*, 1775	3	8vo.
Common Sense, Phil., Jan. 1776	47	do.
Epistle to the Quakers, Phil. 1776	5	do.
The Crisis, 16 numbers, from Dec. 23, 1776, to Dec. 9, 1783, total pages	144	do.
Letter to Abbé Raynal, Philad., 1782	55	do.
Publick Good, Being an Examination of the Claim of Virginia to the Vacant Western Territory, &c. Phil. 1784	31	do.
Dissertations on Government, the Affairs of the Bank, and Paper Money, Phil. 1786	50	do.
Prospects on the Rubicon, London, 1787	32	do.
Letter to the Authors of the Republican, Paris, 1791	4	do.
Rights of Man, part 1. London, 1791	98	do.
Letter to Abbé Seyes, 1791	2	do.
Rights of Man, part 2, London, 1792	122	do.

Letter to Henry Dundas, London, June 6, 1792	11	8vo.
Letter to Lord Onslow, London June 17, 1792	4	do.
Letter to Onslow Cranley, commonly called Lord Onslow, London, June 21, 1792	3	do.
Address to the Addressors, London, July, 1792	42	do.
Letter to Secretary Dundas, on his detention at Dover; Calais, Sept. 15, 1792	3	do.
Letter to the People of France, (on his election to the convention) Paris, Sept. 25, 1792	3	do.
Letter to the Attorney-General of England on the prosecution a against him, Paris, Nov. 11, 1792	2	do.
Reasons for preserving the life of Louis XVI, Paris, Jan. 1793	6	do.
Age of Reason, part 1, Paris, 1794	96	duo
Dissertations on First Principles of government, Paris, 1794	18	8vo.
Speech delivered in the convention against the constitution of 1795	8	do.
Agrarian Justice, Paris, 1796	32	do.
Decline and fall of the English System of Finance, Paris, 1796	23	do.

Letter to George Washington, Paris, 1796	76	8vo.
Age of Reason, part 2, Paris, 1796	199	duo
Letter to the Hon. Thomas Erskine on the prosecution of Williams, Paris, 1797	24	8vo.
Letter to the people and armies of France on the events of the 18th Fructidor, Paris, 1797	52	do.
Discourse to the Theophilanthropists, Paris, 1797	6	do.
Letters to the Citizens of the United States, Washington, 1802	50	do.
Examination of the Prophecies, Essay on Dream, &c. New York, 1807	66	do.

He wrote, in addition, from 1805 to 1808, essays for our newspapers, some of which were decidedly in favour of an invasion of the United States by the French.

His productions in verse are fugitive, and have never been collected. The happiest of them, that I have seen, are his "Death of Wolfe," and his "Castle in the Air," which I have taken into his life.

Index

A

B

C

D

E

F

G

H

I

J

K

L

M

N

O

P

W

Y

www.ingramcontent.com/pod-product-compliance
Lightning Source LLC
Chambersburg PA
CBHW020927310726
48980CB00010B/823/J

* 9 7 8 1 9 0 9 6 0 6 3 2 6 *